A User's Guide to
The Fall

A User's Guide to
The Fall

By Dave Thompson

Helter Skelter
Publishing

First edition published in 2003 by Helter Skelter Publishing
4 Denmark Street, London WC2H 8LL

Copyright 2003 © Dave Thompson

Cover design by Chris Wilson
Typesetting by Caroline Walker
Printed in Great Britain by The Bath Press

All lyrics quoted in this book are for the purposes of review, study or criticism.

Photo credits:

A CIP record for this book is available from the British Library

ISBN 1-900924-57-9

Contents

Acknowledgements

Thanks to everyone whose ideas, thoughts, theories, memories and, most of all, record collections helped to make this book what it is: Amy Hanson, Jo-Ann Greene, James Stevenson, Henry Rollins, Mike Scharman, Rick Gershon, Ella and Sprocket; to Sean Body at Helter Skelter for unleashing it in the first place; and to everybody else who now walks around with 'Telephone Thing' stuck in their heads… Snarleyyowl the Cat Fiend, K-Mart (not the store), Dave Makin, Gaye and Tim, Anchorite Man, the Bat family (and Crab), Blind Pew, Barb East, Gef the Talking Mongoose, the Gremlins who live in the furnace, Geoff Monmouth, Nutkin, Squirrels, a lot of Thompsons, Neville Viking and the Walrus Ball.

'If The Fall were ice cream they'd be Guinness, anchovy-stuffed olives and Marmite flavour. Yum.' – New Musical Express, *1999.*

Author's Note

A User's Guide to The Fall represents the largest and most complete Fall Discography ever published, reviewing and documenting the historical and musical background to more than 70 different LPs (plus reissues) and as many again singles. Based upon 25 years spent following, if not always actively collecting, the band, it also utilises material from two interviews conducted with Mark E Smith back in 1993 and 1994, and an (ultimately unpublished) Fall retrospective written for the American record collecting magazine *Goldmine*, a few years later. Other sources, including quotes and excerpts from Smith's often legendary press encounters elsewhere, are acknowledged in the text and in the bibliography at the end of the book.

HOW TO USE THIS BOOK

For hopefully obvious reasons, **A User's Guide to The Fall** is laid out chronologically by year, with all entries then following, again, in chronological order. Although the emphasis is on material released officially, a small number of bootlegs are also noted. Within these parameters, the following headings should be similarly self-explanatory. But, just in case:

MUSICIANS: The band's line-up(s) during the relevant period.

SINGLES: includes 45rpm, 10-inch, 12-inch, EP and CD single releases, including Smith's collaborations with other artists. Bootlegs are featured, but by no means exhaustively. Original release, reissue and chart data (if any) is also included.

ALBUMS: includes LP, cassette and full-length CD releases, including Smith collaborations with other artists and Various Artist compilations featuring newly recorded Fall material. Again, a handful of bootlegs are noted. Original release, reissue and chart data (if any) is also included.

LIVE: Concert recordings listed by date of original show where known.

STUDIO: Studio recordings subsequently released on compilations and anthologies (detailed in appendix II), listed by date of original recording where known. Undated material is listed either following the main chronological sequence, or where it would seem to fit in regard to the band's repertoire of the time. When in doubt, performances are dated to the year in which the song was first recorded.

BBC SESSION: A number of performances recorded during the Fall's many BBC (primarily John Peel) sessions have been released officially.

For ease of reference/cross-reference, every song is individually numbered according to year (the first two digits – 77, 78, 79 etc) and by the release's position within the above sequence. Unreleased songs known to have been recorded at listed events are noted UNR (UNRELEASED)

Subsequent (live, radio or rerecorded) appearances of the same song receive a new number. However, alternate recordings/mixes from original session, or commercial remixes of a previously released recording, when issued under the original title, retain the original number, suffixed a, b, c etc.

NOTE: Between 1996-1997, the Trojan group of companies released and/or licensed a number of Fall compilations drawing from a stockpile of material dating between 1979 and 1996, the bulk of which comprised previously unreleased live, rehearsal and out-take recordings. Released without any annotation whatsoever, it has not always been possible to determine the exact origins of a performance – even down to whether or not it is a live (as in concert) recording. For the most part, these are treated as alternate versions only, dated to the year of the song's own origin and suffixed accordingly. Should further information come to light, this will be incorporated into later editions.

Further material is included in the appendices: (I) BBC Radio sessions, (II) Compilations and Anthologies, (III) Miscellaneous, (IV) Index of Members and (V) Tape-ography.

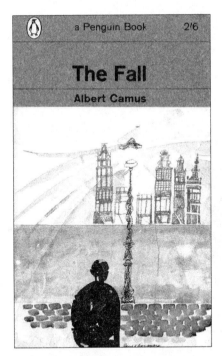

a Penguin Book   2'6

The Fall

Albert Camus

Introduction

"People always reveal more about themselves than anything else when they write about The Fall." – Mark E Smith, 1983.

They were outcasts from the outset. From the moment former office boy Mark E (for Edward) Smith gave up trying to join other people's bands, and set about getting his own underway, the Fall never fit in with what most people assumed was the sound of young Manchester, circa 1977. True, the trendy liberals flocked to their gigs, intrigued by rumours that the Fall espoused a peculiarly streetwise brand of Communism, spellbound by lyrics fired by nightmares of madness and hospitals and, of course, well impressed that they took their name from a book by French author Albert Camus ('oh, haven't you read it? They *so* encapsulate the innermost contradictions').

There was also the cachet of Manchester itself, a hotbed of Punk while London was still merely warming up, machine-gunning its hip-notic names into the trendy critic's grinder – the Buzzcocks, the Worst, the Nosebleeds, Slaughter and the Dogs, the Drones, John Cooper Clarke, Warsaw, Magazine… oh yeah, and the Fall.

Twenty-five years on, they're still not quite accepted. Think of all that Manchester (so much to answer for, as a Peel session sampler proudly titled itself) has spawned in that quarter of a century, and you're looking at a not-even loosely alternative history of British rock. Joy Division and New Order, the Smiths and Morrissey, the Stone Roses, Oasis, the New Fast Automatic Daffodils… oh yeah, and the Fall.

It would be fun one day to sit down and ponder why this should be: how a band that has survived more or less unblemished by commercial considerations for more than a quarter of a century, that has maintained an ever-evolving membership around its never-changing leadership, that has 15 entries in the *Guinness World Records* book of British Hit Singles and has met every high-falutin criterion that rock fans and critics alike can devise, can still be considered an afterthought in any serious discussion of rock's last 25 years. It would be fun, but it would also be futile. When even the group's avowed fans can assert that 'only hardcore fans can differentiate between the Fall's many albums,' as their on-line *All Music Guide* entry declares, what hope does anybody else have of unravelling their impenetrable mythos?

And what would be the use, anyway? If the Fall didn't exist, nobody would have invented them, because nobody would really know what it was that they were trying to invent. Cult bands, after all, are ten-a-penny – maybe even commoner. What does it take, after all, to join that particular club? A few years of banging your brains against the wall, a few years of devotion from some dogged individuals, and a name that a lot of people recognise without actually being able to place a single song in their head.

But, if the Fall really are a cult, then someone has redefined the meaning of the word. They just didn't tell the band's detractors. Or their fans.

Early on, somebody compared the Fall to two of the bands which the young Smith himself acknowledged as favourites, if not inspirations: Can and the Velvet Underground. As far as the authors of most modern rock encyclopaedias are concerned, the Fall themselves could have folded there and then. They'd found their cultural high-water mark and, no matter how many times Mr Guinness added their records to his book, they would never rise any higher.

Smith himself has never had a problem with this, has, if anything, deliberately nudged it along. The Fall are successful, but so much on their own terms that, to the rest of the world, they remain an abject failure – albeit a strangely compelling one, a cracked and crooked mirror that leaves listeners and critics contemplating a bitter harpooning of modern life (rubbish long before Blur came along) viewed through the Rorschach-tinted spectacles of... a curmudgeon! A crank! Mr Grumpy!

Most songwriters of the rock'n'roll era, after all, spend their entire careers aspiring to be deemed 'important', to 'map the zeitgeist', to raise their craft from the realms of mere wordsmithery to the rarefied plateaux of sociological seer. Ever since Dylan first put poetry to the beat (or, perhaps, ever since a handful of American critics decided that that was what he had done), there has been no shortage whatsoever of earnest young laureates desperate to share in his shoe leather, and tell us all exactly what is wrong with the world.

Mark E Smith has never demanded such treatment, has never presumed to imagine he deserves it. Instinctively conscious of the humbug that is inherent in hubris, he punctures pomposity (in himself as in others) as naturally and thoughtlessly as penguins keep their feet warm. And, even when he does appear to be making some kind of pertinent point, you analyse his lyrics at your own peril.

The pat interpretation never sits comfortably upon his pronouncements; nor, as successive tussles with a litany of Isms have proven, do political fashion or correctness. So, to nod in the direction of a handful of Smith's most wordridden contemporaries, Bono, Sting, the young Billy Bragg and the mid-term Paul Weller will have to sup alone tonight. And they all can drink the health of the Voice of the Oppressed Working Classes, the monotone malignancy of the North's Social Conscience: Mark E Smith, the clog-dancing demagogue, a flat-cap and cardigan-clad clash between George Orwell, Arthur Scargill and Brian Clough. Or not.

And then there's his band, the Fall themselves. They are musical but, again, the music they make is the music they want to. When the rest of the British scene got into soulful choruses of horns, the Fall brought out a kazoo. When everyone else was delving into bleeding heart self-introspection, the Fall painted slogans on the wall with the blood. And, when everyone else thought they'd come up with something new and exciting, the Fall could usually find it on one of their old records.

No band (with the possible exception of latter-day labelmates Sparks) has been so widely imitated and so roundly ignored; few artists (with the probable exception of Bowie) have so accurately pinpointed the moods of the future while not appearing to be in touch with the present. Plastic soul, Mr Bowie? Acidic Grunge, Mr Smith?

Indeed, far from all their albums being indistinguishable from one another, beyond the vocals that nothing on earth could change (but which frequently alter themselves regardless), the Fall never sat still long enough to even hint at a formulaic sound, just a constantly shifting aggregation of musical reference points from which Smith draws barbs as the mood strikes. And that's the block over which all attempts to summarise the Fall will stumble. You know exactly what you're going to get from their records – until you actually sit down and listen to them.

That, after a fashion, is what this book does. It sits down and listens. Twenty-five years have seen several times that many albums, singles, live recordings and compilations released by, and in the name of, the Fall. It is a body of work that could easily lay claim to being among the most significant of the past quarter of a century. But it is also among the least orderly and, in many ways, the least understood.

Access any of the many Fall internet sites that have sprouted up over the past five or six years and you will find Mark E Smith's lyrics have been analysed from every direction imaginable. Turn back the pages of the music press: the Fall's music has been dissected with scalpel-fine precision. But walk into your local music emporium and spend a few minutes looking through the shelf where they keep the Fall CDs and, unless you know precisely what you're looking for, it's hard to know even what you're looking at. That is what this book will tell you. But it will also tell you why you're looking at it.

It is not a biography of the band. Although the group's chronology is mapped out, and major events in their career are discussed, the true grit of a biography – the whys and wherefores, the cause and effect – can only be told when Mark E Smith himself is ready to tell it.

Gamely, one could string together 25 years' worth of recordings, sackings, gigs and arguments into a single cohesive narrative, coloured with choice remarks from Fall guys past and purulent, but the best will in the world could only paint the picture as it's seen from outside. Smith himself has made it very clear that the view from within is nothing like that. Attempts to enter that inner sanctum, however, invariably end in failure. Indeed, every time Smith submits to another press interview, we watch one more would-be psyche-cracker come to bitter grief – whether it be the mid-90s *Loaded* journalist who narrowly avoided becoming Smith's ashtray or the late 70s fanzine editor who wasn't granted even that much attention.

Stick to what we know, then, to the facts that cannot be controverted, the truths there in black and white. Of course, the end result is, in its own way, a biography, peppered with references to Smith's own loves and hates, thoughts and opinions, taste and talents, the records he loved while he was still growing up, the music he hated once he'd grown. But it is more than that. It is a biography you have to listen to rather than read. To unfold the story of the Fall through Smith's songs is to unfold the social landscape of England (and that's all of England, not just the tatty corner of a northern pub where popular imagination places him) in a manner that has more in common with Dickens' novels or Orwell's journalism that any of the media in which Smith himself has been embroiled.

This is a factor that Smith himself reiterates via the constant updating and rewriting of his own words. Every song is of the moment it was conceived for; every lyric speaks only for when it was spoken. He admits his words, as captured on record, are starkly ephemeral – one reason why he often seems to loathe any attempt to haul him back to his own past.

Even *Record Collector* magazine, a publication whose very existence is tied to the repatriation of the past to the present, could not draw Smith into more than passing reflection. 'I like to look at the albums like diaries. I'm not one for nostalgia.' It only stands to reason, then, that when the concert setting demands that he open those diaries to read one of their entries, the page alone will remain familiar. The words, however, will be fresh as today, and an evening spent perusing every word written about the Fall's songs will prove that there are as many interpretations of precisely what Smith is saying, as there are interpreters. As another songwriter, another Smith, Adverts vocalist TV, once put it, 'I can only prepare the meal. It's up to you how you eat it.'

This book, then, is the table setting. The meal is cooked and about to be served. All you need to know is, which order in which you should handle the silverware.

And what's the first thing on the menu? Why, it's Guinness, anchovy-stuffed olives and Marmite flavour ice cream. *Yum!*

Before The Fall

Mark E Smith never found Punk Rock. It found him. True, he possessed all the necessary credentials: 19 years old, dead end job, pissed off with everything that then called itself music, and inexplicably excited by the noises that the Punk scene was making. But the sounds he'd been dreaming of were swimming around his own head for years. They had nothing in common with the buzzsaw rush of the new wave other than a shared love of the Velvet Underground, and the belief that music didn't have to be made by real musicians.

That, maybe, was why the Fall never fit into the Manchester scene, even once they were gigging and pulling in shows opening for others among the city's elite. They didn't fit because there was nothing to fit in with. No shared credo of revolution for art's sake, no twisted take on love or death, no right to work or clapped-out city rockers. And, where other bands drew their line-ups from a tangled skein of interconnected rockers, you'd never find the Fall fitting into a Pete Frame-style Family Tree. Or, rather, you would (Paul Barber executed one for *NME*, May 11th 1991), but none of the members were ex-Anyone You've Heard Of, and only a few would go onto anything else, often prior to making their own way back to the Fall once more. And just one of their names has remained a permanent fixture.

Mark Edward Smith was born in the Manchester suburb of Prestwich on March 5, 1957, the first of four children. By the standards of the time and his peers, he enjoyed an unremarkable childhood, the biographical highlights and moments-of-moulding that have piqued the interest of so many subsequent scribes no more-or-less unique to him than to anyone growing up in the same place and time.

Throughout his childhood, Manchester enjoyed a cultural boom of sorts, furiously chasing Liverpool in the musical arena, effortlessly swamping it on the soccer pitch. It was the age of the Mindbenders and the Hollies, Bobby Charlton and Francis Lee, a glorious epoch during which both United and City were at a peak of achievement, there or thereabouts in every competition that mattered. Smith, for his part, supported City, but he worshipped George Best all the same.

Music, on the other hand, played little part in his upbringing. There wasn't even a record player in the house until he was 14, while the radio was perpetually tuned to the BBC, whose popular music output for much of the decade (until the launch of Radio One in 1967) was confined to just a handful of regular programmes, squeezed begrudgingly into a schedule dominated by light entertainment and family favourites. Only when the boy accompanied his plumber father to work would he hear what was going on, sweeping up in the shop while the apprentices blared the pirate stations.

Even they had little immediate impact, however. At school, where everybody else was into the Beatles, Smith reserved his admiration for whichever current band laboured beneath the stupidest name, regardless of what they actually sounded like. One year, in the school's Best Band poll, Smith's vote stood out like a red plastic nose. It was the only one that supported John Fred and his Playboy Band.

But music sank in regardless – few teenage pastimes could pass without someone's transistor providing the soundtrack, even if it was simply a matter of getting beaten up at the youth club while 'There's A Ghost In My House' crackled in the background.

Later, as Glam Rock moved into view, Smith continued moving away from the crowd. The first gig he ever attended was the Groundhogs at Manchester Free Trade Hall in 1971, when he was 14. He told *Melody Maker*'s 'My First Gig' feature, 'I remember that they were very good. At the time I didn't like weirdo music, y'know weirdo long hair stuff. [But] they were sort of like John Lee Hooker on acid. The impressive thing about them was they were these greasers in leather jackets. It was very unusual in those days. They were far more greaser than hippies and the audience were just the same, like an Alice Cooper audience, but about 30 years younger.'

Black Sabbath, Van Der Graaf Generator, Can and the Velvet Underground all followed TS McPhee's crew into his consciousness, drawing Smith into the crowd of elder malcontents that every school of the time seemed to inflict on the Glam-loving brats in the years below. (Years later, Smith and Van Der Graaf frontman Peter Hammill came close to working together. 'It didn't happen in the end,' Hammill told *The Wire*. 'I'm a bit of a control freak.')

Reflecting on how (or even if) the Fall drew upon childhood influences, Smith told *Dazed And Confused*, 'When I first got into music – which was around the ages of 13 or 14 – I very quickly worked my way through every scene from Northern soul to Glam rock to Disco. Later, I got into Lou Reed and Can. I admired Iggy Pop, but he was too American rock and roll to influence me. I liked his music but, at the same time, it felt alien to me. There were no groups around that I thought represented people like me or my mates. No one was speaking to the clerks and the dockers. If I wanted to be anything, it was a voice for those people. I wanted The Fall to be the band for people who didn't have bands, for people who weren't supposed to have bands which related to their lives. I think we achieved that. I think we still do.'

Through his early teens, Smith attended the same academy, Stand Grammar School, as Lord Clive, whose exploits in 18th century India should be familiar to every English schoolchild. Departing in July 1973, Smith then enrolled for his A-Levels at St John's College, where he hooked up with the first of the few who would one day form the Fall, Una Baines.

He left home around the same time, estranged by his prickly relationship with his father. He once reflected, 'I never really liked my dad, I used to hate him, that's why I left [home]. I used to get on really well with my mother, but apart from that I couldn't wait to get out of the house. Other kids used to get a fiver for passing their eleven-plus, all my dad did was call me a bookworm.' However, while he admitted 'I couldn't appreciate it at the time,' in later years the reality of the old man's lessons hit home. Academic achievements themselves are worth no more than the paper they're written on. It's what you do after you achieved them that matters. 'I'm grateful for him bringing me up like that.'

Smith and Baines were typical students, in that they were perpetually broke – so broke that, before long, both quit college to find real jobs. While Baines began training as a psychiatric nurse at Prestwich Hospital, Smith found himself clerking for an import-export business at Manchester Docks. He kept his nose pressed so conscientiously to the grindstone nobody noticed that most of what he produced on the office typewriter comprised short stories and poems – efforts that would, in the earliest days of the Fall, be transmuted into song lyrics and themes. He'd been a voracious reader all his life – a lot of HP Lovecraft, a lot of Philip K Dick – 'and that made me interested in writing. Then I thought, "Why can't I put this writing with the sort of music I like?" It was that natural.'

The Fall began slowly. According to Fall legend (a beast so integral to the band's entire history that it really should be a word in its own right: *fallegend*), Smith tried out for various local Heavy Metal-type bands, only to find that neither his voice nor his lyrics (nor his own ideals of music) gelled with anything the others were trying to do. The notion of forming his own band, however, remained a pipedream until one afternoon when his sister, Barbara, dropped round with a couple of friends of hers, Martin Bramah and Tony Friel.

Both were musicians – or, at least, musically inclined and prone, Bramah told *The Wire* in 2001, to shoplifting instruments while playing truant from school. The pair clicked with Smith and Baines immediately. By spring 1976, a tentative line-up formed: Bramah on vocals, Smith on guitar, Friel playing bass and Baines on drums. There were problems, though. Smith couldn't play guitar and Baines didn't have a drum kit. Smith and Bramah traded roles, Baines began saving for a keyboard. And then the Sex Pistols came to town.

By June 1976, when local students Pete Shelley and Howard 'Devoto' Trafford arranged for the London band to play their first out-of-London show, the Sex Pistols had already consumed more column inches in the music press than many bands twice their stature. It began with a simple warning – 'Don't look over your shoulder, the Sex Pistols are coming!' – bannered atop a *New Musical Express* review of one show, and a dire admonition – 'Terrorise *your* fans the Pistol way' – above another. The band itself, all agreed, was little more than a violent noise, vulgar, raunchy and loud. But there was nothing wrong with that. When Mark E Smith read journalist Neil Spencer comparing their din with the Stooges, he was… if not *sold*, then at least curious enough to go along to see them. The Stooges themselves may have been too American, but an English response to their sound had to be worth checking out.

The Manchester gig, at the Lesser Free Trade Hall on June 4th 1976 was not sold out. But, as Brian Eno once said of the Velvet Underground, not many people heard them, but everyone who did formed a band. Within weeks of the gig, and certainly by the time the Pistols returned to Manchester on July 20th, Shelley and Devoto had the Buzzcocks up and running; the rudiments of Joy Division were preparing to buy their first instruments; a young Steven Morrissey was penning ecstatic epistles to the music press ('it's nice to see that the British have produced a band capable of producing [the] atmosphere created by the New York Dolls'); and Mark E Smith and co were underwhelmed enough by the entire event that it completely kick-started their own ambitions. 'I knew we could be a lot better than they were.'

The first task, of course, was to think of a name. Pre-empting Ian Curtis and co's dice with Teutonic imagery, one of the quartet's early ideas was Master Race and the Death Sense. There was also a flurry of enthusiasm for the Outsiders, from the

English-language title of French author Albert Camus' first novel, *L'Etranger*. Then somebody realized that another band had already beaten them to it, so Friel suggested they go with Camus' sixth book instead, *La Chute* – the Fall. That, according to a possibly less-than-reliable Smith, then gave way to The Flyman And The Fall. 'I was going to dress up as a greenfly and stand in front of the band going "buzzzzzzzzz." Honest I was. When we'd do interviews, if someone asked me a question, I'd reply, "Buzz".'

Over the next six months, it was Manchester that buzzed. The Electric Circus, a long established rock'n'roll club that had fallen on hard times, redesigned itself as a Punk Mecca of sorts: barely scraping by in July, it was filled to the gills by September. The Buzzcocks were regularly hopping up and down to London, supporting the Pistols at every opportunity they got, and preparing to release their own first record, the self-sufficiency manual of *Spiral Scratch*.

Slaughter and the Dogs, Ed Banger and the Nosebleeds, Warsaw, the Worst, the Drones... by early May 1977, when *Melody Maker* made its way into town to take a look for itself at the events unfolding thereabouts, there was even a thriving Indie label on the go, Tosh Ryan's Rabid. It was he who set out the city's stall in the ensuing article: 'The area is so neglected, so economically deprived and full of massive housing complexes, that the mood of the place was right and ready for a new movement in music with markedly different criteria of success. What has developed is peculiar to Manchester and I can only hope that instead of going to London for future deals, the agents and record companies will come here.'

One of the principle forces in this new ferment of musical aspiration was the Manchester Musicians' Collective, a co-operative formed early in 1977 by Trevor Wishart, the composer in residence at the North West regional branch of the Arts Council, Dick Witts, a contemporary classical music promoter who once played with the Hallè Orchestra, and electronic composer Simon Holt.

Taking over the basement beneath the Council's King Street offices, the Collective drew a healthy attendance from the start, the notions of what came to be called 'New Musik' dovetailing with the new frontiers being broached, if not exactly breached, by Punk: it was from organisations such as the MMC, the length and breadth of Britain, that the furthest fringes of the new wave would themselves take flight later in the decade. The Collective would later form its own record label, Object Records, and release a stream of frequently challenging, always intriguing, 45s by various MMC members. In spring 1977, the possibilities appeared boundless.

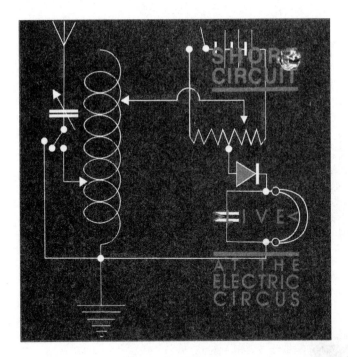

1977

By April, the Fall were firmly committed to doing something. Friel was the first to discover the Manchester Musicians' Collective and, encouraged by his enthusiasm for the fierce independence of this scene, Smith, Baines and Bramah regularly joined him at the Collective's Monday night meetings. There they witnessed acts of the most bizarre bravado, and the most hopeless optimism, a school of experimentation whose one guiding principle was to contort the most unmusical objects imaginable into the stuff of wild symphonies.

It was within these same precepts that Smith's songwriting, raw and unformed though it was, commenced sounding out its own parameters. 'The only real aim was to make the songs very fuckin' odd and particularly English. I wanted them to be a mish-mash of all sorts, particularly a lot of Garage groups of the mid '60s. I used to go to all sorts of different clubs in Manchester, which was why The Fall had to appeal to someone who was into cheap soul as much as someone who liked avant-garde groups like Stockhausen. I even wanted the Gary Glitter fans.'

In early May, the Fall were invited to make their own live debut at the MMC, sandwiched between a Socialist brass band and a performer who created symphonies from taped bird calls. They accepted – and then started to worry.

Despite some nine months of preparation, the Fall were by no means ready to play a live show, even in the presence of friends and like-minded bystanders. Baines was still waiting for the bank to process the loan application that would pay for her keyboard, while the band itself was still without a drummer. But they were not going to spurn the offer. While Baines opted to remain in the audience for the occasion, a drum-playing insurance salesman named Dave was recruited through an ad, and rudely introduced to the fledgling group's repertoire.

But the muting confines of the band's practice space – usually somebody's flat – prepared neither Dave nor the rest of the band for what happened when the Fall hit the stage for the first time. While Bramah, Friel and Dave stuck more or less to whatever passed as the scripted arrangements, Smith let rip with a logorrhoeac howling that Baines later confessed, 'scared me. I don't know what the fuck he was doing. I've never heard him do that before!'

The audience, too, was taken aback. However many people were in the room – and there weren't many – most of them were musicians (many were members, past and present, of the Buzzcocks) and all were well-acquainted with the far musical limits of the MMC's remit. But even they were stunned by the verbal dervish into which Smith transformed himself. No cute spiky-haired whigmaleerry, belching for the flashbulbs and whining on about anarchy and life on the dole, Smith declared open war on everything within earshot – and arm's length: one wildly emphatic finger came perilously close to jabbing itself up a watching Howard Devoto's nose.

Bramah later reflected that the brutality of the performance, though not planned, was probably inevitable. 'It was just welling up inside us all,' he told *The Wire*. 'That was the way we were living, that was the way we felt and that was the way Mark was. I mean, if you went out to a club with Mark, he'd pick a fight with someone. But that was just Mark: irrational and erratic. He didn't practise it, he didn't plan it, he was just like that.'

The performance was short, a clutch of the Smith originals which the band had worked up over the past few months, extended way beyond the confines of their lyric until they merged into a dense, intense barrage of bruises that raged behind Smith's near-incoherent vocals: 'Bingo Master's Break-out', 'Hey Fascist', 'Race Hatred', 'Psycho Mafia' and, most protracted of all, 'Repetition'. Even more disturbingly, Smith recalled, they played almost the entire set in the chord of E. 'It wasn't exactly the Beatles,' he reflected.

Baines' keyboard finally arrived just days before an equipment review in one of the music papers declared her chosen model, the aptly-named Snoopy Piano, to be the very worst instrument available on the market. It was certainly distinctive, however: a couple of years later, Sheree Lawrence of unabashed Fall fans Deep Freeze Mice unleashed the selfsame instrument on that band's own debut album, 1979's *My Geraniums Are Bulletproof*.

The first weekend in June saw the Fall face the general public for the first time, propping up the bill at the Squat Club's *Stuff The Jubilee* festival. Queen Elizabeth II only had 25 years on the clock back then, but the festivities were as grand as could be. Opposition was painstakingly organized, spearheaded by the Punk movement that serendipitously took shape as the royal celebrations loomed, then broke in one great concerted wave over the weekend of the Big Day itself. In London, the Pistols sailed a boat down the Thames and the Ramones raised the roof at the Roundhouse. In Birmingham, the Jam wore their Union Jacks in ironic defiance; in Liverpool, Leeds, and a thousand points besides, the alternative 'God Save The Queen' roared off underground turntables as loudly and as often as any street party could bellow.

The Squat Club was indeed a squat, manned by students of the Devas Street building's former tenant, the Royal Manchester College of Music. While Manchester's contribution to the treason was one of the lesser events on that night of nights, it was heartfelt, the culmination of an impromptu anti-Jubilee protest staged earlier in the day, with the Fall joined by the Worst, the Negatives, Warsaw and, headlining, the Drones, scions of the local hierarchy one and all.

According to Martin Bramah, interviewed in 1985 by *To Hell With Poverty* fanzine, Dave the drummer departed after four shows, never to be called on again. But, with the success (or whatever) of these excursions hanging over them, the Fall immediately sought a full-time replacement. They settled on Karl 'Krunch' Burns, a former member of one of Tony Friel's previous bands, a self-destructive metal act called Nuclear Angel. It was said that they folded after one intensive rehearsal too many ended with them demolishing all their own equipment.

Nevertheless, the Fall remained popular with their peers. When the Buzzcocks travelled down to London to play a Rock Against Racism benefit at the North London Poly, the Fall joined them on the bill. A week later, on July 4th, the two bands were together again, this time at the opening of the latest addition to the London Punk circuit, the Vortex.

Occupying the same Wardour Street space as Crackers Disco of earlier renown and soon to be filling the dance floor with the cream of the capital's Punk Rock cognoscenti on Monday evenings, the Vortex grabbed its first headlines on its very first lunchtime, when Sham 69's Jimmy Pursey was arrested for disturbing the peace by re-enacting the Beatles' 'Get Back' sequence on the building's roof. The nighttime entertainment was a little calmer, but not through want of trying – that was the evening, after all, that Buzzcocks' bassist Garth Smith was ejected for throwing things at the headlining Heartbreakers. And it was also the evening that the Fall, playing only their sixth-ever concert, learned how hard it is to be heard when nobody wants to listen. Barely anyone threw things, barely anyone booed. Barely anyone paid them the slightest attention.

The Fall returned the compliment. It was, Smith later fumed, 'fuckin' terrible. The audience totally ignored us, so fucking cool. Everyone just stood there posing. We were the scruffiest people in the place and we had no money for drinks or owt. And there's all these street kids in bondage suits sipping vodka and orange. It freaked us out.'

Not that the Fall were making too many appearances in London – indeed, you could make a longer list of seminal venues that they didn't play (the Roxy, the Nashville, the 100 Club...) than those they did. Smith admitted as much: 'We enjoyed playing the Marquee with Buzzcocks and the Worst. It was three different sounds all from one place. It blew their heads off.' But, in general, 'the thing down there stinks.'

In fact, Smith recalls the band's first year as involving as many northern working men's clubs as conventional concert venues, one reason why diaries of the band's early days are so patchy. Most reliable Fall gigographies are compiled from tapes of the actual concerts. The pit workers and such who Smith insists comprised the band's most loyal period audiences rarely went out for the night armed with cassette recorders. He told *Volume* in 1992, 'We were doing cabaret circuits at the time, just to earn money. Workingmen's clubs and all that. Fuckin' godawful! Fuckin' terrible! Good though. It toughened you up. They'd be throwing glasses – proper glasses, like – and spitting at you. I see a lot of groups today, and they don't know they're born. But, touch wood, nobody ever walks out of a Fall concert. You've got to keep the fuckers in there. That's how we got half our following. You fuckin' win them over and get their respect. They still come now. Miners from Wakefield and

Newcastle.'

Within the confines of the 'conventional' music scene, however, the Fall did not go completely unheard. At the beginning of October 1977, the Electric Circus finally bowed to police pressure and announced it would close its doors for the final time. Virgin Records despatched a mobile recording studio north to Collyhurst Street to preserve the proceedings for posterity.

Their motives may not have been wholly altruistic: six months earlier, the Harvest label scored a sizeable hit with its own documentary record of the Covent Garden Roxy, recorded at what was widely predicted to be that august venue's final few nights. (In any event, it simply underwent a change of management and, maybe, scruples).

More importantly, Manchester was a musical plum aching to be picked. Though the headlining Buzzcocks were newly signed to UA, their now-errant genius, Howard Devoto, would be unveiling his new band, Magazine, on the Sunday: they were still free agents. So, to all intents and purposes, were the bulk of the other bands filling the bill over that long, last weekend – the Panik, the Negatives, John the Postman, Manicured Noise, the Drones, Big In Japan, John Cooper Clarke, the Worst, the Prefect, Warsaw, the Fall... In the event, Magazine would be the only band on the bill to wind up with a full-length Virgin Records contract, a handful of the others did score abbreviated versions, as the label grabbed six bands, eight songs and ten inches of vinyl, and put them altogether as *Short Circuit*.

Released in April 1978, *Short Circuit* featured two Fall songs – 'Stepping Out' and 'Last Orders' – an indication of just how their profile had grown over the past six months. True, *England's Dreaming* author Jon Savage finds nothing more to say about the Fall in his authoritative history of the era than the awkward observation that they possessed a female organist, but two of the era's genuinely influential rock journalists, Paul Morley (*NME*) and Chris Brazier (*Melody Maker*), adopted the group as a *cause celebrè* for somewhat more cerebral reasons.

The arrival of a full-time manager, Kay Carroll, meanwhile, had opened more doors, as well as freeing Smith, until now the band's *de facto* manager, to concentrate more on the music and less on trying to avoid the endless rip-offs prepared for the young *ingénue*. A nurse at Prestwich Hospital, where she worked alongside Una Baines, Carroll gave up her job and moved into the group's Kingswood Road headquarters around the same time Smith finally jacked in his day job, unable to juggle two careers.

October 1977 saw the Fall take their first steps out onto the national circuit, joining the Worst and the Flys as support for the Buzzcocks' first headlining tour. For the most part, audience response tended to be divided between muted and miserable: attracted by the sharp pop tones of the headliners' debut single, the saucy 'Orgasm Addict', many of the kids flocking to the provincial shows were experiencing their first-ever Punk concert. The last thing they expected, after a year spent practising their pogo and spitting, was to be harangued by an opening act that seemed as disdainful of the audience as the audience was of them.

Back in Manchester the following month, Buzzcocks' manager Richard Boon financed the Fall's first recording session at the local Indigo Studios. The intention was to land a release through the Buzzcocks' label, either on the parent United Artists or via a distribution deal set up for Boon's own New Hormones, and the new year saw Smith announcing an imminent release with what would soon be revealed as characteristic brusqueness: 'Tracks: "Psycho Mafia", "Bingo Master's Break-

Out", "Frightened" and "Repetition". It lasts for 17 minutes. People have tried to tell us volume will suffer and "Frightened" is out of time slightly. If people couldn't turn the volume up, they wouldn't buy it!'

In fact, they didn't get the chance. Six months later, with UA, Virgin and even local hot dog Rabid having passed on it, the tape was still languishing on the shelf.

The Fall continued making occasional appearances at the Musicians' Collective, now operating out of the Band on the Wall club. Moved to quote Nico ('frozen warnings on the borderline'), local writer Ian Wood reviewed one of their shows in November, remarking, '[They] avoid the current commercial clichés of the bandwagon, and disown the poseurs that inhabit Manchester's hipper clubs. Taking Minimalism closer to logical extremes, ludicrous rhymes and repeats come often and frequently. They look totally nondescript, cleancut even. [That's] probably why their impact surprises so much.'

The band also turned out for Rock Against Racism on several occasions. One show, back at the Squat Club, is remembered as the first gig that legendary Garage deconstructionist/GPO mail carrier John The Postman ever played with a band (the Fall lent their equipment); another, headlining over both John the Postman and John Cooper Clarke, took place at the Stretford Civic Centre on December 23rd.

The Fall were not, however, altogether happy with their continued participation in the RAR carnival. Although the cause was one that the band happily espoused, RAR could also be incredibly self-serving and insultingly patronising. As Smith mourned to *NME* writer Ian Penman the following August, 'I was disillusioned very quickly. I'd always equated left-wing politics with revolution... [But] what happens is, before you go on they say, "Will you hold this poster up?" and it's a picture of Belsen. "DON'T LET IT HAPPEN AGAIN." I would say, "We're a political band, that's what we sing about." But they want you to make announcements between songs; they see you as entertainment. You might as well be singing Country & Western.'

The group's early stance against political entanglement had further consequences. Fêted by *NME* writers Julie Burchill and Tony Parsons as the 'real' voice of the downtrodden working class, the Fall were offered an *NME* cover in return for posing as the poster children of the anti-Fascist movement, beneath the headline 'The band that stands against the National Front.' They turned it down. A decade later, Smith recalled, 'Burchill... was going on about the working class, and I was trying to catch her out, saying, "What about these National Front skinheads that are working class?" She's going, "You fucking liberal, you fucking liberal." It was crazy, we just got on the coach and went home.'

The Stretford RAR show is most significant, then, in that – their brief Electric Circus appearance notwithstanding – it represents the earliest available recording of the Fall in concert. It also marked the end of Tony Friel's tenure with the band he named, as he departed to form his own group, the Passage.

It was not a happy parting, at least for (some of) those he left behind. Martin Bramah told *The Wire*, 'When Mark and Kay [Carroll] became a team, it became a bit of a dictatorship and that changed the band because we'd started as equal friends. Kay was his enforcer, his strength and his mouthpiece within the band. We all recognised his talent and just put up with things, but I think Kay made it harder to be in the band, especially for Tony, who thought the Fall were as much his vehicle as Mark's. He'd thought of the name and was the primary musician within the band.'

Bramah himself would be out of the band just a few months after Friel, but Smith was neither concerned nor surprised. 'I didn't like any of them,' he told *Volume* 15 years later. 'I never thought the line-up would last. Tony Friel wanted to be like Weather Report. He used to want to do bass solos and all that. Martin was into Television. [Even] Karl was into Rush. I was into Can, more into sound than music – noise, you know.'

(MUSICIANS)
LINE-UP #1 (May 1977): MARK E SMITH (vocals), MARTIN BRAMAH (guitar) TONY FRIEL (bass), DAVE (drums)

LINE-UP #2 (June-Dec 1977): MARK E SMITH (vocals), MARTIN BRAMAH (guitar) TONY FRIEL (bass), UNA BAINES (keyboards), KARL BURNS (drums)

(STUDIO) Summer 1977
7701. Dresden Dolls
7702. Industrial Estate
7703. Psycho Mafia
ORIGINAL RELEASE: Total Eclipse DRD 1 (7-inch) undated
COMMENTS: The earliest known Fall recording comprises a rough rehearsal tape that crept out on a bootleg single a few years later; 'Dresden Dolls' then reappeared on the 1994 *Backdrop* compilation bootleg. Apparently recorded in Smith's living room (an irate neighbour banging to complain about the noise is readily apparent), a slovenly-sounding Fall clatter behind a Smith sneer that's closer to the 'Punk' ideal than anyone would thank you for noticing. Awkwardly noticeable, too, is the ghost of Siouxsie and the Banshees that hangs none too complimentarily over the insistently stop-start arrangement: 1977 was the height of the Banshees' perceived flirtation with Nazi chic and, whether 'Dresden Dolls' was intended as support, condemnation or merely observation, the linkage really isn't too far a stretch.

(LIVE) October 2, 1977, Electric Circus, Manchester.
7704. Stepping Out
7705. Last Orders
UNR. remainder of set unknown
ORIGINAL RELEASE: various artists live album *Short Circuit: Live at the Electric Circus*: Virgin VCL5003 (10-inch LP) April 1978.
REISSUE: Virgin CDVCL 5003 (CD)
COMMENTS: Poorly conceived, badly recorded and messily sequenced, *Short Circuit* is another in the long line of *One Night At The Wherever*-type live albums that the majors threw at the Punk audience during 1977-78, in the hope of emulating the success of the original *Live At The Roxy*. But the Roxy album worked because at least half of the bands actually meant something to some folk, and would go on to mean a lot more to many. Buying it meant buying into a musical adventure that was still to reach its peak.

Subsequent sets, honouring such stately piles as the Hope & Anchor, the Vortex, the Roxy (again) and, now, the Electric Circus, could not make the same connection – either you already knew who the bands involved were, or you'd already decided you didn't care. *Short Circuit*, with its Mancunian meld of Punk, pop and poetry interrupted amidships by Brummie reggae band Steel Pulse, would subsequently achieve a form of immortality (and modern-day collectibility) thanks to its discriminating inclusion of the very early Joy Division, but only for as long as it took to play their contribution. Like everybody else in this shoddy shop window, they would never sound so bad again.

With two songs on the eight-track album, the Fall's fall from grace is even more pronounced, providing twice as many reasons *not* to go and see them as the Drones or the Buzzcocks supplied. The opening 'Stepping Out' is the murky merging of two scratchy rhythms – bass and a Wire-y guitar – over which Smith's yowling vocal is little more than a repetitive irritant. 'Last Orders' is better, although Karl Burns' drums are higher in the mix than they need be and fussier than you could want, subverting the Modern Lover-ish keyboards and guitar interplay beneath the neat co-ordination of a western front barrage. On this evidence, it would be astonishing if the band lasted another 25 minutes. 25 years is completely inconceivable.

(STUDIO) November 9, 1977
    7706. Bingo Master's Breakout
    7707. Psycho Mafia
    7708. Repetition
    UNR: Frightened
    ORIGINAL RELEASE: *Bingo Master's Break-out* EP, Step Forward SF7 (7-inch) August 1978
    COMMENTS: The Fall's first single would be close to a year old by the time it was released, and still it represented a blur of demented adrenalin that leaves one breathless, no matter how many times the opening flagship, 'Bingo Master's Breakout', has turned up on cheapo compilation albums. 'Excuse me while I get up off the floor,' begged *Melody Maker*'s Colin Irwin. 'This is amazing. A Manchester band with the musical intensity of Suicide, coupled with a truly inspired feel for the quirky.'

It was, in the light of the next 25 years' worth of press commentary, a key observation. The urgency with which the recursive riot of Smith's lyrical imagery has been transcribed and analysed has consistently overwhelmed his equally (and, perhaps, more important) talent for harnessing cadences that, in other hands, might easily fall flat.

It is a talent that has allowed the Fall to continue moving forward throughout their career; one that has prevented them from ever sitting comfortably within any of the multitude of musical genres and fashions that have risen up alongside them. But, most crucially, it is the one that separates them from the myriad bands that declare them an influence, yet whose own music is concerned more with the cacophony that exists on the surface of the Fall, than with the melodies, tunings, rhythms and manipulations that lie beneath.

As late as 1992, in an interview with *Volume*, Smith was insisting, 'The only thing that keeps me going is I want to put things in rock music that aren't there. I don't think a guitar's even been explored yet. Or a bass, or a drum kit. Or vocals. Everybody seems to play it safe. I fuckin' went into it blind, man, I'm telling you.'

In 1977-78, little of this ambition was evident: one heard the Fall and they offered just one more spastic riff-twitch in a sea of the things. Only when one stood back was anything more apparent: in 1982, 'Bingo Master's Breakout' was included on one of the earliest of all Punk anthologies, Cherry Red's *Burning Ambitions*. There, amid a plethora of prime movers (the song falls between the Buzzcocks' 'Boredom' and Wire's '12XU'), the Fall slur, lurch and ultimately explode with an unconscious ferocity that is as jarring as it is exhilarating. Hindsight confirms that, even from the outset, the Fall were for life, not for Christmas.

Go back, then and flip the original single. Echoey and churning, 'Psycho Mafia' was a condemnation 'of the way mental hospitals are run... the psycho mafia is a chemical Mafia.' It's a powerful performance. Best of all, though, was the lazy, hypnotic 'Repetition', the band's set-closing statement of intent and a number that was capable of simply drawing out forever. On record, it lasted just five minutes, but from Smith's opening demand for 'white noise' on through the second-son-of-'Sister Ray' mantra that drifted round and round beneath his half-demented, half-Devoto yowl, and on to the invocation of a 'Blank Generation' that really shouldn't be too pleased at finding itself included here, time could easily stand still.

(LIVE) Dec 23 1977, Stretford Civic Centre
    7709. Psycho Mafia
    7710. Last Orders
    7711. Repetition
    7712. Dresden Dolls
    7713. Hey! Fascist
    7714. Frightened
    7715. Industrial Estate
    7716. Stepping Out
    7717. Bingo Master's Breakout
    7718. Oh Brother
    7719. Copped It
    7720. Futures and Pasts
    7721. Louie Louie – featuring JOHN THE POSTMAN.
    ORIGINAL RELEASE: *Live '77*: Cog Sinister COGVP114CD (CD) 2000
    COMMENTS: *Live 77* is a fascinating document, the only readily available source for several of the Fall's earliest songs which presents an eagle's-eye view of the perils of playing live at the height of Punk. Cries of 'you immature bastards' do nothing to halt the hail of gob raining down on the band. The sense of confrontation between musicians and onlookers is palpable. Visceral versions of 'Oh Brother', 'Copped It' and the bare bones of 'Hey! Student', 'Hey! Fascist', are also fascinating: it would be several years before the Fall would record studio versions.

Unfortunately, if high fidelity is your main concern, this is one to avoid. While the show itself has some historical interest as Tony Friel's final appearance with the Fall and the performance is executed with all the dismissive flair and aggression for which the early Fall were renowned, the sound quality is such that listening to the actual disc is an experience best reserved for wrapping up those parties when the guests refuse to leave.

1978

'Harsh, commendably unadorned; at present undeveloped. Torn between moral resolve and the paraphernalia of a medium which they ultimately despise, [the Fall] could prove – with ATV and the Slits – to be strict fulfilment of the original promise and premises of New Wave' – NME Book of Modern Music, *1978*.

An early 1978 press communiqué from Smith sums up everything else that the Fall represented. 'Despite [our] "reputation", [we've been] struggling for a year – we don't dig promoters, backhanders, publicity (bought that is), backers, agents etc. Our aims vary – we would like to be self-sufficient and alter the DNA of the nervous system (you did ask us to write what we liked!). We are opposed to compromise, fascists, rich revolutionaries and cars. Our message is not contrived nor preached, it just comes out that way! We think 90% of the New Wave is crap, though we don't like to adopt a superior attitude. A lot of the bands who fancy themselves as "alternative" are developing. No offence, but the bulk of the vinyl shit seems to come out of London. The Pistols are OK – especially McLaren's great pisstake of the media.

'Success, Una'd hate it, Martin ignore it and Karl think it shit hot. We are managed by Kay Carroll who feels insignificant amongst those "hypnotic merry innovators" and whose main aim is to fend off bullshitters.'

Even to industry figures who'd finally got a handle on these safety-pinned snotnoses who called themselves Punk Rockers, it was the Manifesto from Hell, the self-obsessive pronouncements of a band who really were as awful as the rest of the Punk pack pretended to be. Indeed, Punks themselves weren't too sure about the Fall, especially when it became painfully obvious that the misgivings were mutual.

For all its earlier protestations of amateurism and enthusiasm, Punk grew up to be no less tied to some ungodly (and certainly impractical) principle of musicianship as any of its horse-headed proggy predecessors: wasn't it the Punk community which rounded on Sex Pistols' bassist Sid Vicious, accusing him of not being able to tune his own instrument? The Fall never quite entered that particular trough, but still there was a sizeable gulf between their concept of a well-played number, and that of the increasingly volatile audiences they were now facing.

The departed Tony Friel was replaced by Johnnie Brown, just three days before the Fall's next show, in Huddersfield in late January 1978, the opening night of a misfit tour with the Doll, the Prefects and Sham 69.

It was a fraught occasion, as the Doll's Christos Yianni subsequently recalled. No sooner had his band – scheduled to appear immediately before the bill-topping Sham – arrived at the venue than 'we walked straight into a row. Mark was strutting around like a major rock star, very obnoxious and very, very pissed. Basically his attitude was, "We're the Fall. We're the local boys. We're the stars up here. We should be second on the bill."' He wouldn't drop his demands, even after the headliners' Jimmy Pursey joined the debate. Pursey finally decided to give him what he wanted. Sham would play before anybody else, effectively bumping the rest of the bill up one notch – and offering a nice early night to anyone who was there just to see the headliners. So the Fall were second on the bill after all. But the Doll were still on after them.

Not that it did them any good. Despite Smith's protestations of local stardom, the Fall's performance fell on the stony ground you'd expect an audience raised on Sham to be treading, as Danny Baker recorded in *Zig Zag*: 'The effect of a five-piece playing quirky, cutting, fuck it, INTERESTING ten minute songs was, as far as Oooodersfeeld was concerned, farting in class.' Not until it came time to introduce the band did Smith finally crack a smile from the crowd. 'Let me introduce you to our new bass player,' he announced. 'He's from Yorkshire. And I am a patronising creep who will go to any lengths to win an audience.'

The ever-supportive Buzzcocks notwithstanding, gigs with the so-called Punk elite were never among the Fall's favourite outings. While other bands were already forging the identities that would come to haunt them, the uniforms and imagery that could sum them up in a glance, the Fall remained determinedly nonplussed by the attendant circus.

Their self-sufficiency led to some memorable verbal confrontations. Siouxsie and the Banshees' manager Nils Stevenson recalled, 'We loved playing with the Fall, because they didn't take any of it seriously. They were very serious about their music but, whereas other bands would dress up for the stage, and audiences would dress up to watch them, the Fall would dress down. They'd come out in pullovers and corduroys, it was the ultimate role-reversal. The audience would all be dressed like a band; the band would be dressed like an audience. And the big insult was to call someone an art student. Anyone who dressed up, the Fall would call them art students. They were great.'

Julian Cope, in 1978 merely one of the Liverpool crowd who would turn out to see the band whenever they played locally, agreed. 'Mark Smith was right. Get your V-necked sweater on.' That year, Cope averred, he saw the band play 28 times, usually in the company of friends Ian McCulloch and Dave Pickett. He recalled in his *Head On* memoir, 'The Fall shot through us all. But not like they hit [McCulloch, Pickett and I]. We were goners. They didn't even have records out. You had to see them live to hear them... and that was the brilliance of Mark E Smith. His proximity.'

For a time, Cope and Smith were regular correspondents. '[Smith's] girlfriend Kay [Carroll] writes hippy poems at the end of his letters. He addresses me "Dear Jules Verne".' Smith's view of his starry-eyed young acolyte would change: he once described the Teardrop Explodes as 'fucking escapist crap'. For now, however, Cope admitted, 'McCull and I were in awe of Mark... and he pulled a lot of shit out of us that we were scared of with the others. All the uncool thoughts you'd have, he'd say. With hindsight, I'll say that the main reason anything started to happen was because of Mark. He had very shamanistic qualities, a particular ability to draw the best from people.'

The Fall's line-up remained unstable throughout the first half of 1978. Having contributed what would become the sleeve design for the Fall's first single, 'Bingo Master's Break-out', Jonnie Brown had by now faded away; so, after a similarly brief spell, had such replacements as Eric (ex-John Cooper Clarke's Curious Yellows) and a character that the Fall's 16-year-old roadie Marc Riley remembers only as 'an oily little beast called Ferret.' Gone, too, was Una Baines, edged – willingly or otherwise – from the Fall by Smith's relationship with Carroll, and his increasingly firm grip on the band's lyrical content. She moved onto a new band of her own, the Blue Orchids, to be replaced in the Fall by arch-Nico fan Yvonne Pawlett.

Despite such turbulence, the Fall continued turning heads in high places. In May, they appeared on Manchester television's *So It Goes*, performing 'Psycho Mafia' and 'Industrial Estate'. The same month, they made their debut on the John Peel show, after producer John Walters caught them supporting Siouxsie and the Banshees at the Croydon Underground.

Yet, for all the plaudits raining down on them, the band remained unsigned, seemingly unsignable. They nearly lost their first chance of scoring on vinyl: when Virgin delivered the contracts for the *Short Circuit* album, they were promptly accused of trying to short-change the band. Carroll returned the paperwork unsigned. Either the Fall were offered the same deal as the Buzzcocks, or they wouldn't be appearing on the album at all. They got their way.

But still, to a music industry which remained locked into the practices of the pre-Punk (and, in some cases, pre-rock'n'roll) era, bewildered by the ever-changing succession of critical favourites, the Fall were simply one more in a long line of acts awaiting inspection. Even Peel's patronage was no indication of quality or craft. Of the bands aired in session over the previous couple of months, who cared half a hoot for the White Cats, the Smirks, the Crabs, the Zones or the Hits? The long-awaited release of *Short Circuit* offered little more than a muddy rumble that may or may not have resolved into something of more commercial value. A handful of labels went to look at the Fall, all of them passed.

The Fall themselves all but abandoned any hope of securing a record deal – the latest plan was to issue the months-old Indigo Studios tape themselves. Elsewhere, however, eternal cheerleader Danny Baker was still hard at work, nudging Illegal Records head Miles Copeland to give the band a go. He had three imprint labels on the boil at the time: Step Forward, Illegal and Deptford Fun City. Surely there was room on one of them for the Fall? (Years later, when Baker laid claim to 'inventing' the Fall in an *NME* article, Smith mailed him his share of the earnings – a 10p piece.)

Like so many others, Copeland was not initially convinced, although the fact that the band had already recorded its first release surely helped sway him. Though the Fall themselves knew that it scarcely represented the sound of the band in summer '78, August 11 saw Step Forward release three tracks from the previous autumn's four-track tape, opening with the now-seminal 'Bingo Master's Breakout'.

It was an intriguing release, the vinyl confirming the Fall's distance from everything else in the Punk spectrum let alone their newfound labelmates, the traditional Punk postures of Chelsea, the Cortinas, the Models and the early Sham 69. Indeed, it was a field which Smith felt no compunction whatsoever about slamming.

'The new wave is a sell-out. I mean, compared to the old wave, it's all so tame what they actually do.' He invoked the names of his own musical heroes, and suggested that there was no comparing what Captain Beefheart, the Velvets and Dylan had accomplished in their heyday with the one-dimensional scratch'n'riffing of the Punk parade. Soon, the Fall were saddled with another attractive tag. They were the 'Henry Cow of the New Wave'.

With the problematic empty bass space finally filled by the promotion of roadie Marc Riley, the Fall played their biggest show yet on August 20, joining Penetration, Punishment of Luxury and fellow Mancunian Ed Banger on one of the London Lyceum's Sunday night Punk parades. On September 8, they headlined the Marquee for the first time and, a fortnight later, Step Forward sent them out to play a couple of shows with Chelsea, including a tremendous performance at London's Music Machine.

Poised on the brink of the venue's then-infamous over-head-height stage, gazing down on the faces that strained upwards to see him, Smith seemed imperious, imperial. He knew he'd be antagonizing the audience with a live set that disdained any reference to the newly released EP, but he went ahead all the same, swatting aside cries for 'Repetition' and 'Bingo Master' with palpable disinterest. He'd leave the golden oldies to the headliners.

The contrast between the Fall and what passed, especially in the provinces, for 'Punk Rock' could not have been more pronounced, but it wasn't an act. So many bands, over the years, have affected disdain for their audience – the Fall didn't do that. Indeed, if anything, they went the other way entirely, viewing the audience with *too much* respect – certainly crediting it with too much intelligence. It seemed beyond Smith's comprehension that the serried ranks of identi-Punks arrayed before him on a nightly basis did not share the Fall's belief that they were being taken for a fashion-frenzied ride; it never occurred to him that herds maybe form because they enjoy being a herd.

Early in 1979, analysing the fall-out from another bout of intensive Fall shock treatment, *NME*'s Charles Shaar Murray mused, 'The Pistols could be incredibly comforting if you identified yourself with their threat rather than their targets: "Yeah! We're all Punks together! Bugger the Queen!" This response is not possible with the Fall. [They] are not comforting in the way that even the most bad-ass conventional rock act is.'

And why? Because 'comfort' was the last thing the Fall believed their audience needed. Writing in *Melody Maker* at the end of the year, journalist Oliver Lowenstein elaborated, '[Smith's] movements and expressions give his thoughts away, the sham of the spectacle, a disillusion that people can still believe in the shamanism the stage provides.'

Smith shrugged off such philosophising. 'We could go out with a set of stuff we've recorded and go down a storm. But we don't wanna do that. Nobody's got a right to lay that on us. Every band does it and it's the death of every band. We don't wanna die like that.'

He would not change, no matter how many times his faith took a beating. James Stevenson, mercurial guitarist with Chelsea throughout the years of their most savage import, remembers 'Mark walking around Miles [Copeland]'s office, offering everyone a swig out of his carton of orange. Didn't he know beer was the rock and roll staple?'

Yes, he probably did.

If the Fall found any soulmates on the scene, they were those that existed, similarly, far from the madding crowd: former *Sniffin' Glue* fanzine editor Mark Perry's Good Missionaries successor to the earlier ATV; Wilful Damage, described by Smith himself as 'the only Manchester band doing anything positive once they drop Punk influence. Come across like the best of The Worst with touch of Zappa and rock'n'roll'; and Here and Now, a loose aggregation of musicians, misfits and madmen put together by ex-Gong maestro Daevid Allen.

The Fall first came into contact with Here and Now when the two bands were booked to appear at that summer's week-long Deeplyvale Free Festival, with the Fall joining Durutti Column, the Ruts, reggae band Misty In Roots, Wilful Damage and a clutch of other local talent on the Saturday's New Wave Afternoon. Compered by *So It Goes* TV host Tony Wilson, their share of the event attracted around 10,000 fans (headliner Steve Hillage played to twice as many), the biggest audience the Fall had yet appeared before, and one of the most enthusiastic.

The band had barely left the stage before they were agreeing to join Here and Now on their own tour, a series of free indoor concerts, with expenses covered by donations and passing the hat. Chris Hewitt, one of the crew on the tour (and now head of Ozit Records), recalls two shows with especial fondness, at Salford University and The Tower Club in Oldham: 'I seem to remember another date with The Fall and The Smirks and China Street at New Planet City in Lancaster.'

That outing completed, work began on the bellicose clatter and chilled experimentation of what would become their debut album, *Live At The Witch Trials*, recorded and mixed in two furious days in late November with producer Bob Sergeant. A new single had already emerged, 'It's The New Thing', but it would not be appearing on the album: not just because 'we wanted to... get out all the stuff we can't do as singles.' It wouldn't really have fit.

The gigs continued, too – so many that, by Christmas, the band members were finally able to sign off the dole and reward themselves with a salary of ten pounds a week. Most of these shows took place in the north, on the Manchester/Liverpool axis that was fast establishing itself as an alternative to the increasingly disgraced London circuit. But the capital proved irresistible. On November 27, the Fall returned to the BBC's Maida Vale complex to record their second Peel session; three weeks later, they were back to headline the Marquee with a live show dominated by the imminent *Live At The Witch Trials*, but tenderly taking the audience back a few months, with a rare airing for the now-veteran 'Stepping Out' – and a dishevelled 'Psycho Mafia' too.

Tapes of the occasion are revealing. After so much had been said about the band's stubborn charmlessness, after all the media snipes and outsiders' gripes that the band courted opprobrium, the Fall were welcomed on stage like conquering heroes – and fêted ever more wildly as the evening wore on. The Punk cognoscenti might have regarded them as a band of outsiders. But at least they were breathing fresh air.

(MUSICIANS)

LINE-UP #3 (live only, Jan – spring 1978): MARK E SMITH (vocals), MARTIN BRAMAH (guitar) JOHNNIE BROWN (bass), UNA BAINES (keyboards), KARL BURNS (drums)

LINE-UP #4 (live, John Peel, spring/summer 1978): MARK E SMITH (vocals), MARTIN BRAMAH (guitar, bass), YVONNE PAWLETT (keyboards), KARL BURNS (drums), STEVE DAVIS (congas)

LINE-UP #5 (live only, spring 1978): MARK E SMITH (vocals), MARTIN BRAMAH (guitar) ERIC ? (bass – replaced by Ferret?), YVONNE PAWLETT (keyboards), KARL BURNS (drums)

LINE-UP #6 (remainder of year) MARK E SMITH (vocals), MARTIN BRAMAH (guitar) MARC RILEY (bass), YVONNE PAWLETT (keyboards), KARL BURNS (drums)

(ALBUM) *John The Postman's Puerile* by JOHN THE POSTMAN
7801. Louie Louie
ORIGINAL RELEASE: Bent Records BB2 (LP) March 1978
REISSUE: Overground OVER 72 (CD) 1999
COMMENTS: The legendary Postman's debut mini-LP was recorded in February 1978, and discreetly released wrapped a brown paper bag. Half a dozen tracks included two versions of the Postman's signature disembowelling of 'Louie, Louie', plus similarly irreverent stabs at the Stooges' 'Not Right' and the Postman's own 'Kawalski Of The Seaview Has Got The Best Hairstyle I've Ever Seen', 'Flaming Aeroplane' and 'PJ Meets TD'. Best described as a chaotic cousin to former Frank Zappa protégé Wild Man Fischer (one of the Postman's own heroes), largely involving non-musician friends, it is nevertheless an historic release. With the release of *Short Circuit* still three months away, the introduction to the first 'Louie Louie' represents Mark E Smith's first appearance on vinyl.
   Of incidental note, the Postman's second album, 1979's *Steppin' Out (Of Holt's Brewery)* was titled at least partially in tribute to his favourite Fall song.

(BBC SESSION) 15 June, 1978
7802. Rebellious Jukebox
ORIGINAL RELEASE: *The Peel Sessions* (1998)
COMMENTS: see appendix I/BBC sessions

(LIVE) August 22 1978, Mr Pickwick's, Liverpool
7803. Like to Blow
7804. Stepping Out
7805. Two Steps Back
7806. Mess of My
7807. It's the New Thing
7808. Various Times
7809. Bingo Master's Breakout
7810. Frightened
7811. Industrial Estate
7812. Psycho Mafia
7813. Music Scene
7814. Mother – Sister!
ORIGINAL RELEASE: *Live In Liverpool '78*: Cog Sinister COGVP118CD (CD) 2001

COMMENTS: The Fall were regular visitors to Liverpool at this time. Between November 18th 1977 and November 8th 1979, they played the city at least nine times, usually touching down at the now-legendary Eric's. It is their appearance at Mr Pickwick's, however, that lives on, courtesy of a bootleg cassette purchased at a street market and mastered to CD for this archaeological treasure.

The performance itself smokes, with Mark E in dynamic (if somewhat incoherent) form throughout, while the set offers a fair representation of the band's then-current repertoire. (Just one song from this period, 'My Condition', remains officially unreleased.) Liverpool provides the ideal surrounding for the performance of 'Two Steps Back' – the Julian namechecked in the song was future Teardrop Explodes mainman Julian Cope. 'I was pleased as hell,' Cope reflected.

Unfortunately, the sound quality is distinctly lacking in listenability. The audience is more prominent than the band. After a few minutes, listening to a distant rumble interspersed with a booming rant loses even its academic interest.

(SINGLE) It's the New Thing
    7815. It's The New Thing
    7816. Various Times
    ORIGINAL RELEASE: Step Forward SF9 (7-inch) November 1978
    COMMENTS: Recorded earlier in the autumn, the vaguely autobiographical 'It's The New Thing' was a hasty concoction, leading with a childishly Christmassy keyboard line while the band raged more or less incoherently around it. It was certainly arresting, though, especially once one unscrambled Smith's purposefully incoherent lyric into a discussion of the Fall's own *modus operandi*, crossed with a bandwagon-berating condemnation on the current scene ('the Worst died for you').

Coming from a similarly understated place as early Joy Division, rhythm and vocal merging into an almost poetic whole, 'Various Times' was an exercise – as were many of Smith's early writings – not in condemning a problem, but in musing upon where (and, more importantly, how) it might have arisen. The wry comparison between anti-Semitism in pre-Holocaust Germany and racism in modern Britain is laboured but powerful, a chilling number that reminds us that the Punk-era battle cries of 'young and broke and on the dole... no future' weren't simply the hollow headlines of tabloid tattle. Not always, anyway.

(BBC SESSION) December 6, 1978
    7817. Put Away
    7818. Mess Of My
    7819. No Xmas For John Quays
    7820. Like To Blow
    ORIGINAL RELEASE: Strange Fruit SFPS 028 (12-inch) May 1987
    COMMENTS: see appendix I/BBC sessions
    UK INDIE CHART PEAK: #3

1979

As Smith liked to say of the Fall themselves, reviews of *Live at the Witch Trials* – released in January 1979 – were predictably unpredictable. But he probably expected the papers to slam it. Instead, they praised it high.

'Crash! Smash!' announced the *NME* summary. 'It's The Fall. The missing link between The Doors and Spherical Objects (sound), the Velvet Underground and O Level (vision). The accessible face of modernistic pop. Not quite in the mainstream, not very far away. You can dance to it and pretend it's avant-garde. Mark Smith knows; "Eggheads and Boneheads queue".'

Record Mirror was on the ball, too, despite Chris Westwood's admission that 'the Fall's erratic complacency at the recent [March 1st] Nashville gig worried and angered me. [But,] if they have the ability to move on, side-stepping that dour, dire formularisation syndrome, capitalising on the excellence of this vinyl statement, the future will be optimistic. People acquainted with them will not be bemused, startled or surprised by this record; they will, instead, accept and love it. *Witch Trials* is not brilliant, revolutionary, activist, radical. It is complete and representative, and good.'

What Westwood didn't know, as he viewed that Nashville show, was the root of that 'dour, dire formularisation,' the chaotic struggle that was ripping the last elements of the founding Fall line-up asunder. Though the group would continue to tour intensely over the next couple of months, by early May both Martin Bramah and Karl Burns would have departed, leaving Smith to redesign the Fall around two members of the Nashville night's support band, Staff 9, Steve Hanley and Craig Scanlon, themselves former bandmates of Marc Riley in the Sirens.

Burns was out first, to be replaced by Mike Leigh in February, and it was that which precipitated Bramah's departure. Leigh was a very different drummer to his predecessor: in Smith's words, '[a] big sort of chubby Teddy Boy who used to stand up and never play his bass drum. People in the audience wanted to kill him!' But, 'he plays his drums, he doesn't knock shit out of them.'

Leigh also possessed what, in Fall terms, might have been considered an unconventional background, a past spent languishing in a string of rock'n'roll revival bands. Now he found himself pounding his way through the last days of the dying empire – a sequence of gigs that were almost uniformly uncomfortable, with the low point coming on March 25th, at the London Lyceum's unfortunately named Gig of the Century.

Sharing a bill with Stiff Little Fingers, the Gang Of 4, the Human League, the Mekons and Mark Perry's Good Missionaries, it was the Fall's chance to measure just how close they had come to dispatching the 'difficult' tag, to measure themselves against an audience gathered for what *NME*'s Charles Shaar Murray belatedly, but accurately, described as 'a Clash-surrogate late seventies Punk gig.' They came up shorter than short.

A month earlier, opening for Generation X at the same venue, the Fall came close to igniting a riot when they reacted to a can-throwing onlooker by throwing the cans right back at him. Tonight, the debris started flying before they'd even begun playing – followed, while the opening 'A Figure Walks' was still taking shape, by the phantom can-chucker from the previous gig: he leapt onstage to pound Smith with his fists. By the time the performance was over, even the most optimistic Fall fan (a few were present) knew there'd be no curtain call: the Fall were the only band on the bill who wouldn't be playing an encore. Which was a shame because, as Murray concluded, 'They were the band who deserved one the most.' Live at the witch trials, indeed.

'The witch trial is very relevant to me,' Smith told the *NME* the following day. 'The witch trials got rid of all the creative people and I think that's why you get people like they are now, because their culture is taken away from them, they're smashed down. It's not so much that we're persecuted, but we are part of that voice. And there are a lot of people – like that psycho last night – who think the Fall should not be allowed to exist, which is ridiculous. I can understand anyone not liking the music – it grates on me now and again. But to say "you can't do it" is wrong.'

Martin Bramah left in early May, forcing the cancellation of a handful of shows while new members Hanley and Scanlon settled in. With Hanley taking over bass duties, and Scanlon joining Riley in a vicious two-guitar commando raid, the Fall resumed action in Aberdeen on May 9.

Leigh, at least, regretted the recent rupture. 'Martin... was a great guitarist,' he told Cambridge fanzine *Harsh Reality*. 'He really worked well with Marc Riley. He's gone and got a bloody hippy band together now!' In fact, he fled to Una Baines' Blue Orchids, as they commenced their own admittedly Fall-like, but nevertheless defiantly individual, assault.

The new line-up gelled quickly. Supported by Ian McCulloch and the infant Echo and the Bunnymen, fervent Fall cheerleaders in their own early interviews, the Fall played Manchester's newly opened Factory in July and were promptly proclaimed, by *Melody Maker*, to have attained 'their zenith' – a plateau that was promptly revisited when the Fall appeared alongside Joy Division and the young Mick Hucknall's Frantic Elevators as headline attractions at the Manchester Mayflower club's *Stuff the Superstars Funhouse Special Festival*, at the end of month.

July also brought the Fall's third single, the compulsive 'Rowche Rumble (Look At What The People Around You Are Taking)'. It scored magnificent reviews but, once again, the release was a deceptive feint. Weeks after recording 'Rowche Rumble', but just days before the Fall were due to begin work on their second album with producer (and Here And Now mainstay) Grant Cunliffe, Pawlett quit by simply failing to turn up at the band's Marquee gig in August. Smith scarcely shrugged.

'Musicians go cranky once they get around a bit,' he told the Stevenage-based *V-Sign* fanzine in the New Year. '[They] start believing everything that's written about them: "I am a musician and I quit".' One thing he'd learned since forming the band was, 'it's not just the biz that fucks music up, but also the musicians. I have seen much stupidity and lost most of my faith in human nature...'

With Riley taking over keyboard duties in the studio, the Fall opted not to replace Pawlett as *Dragnet* was hauled into shape. By the time the group played the first Futurama festival in Leeds in September, new material was already squeezing older songs out of the live show, although Futurama itself saw the group at least nodding towards a friendlier reputation, with a set that at least one onlooker recalled as 'the greatest hits show you never imagined you'd see.'

The Fall were not the headliners. In the months since the release of their own *Unknown Pleasures* debut album, the Artists Formerly Known As Warsaw had streaked as far ahead in the public eye as the Fall once stretched the critical gaze. Joy Division closed the first night, space rock veterans Hawkwind, enjoying a new lease of life as parents of a neo-psychedelic strand of Punkoid offspring, headlined the second; lurking elsewhere on the billing were Cabaret Voltaire, the Expelaires, Orchestral Manoeuvres In The Dark and Public Image Ltd, playing their fifth-ever live show.

Joy Division triumphed over all-comers on the Saturday, but the Fall certainly swept the board the following evening, at least so far as Smith was concerned. 'We were the only band who did something different with each song, the others were "brrr-stop-clap-thankyou".' He admitted, however, that the audience for the Fall was one of the smallest of the day. '[We got] one tenth of an audience,' he told *NME* in the New Year. 'The rest were watching Hawkwind's gear being set up.' It was at Futurama, incidentally, that the band first encountered Rough Trade head Geoff Travis, soon to lure the band away from Step Forward to his own label.

Futurama was not the band's only festival appearance that summer. They also returned to Deeplyvale, appearing alongside the Frantic Elevators, the Fast Cars, Here & Now, Spizz Energi, the Ruts and Misty in Roots. But the Fall's love affair with free concerts was fast coming to a close. 'I think Here & Now do free gigs 'cos nobody'd pay to see them,' Smith told *V-Sign*. 'Also, why should we be the only ones penniless at end of night? Rip-off clubs LOVE free gigs as they save on staff, don't have to give band anything and make a fortune on the bar. Also, like a lot of the new wave and hippy movements, it means that only kids with loads of dough from mum and dad, or jobs, can get up and play OR form their own record label. I get 15 [quid] a week which must be 50% lower wage than the majority of my audience.'

The Fall gigged constantly around the UK to mark the October release of *Dragnet*, playing no less than five London shows in the space of a month. It was an intensive schedule, but with good reason. The end of November would see the Fall making their first visit to the USA.

An American himself, Step Forward label chief Miles Copeland had first started touring the British new wave through America the previous year. Among the immediate family from his own labels, Squeeze, Chelsea and the Police were all veterans of his trans-Atlantic ambitions, with the latter (featuring Copeland's little brother, Stewart) reaping the rewards with a Stateside status that absolutely dwarfed any headway they'd made in their homeland.

Whether or not the Fall were ripe for a similar breakthrough was not necessarily the issue. With another brother, Ian, manning the booking agency side of things, the Copelands were empire-building, creating a profile that would, within a few short years, see them holding great swathes of America's own new wave scene in their hand.

The Fall tour did not exactly hit the heights. Opening in rural Cherry Hill, New Jersey, the band's van made the short skip down to Philadelphia, then doubled back for shows in New York and Boston, before everybody boarded a flight for the west coast and a handful of shows around Los Angeles.

Of those concerts that they headlined in their own right, none were well attended, few drew anything more than a handful – sometimes literally – of curious locals, who knew the Fall's name simply from the English inkies they imported every week. The New York show, staged with grand bravado at the Palladium, was well-enough received. *NME*'s New York-based Richard Grabel described the performance as 'effortlessly, automatically revolutionary.' But, according to American journalist Jo-Ann Greene, the Boston show – which, strictly speaking, took place in neighbouring Cambridge, at a venue scarcely renowned for anything other than bar band fare – saw no more than two dozen onlookers. That figure included bar staff.

A breakdown in the band's financial arrangements added to their difficulties, although it wasn't simply the locals' lack of familiarity with the Fall that was disappointing. One of the most overworked clichés in music journalism is that, no matter how much America might love English music, Americans have a very hard time understanding it – that's the reason why, for every hard rockin' Brit butt-kicker who stuffs the country's stadia, there's a dozen cerebral satirists drowning in their pretzel-strewn wake.

So far, Copeland had enjoyed a remarkable run of success, as the ultra-cuddly Police and Squeeze laid the groundwork for subsequent stardom, and Chelsea at least appealed to everyone who'd read about Punk Rock. But even English audiences had a hard time dealing with the Fall. America, paying good money to see a band that didn't think twice about repeating songs they'd already played with a singer who habitually turned his back on the crowd while spewing forth impenetrably accented colloquialisms during and in-between songs, didn't stand a chance.

That said, the audiences that did understand *really* understood. 'I thought it was great,' Smith reflected a year later, 'I think the Fall stand more chance over there – we were getting really good support. And we nearly sell as much in America as we do over here, and we get loads of mail. Y'see, the thing about America is that their scene's so crappy that, when they do see something pretty different, it filters through the crap.'

Nevertheless, opening for local heroes X and the Germs at the sweat and blood-filled pressure cooker of Los Angeles' Hope Street Hall on December 14th was difficult. The word 'mismatch' barely describes the cultural distance between Mancunian rage and California nihilism but 'furious' is perfect for an audience which has just realised that you can't pogo to 'No Xmas for John Quays'. It was with undisguised relief that the band left the venue as soon as they'd completed their allotted slot for the last stand of their American adventure, at the Anti-Club later that same evening. In later years, Marc Riley would describe that particular performance as his favourite ever Fall gig. After what he'd been through earlier in the evening, it probably was.

(MUSICIANS)

LINE-UP #6 (Jan-Feb) MARK E SMITH (vocals), MARTIN BRAMAH (guitar) MARC RILEY (bass), YVONNE PAWLETT (keyboards), KARL BURNS (drums)

LINE-UP #7 (Feb-May) MARK E SMITH (vocals), MARTIN BRAMAH (guitar) MARC RILEY (bass), YVONNE PAWLETT (keyboards), MIKE LEIGH (drums)

LINE-UP #8 (June-May) MARK E SMITH (vocals), MARC RILEY (guitar), YVONNE PAWLETT (keyboards), CRAIG SCANLON (guitar), STEVE HANLEY (bass), MIKE LEIGH (drums)

LINE-UP #9 (remainder) MARK E SMITH (vocals), MARC RILEY (guitar, keyboards), CRAIG SCANLON (guitar), STEVE HANLEY (bass), MIKE LEIGH (drums)

(ALBUM) *Live At The Witch Trials*
 7901. Frightened
 7902. Crap Rap 2
 7903. Like to Blow
 7904. Rebellious Jukebox
 7905. No Xmas for John Quays
 7906. Mother – Sister!
 7907. Industrial Estate
 7908. Underground Medecin
 7909. Two Steps Back
 7910. Live at the Witch Trials
 7911. Futures and Pasts
 7912. Music Scene
 (*) BONUS TRACKS
 7706. Bingo Master's Breakout
 7707. Psycho Mafia
 7708. Repetition
 ORIGINAL RELEASE: Step Forward SFLP1 (LP) January 1979
 REISSUE (1): IRS SFLPCD1 (CD), SFLP1 (LP) 1989
 REISSUE (2): Cog Sinister COGVP103CD (CD) 1997
 REISSUE (3): Turning Point TPM02208 (LP) 2002
 REISSUE (4): Cog Sinister COGVP138CD (CD) 2002 with bonus tracks (*)

(ALBUM) *Live At The Witch Trials* (USA edition)
 7901. Frightened
 7902. Crap Rap 2
 7903. Like to Blow
 7904. Rebellious Jukebox
 7905. No Xmas for John Quays
 7816. Various Times
 7908. Underground Medecin

7909. Two Steps Back
7910. Live at the Witch Trials
7911. Futures and Pasts
7912. Music Scene
ORIGINAL RELEASE: A&M SP 003 (LP) 1979
COMMENTS: As uncompromising as early Fall gigs were – in terms of both presentation and perception – *Live At The Witch Trials* offered little respite from the band's reputation. The absence of the band's singles-to-date was only the first step towards a work of utter dislocation, as songs familiar from the live performance were utterly transformed.

They were working with producer Bob Sargeant, one of the John Peel show's regular producers at the BBC's Maida Vale studio complex – indeed, it was Sargeant who oversaw the Fall's November 1978 Peel session. His experience handling other bands for the same programme gave him an understanding and experience that few, if any, 'regular' producers could match: 'I had a new band in every day to do four songs, and I had ten hours to record and mix those songs for broadcast,' Sargeant reflected later. 'It really taught me discipline and helped me learn the planning and logistics side of production.'

Sargeant did more than oversee the recordings, then. He also marshalled the Fall's resources into a whole that is utterly a child of its time – for better and for worse. It was the age, after all, of the random precision of the Pop Group, Public Image Ltd and the (early) Gang of 4, role models that the Fall might not have chosen (Smith famously avoided any attempt to group them together on the same live bill), but they matched them anyway, note for jarring note. The stop-start modern-dance jerkiness of 'No Xmas for John Quays' and 'Industrial Estate' certainly reveals the Fall to be less out on a limb than their detractors may have hoped, while the venom-drenched eight-minute epic 'Music Scene' was built around a bass line that clung gleefully to the coat-tails of 'Fodderstompf' from PiL's first album – and worked just as effectively because of it.

The PiL link, at least, was not entirely unexpected. 'I feel a bond with PiL,' Smith admitted. 'PiL are doing a lot of what we've always wanted to do. They've got the power as well. PiL's stuff is really good stuff in my estimation – turning it all round, which is about time. That's what I mean about having your own style. Can were a perfect pop/rock 'n' roll band. A lot of people don't see Can as rock 'n' roll, or PiL as rock 'n' roll, but I do, because it's music you'd never get on the television. There's something out that your parents would not sit through. I'm into a lot of oddball stuff that irritates people.'

Considering the speed with which the album was completed – two days from start to finish – Smith continued, 'We tried to do [each] track in one or two takes. If you do more, people begin to speed up, just to get through it, and that's not good for our band because we're not disciplined musicians. If we do a take and half of it is really good, I'd rather leave it like that. If we tried to get it all good, it'd just turn out average.'

All of that aside, *Live At The Witch Trials* is a more accessible album than the band's past might havr led one to expect. Even at the time of release, Pawlett and Bramah's contributions had a musicality that defies the harsher elements of the group's experimental rep ('Two Steps Back' is inescapably atmospheric, 'Frightened' is nearly melodic). Smith's vocals, though never less than bullish, captivate via their very atonality. Broader-minded listeners were also quick to pinpoint Smith's evident debt to Kevin Coyne, one of the more idiosyncratic artists operating in the grey area between the mainstream and the avant-garde during the 1970s and, consequently, one of the few unscathed by Punk's firestorming purge of rock's old guard. In conversation, of course, Smith seldom responded to such comparisons, but clues aplenty would appear to be scattered through the early Fall albums.

It is tempting, but ultimately futile, to view *Live At The Witch Trials* in the context of the rest of the band's catalogue – and not just because the line-up which created it proved so short-lived. Unlike any of its successors, *Live At The Witch Trials* is a reactionary record, forged and designed around all that the band experienced through its first two years of activity, and making its points accordingly. From here on in, however, they would not be so easily led.

(SINGLE) Rowche Rumble
    7913. Rowche Rumble (Look At What The People Around You Are Taking)
    7914. In My Area
    ORIGINAL RELEASE: Step Forward SF11 (7-inch) July 1979
    UK INDIE CHART PEAK: #31
    COMMENTS: Almost certainly penned by Smith, Step Forward's press release for the Fall's third single was a masterpiece of deceptive homily. 'This is a great dance number and combines a cheek-in-tongue putdown of a popular sweetie with the Fall's tribute to Racey. Dig it.' The reality, however, was somewhat harsher.

A hollow military tattoo – which leads into an even hollower-sounding wall of guitars – underlines a (surely) deliberate nod to Public Image Ltd, the querulous echo on the repeated title borrowing one of the erstwhile Johnny Rotten's most familiar trademarks, even as the stated tribute to Racey, a keyboard tinkle hinting at the popsters' recent 'Some Girls' hit, threatens to tip the whole thing into turbulent chaos. The 'popular sweetie', meanwhile, was a popularly-prescribed anti-depressant (manufactured by Roche Products Ltd of Welwyn Garden City), whose invocation gives the song a lyrical tint not at all dissimilar to the Stones' 'Mother's Little Helper' – which might well have been the intention.

On the other side, 'In My Area' suggested a quieter side to the band, an unplugged air over which Smith's vocal evokes a wistful, almost contemplative mood, cut through with one of the greatest threats of a singalong chorus in the entire history of the Fall. Dig it!

(ALBUM) *Dragnet*
    7915. Psykick Dancehall
    7916. A Figure Walks
    7917. Printhead
    7918. Dice Man
    7919. Before the Moon Falls
    7920. Your Heart Out
    7921. Muzorewi's Daughter
    7922. Flat of Angles
    7923. Choc-Stock
    7924. Spectre vs Rector
    7925. Put Away
    (*) BONUS TRACKS

7913. Rowche Rumble
7914. In My Area
8001. Fiery Jack
8002. 2nd Dark Age
8003. Psykick Dancehall 2
ORIGINAL RELEASE Step Forward SFLP4 (LP) October 1979
REISSUE (1): IRS Records SFLPCD4 (CD) 1990
REISSUE (2): Cog Sinister COGVP113CD (CD) 1999
REISSUE (3): Turning Point TPM02209 (LP) 2002
REISSUE (4): Cog Sinister COGVP140CD (CD) 2002 with bonus tracks (*)
COMMENTS: The ugly duckling of the early Fall catalogue for reasons, as Smith told *Printed Noises* fanzine early the following year, that weren't too far away from the band's own limitations. '*Dragnet* has, if there's anything wrong with it, a balance towards songs about the band. It's very introspective. I get really psychotic in life, bring out loads of songs about the music business but who wants to know? It's a bad thing, but I think it should be told. 'Printhead' is like that – a lot of people don't realise about print, and what the papers do. A lot of bands live by the papers, y'know? They get stomach upsets in the morning. I went through it for a short while, but I think it's very funny. I've met loads of people who were crying their eyes out because they'd just had a bad review from someone that's just learned to write. In my mind, it's just pathetic.'

The other end of the scale, he continued, were the likes of the high-hat heavy 'Flat of Angles', and the deliriously word-playing 'Spectre vs Rector'. '"Flat of Angles" I like because it's an objective, story song. I only write a song like that once in a while. It's difficult to be objective.'

Intriguing, too, was 'Dice Man', a study of maniacal contrasts and extremes hammered out around a bastardised approximation of the old 'I Want Candy' rhythm. Inspired by the Luke Rhinehart novel of the same name, it also proclaimed Smith's own future role in the music industry: 'I like to take a chance.' Looking back from 1984, Smith reflected, 'That song was one of the most truthful. I based it on the book because I loved the idea that this guy would throw dice in the morning to decide how he'd be that day. I believe you have the right to change. We don't have a deliberate policy of keeping people guessing – that's just the way I am. You only look at life through your own eyes. I thrive on being outside the pop mess but not many people see that. I'm dead proud that The Fall aren't just another branch on the tree of show biz. Basically, rock music isn't very interesting, so it's only people like me who can make it interesting.' Only by taking chances could he ensure that remained true.

Despite such definite highlights (or maybe because of them: the lyrics are consistently more intriguing than the music), the most sympathetic interpretation of *Dragnet* is that it was a dead end. The turbulent nature of the band's line-up, forcing the constant reinvention or retirement of material that could, in earlier forms, have produced a truly dynamic album, certainly leaves its mark on the record, with too much of it descending into simple droning rants – Fall-by-numbers, if you will.

Genuine gems nevertheless explode with a regularity that utterly belies the album's reputation: 'Spectre vs Rector', of course; 'Muzorewi's Daughter' with its storm-tossed spaghetti western-meets-gypsy dance arrangement; and, best of all, the formative classic 'Psykick Dancehall'. It is no accident, however, that the best available representations of the *Dragnet* material are those that appear within the

Fall's live canon, with *Totale's Turn*, much of it recorded just as *Dragnet* hit the shelves, offering an alternate listen that surpasses anything the album can offer.

(LIVE) Oct 27 1979, Bircoats Leisure Centre, Doncaster (and others?)
  7926. Intro – Fiery Jack
  7927. Rowche Rumble
  7928. Muzorewi's Daughter
  7929. In My Area
  7930. Choc-Stock
  7931. No Xmas for John Quays
  UNR. remainder of set unknown
  ORIGINAL RELEASE: *Totale's Turns* 1980

(STUDIO) out-take
  7932. E.S.P. Disco
  ORIGINAL RELEASE: on *Oxymoron* compilation (1997)
  COMMENTS: New lyric, old song – a punchy period revision of 'Psykick Dancehall'.

1980

After the tumult of earlier years, 1980 offered a period of relative quiet for the Fall, a consequence, perhaps, of the comparative stability engendered by a new record deal. After two years with Step Forward, during which band and label eschewed a conventional contractual agreement in favour of taking each record as it came, the Fall signed with Rough Trade, fast establishing itself as the key indie on the UK scene. Smith explained that the move was almost wholly driven by finance. 'Step Forward, for whom we did those first singles and first two albums... we never saw a penny. That's a fact. We were bloody starving to death. "It's The New Thing" was single of the year and we had no fuckin' money in our pockets.

'We [are] our own bosses, we can do it on our own. But we're in a very insecure position. Presswise, we get a lot of coverage, but we're still only on ten notes [ten pounds a week]. We've got no driver, just two guys who help out as roadies. The Fall on the road is just nine people and we're out on our own. We're not academically outstanding or even especially practical. There are millions of kids like us, who have got something to offer if they could do the thing. We're just saying you can do it.'

At first glance, Rough Trade looked a perfect home for the Fall. A small-time concern renowned for rewarding adventure rather than avarice, art over commerce and chaos over choruses, the Rough Trade label grew out of what was originally a record store, branching out after finding success with a string of imported European Punk 45s: France's Metal Urbain were the new label's first release. Since that time,

Rough Trade had snapped up an impressively disparate catalogue of groups, most of whom seemed to operate on much the same plane as the Fall: America's Pere Ubu and the Residents, Ireland's Virgin Prunes as well as the Slits, Swell Maps, Scritti Politti and more.

The first fruit of the label's relationship with the Fall was the live album, *Totale's Turns (It's Now or Never)*, released in May, shortly after Steve Hanley's brother Paul replaced Mike Leigh in the band's engine room. Reprising songs dating back to 'No Xmas for John Quays', and highlighting the very best of *Dragnet*, it also delivered a physically bruising portrait of the Fall in naked splendour, fighting for the audience's attention, and then fighting those attentions off. It was also the final opportunity to witness the band wrestling with that contradiction.

In April, the group embarked on a British tour which confirmed on a national level what had previously been a regional phenomenon: the band began attracting informed audiences as opposed to the muddled masses simply looking for a new place to pogo. A sea change had taken place over the past year or so, as the all-consuming firestorm of Punk finally died down to a handful of isolated brush fires: the Mod and ska revivals, the street Punk resurgence of Oi!, the manicured electronics of the Futurists... So many bags, so many pigeonholes: none could contain the Fall. Inevitably, audiences who shared their dislocation flocked to the banner.

'We're having a bit of a difficult time,' Smith confessed facetiously. 'People are coming along and sort of liking us, as opposed to the last two years, where it's just been getting up everybody's backs. We're getting more and more of your average rock audience.' What remained to be seen was, would the band subvert them? Or would the acclaim subvert the band? 'You've got to watch it,' Smith continued, 'or you're just preaching to the converted all the time. There's no way I'm gonna go on now and just fuckin' barrack 'em, 'cos you're getting 500 people in a hall and they've all come to see you. It's no use just saying "Fuck it!" like we used to be able to.'

It was that conundrum which flavoured the handful of interviews the band submitted to that summer, particularly their encounter with long-time cheerleader Dave McCulloch of *Sounds*. McCulloch wrote the ensuing article more or less as an obituary to his love for the band, noting not only the yawning gulf between Smith and the audience that hung on his words but also – and this, apparently, was something the young Bono had remarked upon as well – a sense that he, Smith, had been hanging around the music biz a little too long: 'The Fall have hardened. They are more severe...'

There was a cryptic belligerence to Smith's words that had not been there before – or, at least, had never been taken so seriously. But, if McCulloch (and Bono) mourned it, Smith accepted it as an inevitable consequence of the band's growth, and one that experience alone would allow him to expel. 'The reason for this attitude that you're hearing now is, we're dulled by [the industry]. I'm sick of laying my heart on the line and getting it stepped on and, like, two years later some band rips your ideas off, waters them down and gets in the fucking chart.'

The first roar from this new mindset, the sense that, though the Fall remained the voice of the outsider, they were going to pick their champions very carefully, arrived in July with the release of the single, 'How I Wrote *Elastic Man*'. It was followed, two months later, by the randomly conversational 'Totally Wired'. When the Fall made their third session appearance for John Peel that same month, the emphasis was once again on new material: two tracks from their forthcoming third album (the murderous, and preternaturally scream-broiled, 'Container Drivers' plus 'New Face In Hell'), *Grotesque*, one re-recorded from the live album ('New Puritan') and one that would not see a vinyl release for another 18 months, 'Jawbone and the Air Rifle'.

Grotesque duly followed in November, receiving a less than enthusiastic welcome. While the *NME*'s review proclaimed it the band's least flawed album, it also highlighted the dangers that attended the Fall as they revelled in their uniqueness, the possibility that 'they'll drift too close to the self-consciously cryptic and merely sneer at the world from a pit of cosy cultishness.' In fact, concluded writer Graham Locke, 'I've got a creeping suspicion it's already too late for them to stop.'

(MUSICIANS)
LINE-UP #9 (Jan-June) MARK E SMITH (vocals), MARC RILEY (guitar, keyboards), CRAIG SCANLON (guitar), STEVE HANLEY (bass), MIKE LEIGH (drums) (STEVE DAVIS for Dutch tour in June)

LINE-UP #10 (remainder) MARK E SMITH (vocals), MARC RILEY (guitar, keyboards), CRAIG SCANLON (guitar), STEVE HANLEY (bass), PAUL HANLEY (drums)

(SINGLE) Fiery Jack
    8001. Fiery Jack
    8002. 2nd Dark Age
    8003. Psykick Dancehall 2
    ORIGINAL RELEASE: Step Forward SF13 (7-inch) January 1980
    UK INDIE CHART PEAK: #4
    COMMENTS: Co-produced by Rough Trade label head Geoff Travis and Mayo Thompson, the former Red Crayola mainman now established as one of the label's house producers, 'Fiery Jack' locked into a metronomic rockabilly groove that would provide a blueprint for a lot of what the Fall would accomplish over the next year or so. Smith's deconstruction of life on the wrong side of the nutrition shelf was only one of what he called the '20 different things' that the song was concerned with.

Fiery Jack himself, Smith explained, was 'someone I know. That song's an attempt to get back at the ageism thing, where people are supposed to be screwed after they're 29. I mean, the people in the pubs where I go are 48 or 50, but they've more guts than all these other preeners. In every generation, you get this core of spirit, and they never lose it.' On another occasion, however, he mused, 'in a mystical way, Fiery Jack is the sort of guy I can see myself as in 20 years,' he said at the time. And, twenty years later, he might well have succeeded.

Of the b-sides, the otherwise disposable '2nd Dark Age' is noteworthy as the song that introduced Smith's subsequent alter ego of Roman Totale XVII, the outrageously outspoken illegitimate lovechild of King Charles I and the Greek God Pan.

'Psykick Dancehall #2', meanwhile, continues – as its title suggests – the thrust of the *Dragnet* gem, with the spirit of the witch trials still vividly present; essential to the lyric is Helen Duncan, a Scots medium who, in 1944, became the last person to be found guilty of contravening the Witchcraft Act of 1735. In fact, the charge was drummed up only after other legal attempts to halt the activities of a shamelessly fraudulent medium failed. But the anachronism was remarkable nevertheless, and remains even more so today.

(LIVE) February 29 1980, Palm Cove, Bradford.
   8004. Spectre vs Rector
   UNR. Printhead
   UNR. City Hobgoblins
   UNR. Rowche Rumble
   UNR. 2nd Dark Age
   UNR. Impression of J. Temperance
   UNR. English Scheme
   UNR. How I Wrote Elastic Man
   UNR. Your Heart Out
   UNR. Fiery Jack
   UNR. A Figure Walks
   UNR. Dice Man
   UNR. Muzorewi's Daughter
   ORIGINAL RELEASE: *Totale's Turns*(1980)

(LIVE) unknown
   8005. That Man
   8006. New Puritan
   8007. Cary Grant's Wedding
   ORIGINAL RELEASE: *Totale's Turns* (1980)

(ALBUM) *Totale's Turns (It's Now Or Never)* (live)
   7926. Intro – Fiery Jack
   7927. Rowche Rumble
   7928. Muzorewi's Daughter
   7929. In my Area
   7930. Choc-Stock
   7931. No Xmas for John Quays
   8004. Spectre vs Rector 2
   8005. That Man
   8006. New Puritan
   8007. Cary Grant's Wedding
   RECORDED: Oct 27 1979, Bircoats Leisure Centre, Doncaster (tracks 1-5), Feb 29 1980, Palm Cove, Bradford (track 6) and others.
   ORIGINAL RELEASE: Rough Trade ROUGH10 (LP) May 1980
   REISSUE (1): Dojo DOJOCD83 (CD) 1992
   REISSUE (2): Castle/Essential (CD) 1998
   UK INDIE CHART PEAK: #1
   COMMENTS: The first official Fall live album, recorded with the *Dragnet* line-up of the band, ignites in suitably inflammatory fashion, with 'Fiery Jack' following Smith's introductory taunt: 'The difference between you and us is that we have brains.' His liner notes go on to describe the onlookers as 'an 80% Disco weekend

mating audience,' and the ensuing conflict is well-captured on the disc – so much so that Rough Trade's own subsequent *Totally Wired* anthology describes *Totale's Turns* as 'one of the worst quality recordings ever committed to vinyl.'

It isn't but, like most early Fall live recordings, nor is it an album for the faint-of-heart. The group's determined anti-sheen transforms what was, *in situ*, an excellent gaggle of gigs into something approaching a public rehearsal. Although a slick track-listing avoids the false starts and repeat performances that have long been a Fall concert characteristic, even repeat plays never quite dispel the suspicion that trouble's coming. The recording also contains fewer of Smith's acerbic asides than one might have hoped – his reminder that "last orders are at half-past-ten" could as easily be a jab at any bar-flies in the room as a public service announcement.

Of the performances, 'Rowche Rumble' is a genuine highlight, shattered by bass and drums, but kept forever on track by that hypnotic riff – easily superior to its studio counterpart, this might be one of the best live Fall performances ever released. 'Muzorewi's Daughter' and 'Spectre vs Rector' are also quite dazzling, with the latter flapping around Smith's barked vocals like some kind of predatory bat. The closing 'No Xmas for John Quays', on the other hand, is passionately tight and controlled, at least until the closing moments, when keyboards slice across the entire landscape like an avenging axe.

Smith himself viewed the album with some misgivings. While not quite writing *Totale's Turns* off as a backwards step, he at least acknowledged it could have been better. '*Totale's* is great, there's a lot of sweat and pain in that, it is great. But… we're not blowing our fuses. We held the best stuff back. A lot of bands don't do that. But the Fall have grown up [and] the people aren't really ready for what we can do.'

(SINGLE) How I Wrote *Elastic Man*
    8008. How I Wrote *Elastic Man*
    8009. City Hobgoblins
    ORIGINAL RELEASE: Rough Trade RT048 (7-inch) July 1980
    UK INDIE CHART PEAK: #2
    COMMENTS: The rubbery rockabilly 'How I Wrote *Elastic Man*' remains one of the Fall's most venomous releases – and one of their most memorable. Its listener-friendly bounce and whimsically mystifying lyric place the Fall on such a deceptive plateau that both Robyn Hitchcock's Soft Boys and Julian Cope's Teardrop Explodes must have been wondering how they avoided composing and recording the record themselves. Or maybe they had. Smith never wrote a song called '*Elastic Man*', but Julian Cope wrote 'Bouncing Babies', and there's certainly a link there some place. Wry, too, is Smith's insistence on singing 'Plastic' instead of 'Elastic', a jab at fans (and critics) who were already taking his words so far out of context that they often changed the meaning entirely.

Originally (if irrelevantly) titled 'Case For The Jews', 'City Hobgoblins', meanwhile, is a shouted, Punk-powered tale of the supernatural, musically more-or-less disposable, but lyrically entertaining, with references to French playwright Alfred Jarry's *Ubu Roi* and the nightmarish vision of Queen Victoria living out eternity as a large black slug in Manchester's Piccadilly.

(BBC SESSION) Sept 24, 1980
    8010. Container Driver

8011. New Puritan
8012. New Face In Hell
ORIGINAL RELEASE: 8010/8011 on single Rough Trade RT 143, 8012 on *The Peel Sessions.*
COMMENTS: see appendix I/BBC sessions

(SINGLE) Totally Wired
8013. Totally Wired
8014. Putta Block
ORIGINAL RELEASE: Rough Trade RT056 (7-inch) September 1980
UK INDIE CHART PEAK: #2
Sneering and snotty, 'Totally Wired' is the sort of statement (delivered in the sort of voice) you'd expect to hear from Rik in *The Young Ones*, a self-reverential celebration of drinking/smoking/swallowing/whatever-ing too much of something, that only subtly justifies its jerky agitation. Just because you're paranoid, it doesn't mean *etc.* Perhaps mistakenly, 'Totally Wired' made #57 in *Mojo* magazine's Top 100 Drug Songs in 2002: the song's nervous hyper-tension would be more appropriate to a catalogue of songs that make you need drugs instead.

A 'Totally Wired' sample appeared on 'Next', a cut from KLF's legendary 1987 album *(What The Fuck's Going On)*. As the only legally cleared sample on the entire album, it was thus the only one to survive onto the suitably edited *The JAMS 45 Edits* EP – all the others were replaced with silence.

(ALBUM) *Grotesque (After The Gramme)*
8015. Pay Your Rates
8016. English Scheme
8017. New Face in Hell
8018. C'n'C-S'Mithering
8019. The Container Drivers
8020. Impression of J. Temperance
8021. In the Park
8022. W.M.C.-Blob 59
8023. Gramme Friday
8024. The N.W.R.A.
(*) BONUS TRACKS
8008. How I Wrote *Elastic Man*
8009. City Hobgoblins
8013. Totally Wired
8014. Putta Block
ORIGINAL RELEASE Rough Trade ROUGH18 (LP) November 1980 (LP)
REISSUE (1): Castle CLACD391 (CD) 1993
REISSUE (2): Cog Sinister COGVP106CD (CD) 1998
REISSUE (3): Castle/Essential ESMCD640 (CD) 1998 with bonus tracks (*)
REISSUE (4): Turning Point TPM02210 (LP) 2002
UK INDIE CHART PEAK: #1
COMMENTS: The centrepiece of *Grotesque (After The Gramme)* was the closing 'the N.W.R.A.' – 'the North Will Rise Again'. When discussing the album's generally lukewarm reception, it was the manner in which this track was overlooked that bothered Smith the most. Built, he claimed, around the dreams he often had

after northern gigs, the song looked at the aftermath of a Britain sundered by an armed rebellion delineated by the so-called north-south divide.

'Of course, everybody's gonna go, "Huh? The North? Here we go again – Smith talking about flat caps and all that clichéd rubbish." Actually, the message in it is that, if the north did rise again, they would fuck it up. Not that they ever rose before. It's just like a sort of document of a revolution that could happen – like somebody writing a book about what would have happened if the Nazis had invaded Britain. It's the same concept as that. Not a lot of people have gleaned that, probably because it's the last track on the LP.'

In fact, much of the uncertainty that surrounded *Grotesque* was rooted in the suggestion that it was the most comfortable-sounding of all Fall records to date – a suggestion that was, for the most part, spot on. Working with a succession of producers, again including Grant Cunliffe (now operating under the surname Showbiz), Geoff Travis and Mayo Thompson, the Fall struck a balance between purposeful chaos (borrowing one of John The Postman's most fearsome instruments, the kazoo which punctuates the Modern Loverly 'New Face In Hell') and order (the disciplined lope of 'Gramme Friday') that was all the more invigorating for appearing so natural.

Indeed, if the three singles released already in the year – 'Fiery Jack', 'How I Wrote *Elastic Man*' and 'Totally Wired' – represented the most lovable sonic faces of the Fall, *Grotesque* was precision-tooled to paint each one.

From the rollicking humour of the opening 'Pay Your Rates' through the deliberately low-fi 'W. M. C.-Blob 59' and onto the almost folky (well, it has acoustic guitars) 'C'n'C-S'Mithering', examining the band's American experiences through local Punkoid eyes, *Grotesque* was the album converts most readily recommended to newbies they met, people who innocently asked what the Fall really sounded like. Its Independent chart placing suggests that there were a lot who wanted to know.

(LIVE) 11 December 1980, Acklam Hall, London
    8025. Middle Mass (*AKA* Middle Mass – Crap Rap)
    8026. English Scheme
    8027. New Face In Hell
    8028. That Man
    8029. [An] Older Lover
    8030. Slates (*AKA* Male Slags)
    8031. Gramme Friday (actually Prole Art Threat)
    8032. The Container Drivers
    8033. Jawbone And The Air Rifle
    8034. In The Park
    8035. Leave The Capitol
    8036. Spectre Vs Rector
    8037. Pay Your Rates
    8038. Impression Of J. Temperance
    ORIGINAL RELEASE: as *Live In London 1980*, Chaos Tapes LIVE 006 (Cassette-only limited edition of 4000 copies) 1981
    REISSUE (1): as *The Legendary Chaos Tape*, Scout Releases/Rough Trade SAR1005 (CD) 1996
    REISSUE (2): as *The Legendary Chaos Tape*, Cog Sinister COGVP101CD

(CD) 1999
UK INDIE CHART PEAK: #7

COMMENTS: Touring to promote the newly released *Grotesque (After the Gramme)* and thus retiring much of their previous repertoire, the Fall touched down for two nights at west London's Acklam Hall in December. The first found its way onto the streets as a limited edition semi-bootleg cassette that stunned everyone by charging up the Independent chart. (Subsequent CD reissues were titled in memory of the cassette and bore occasionally revised song titles, as above.)

Of all the early Fall's less-than-official live recordings (*Totale's Turns* thus excluded), *Live In London 1980* probably comes closest to capturing the sheer majesty of the pre-Beggars Banquet band, both in terms of undiluted energy and non-intrusive (albeit distinctly less than perfect) sound quality.

The band members – Smith included – are in high spirits throughout. As a confrontational 'Middle Mass' moves into its 'Crap Rap' segment, Smith both trips over the words and laughs at himself for doing so, while a rambunctious 'New Face In Hell' not only unleashes an absolutely brutal kazoo solo, but also catches Smith squawking and clucking like a Christmas turkey.

It isn't all hi-jinks, however. 'An Older Lover, Etc' is certainly tinged with an edgy anger, while 'Leave the Capitol' is positively bipolar, as the sympathetic verses move into bilious chorus and then swing back again. 'Prole Art Threat', too, has a dramatically sneering quality to it, and 'Male Slags' (*aka* 'Slates, Slags etc') surely set some ears burning at the back of the room. There's also a Mach ten race through 'That Man' that merges Punk power with the spectre of a 60s beat song. Great chorus! Best of all, however, is an extended 'Spectre vs Rector', ten minutes that close with Smith thanking 'all the people who've helped me with my vendetta tonight.'

1981

Although the Fall remained uncharacteristically quiet on the recording front, with just an EP and a single bookending the year, 1981 proved to be one of their most active yet. The band recorded two new John Peel sessions in March and September, undertook a string of British dates, returned to the United States and made visits as far afield as Holland, Germany and Iceland. April – the one gig-less month of the year – was spent searching for a new record label.

The band's link with Rough Trade simply hadn't worked out, reaching any number of flashpoints before Smith's patience finally snapped: 'I'd had enough of them and they're all middle class. They didn't know what the Fall was about and they were signing all these bands that sounded like the Fall.' The failure of the 'Totally Wired' single the previous autumn was the final straw. Although onlookers who considered the Fall some kind of talismanic epitome of cultish obscurity may have thought him deluded, Smith viewed the song as a potential hit single – as, indeed, it was.

Unfortunately, Rough Trade disagreed. Smith explained, 'They had loads of bands and they were pressin' the same number [of records] for every band, and we were sayin', "Look, the Fall's bloody unique and you should be backin' us." And they would say, "Oh, so you want to be a pop star now?" And I'd say, "No, I don't want to be a pop star, but I want the bloody respect I deserve. I'd ask why wasn't the record in that shop and why are you sending it to some stupid left wing magazine and not to a daily paper! And they say, "Oh, that's selling out."' It was telling that only one Rough Trade band, the slowly metamorphosing Scritti Politti, had yet landed a national chart hit (1981's 'The "Sweetest" Girl' reached #64).

There was more. The band's relationship with the media, too, was causing alarm as Smith's liner notes to the forthcoming 'Lie Dream Of A Casino Soul' single mused. 'Early this year, things were too gruesome to behold... The Fall had been diluted into part of an almost Betrayal environment; anti-fashion shtick, backs to the audience, mate; pass us the hair dye, wack – Mere Grubby Pseuds making capital out of the Fall sweat and pre-cog.' With discomforting echoes of the *NME* cover scam four years before, the music press thought of the Fall as a plaything for its own schemes and beliefs. Smith had no intention whatsoever of living up to those ideals.

Amid these wranglings, the Fall's next American tour began taking shape; it, too, seemed somehow ill-starred. Immigration regulations stunned the band with the news that 17-year-old Paul Hanley was too young to accompany them on a tour comprising mainly venues restricted to the 21-and-over crowd. The band replaced him with the returning Karl Burns, more than two years after he was unceremoniously dismissed and just weeks after he'd decided to give up music altogether.

Opening far from the spotlight in Oklahoma City at the end of May, the tour wound its way around the US until well into July, with the official first night, at New York's Underground on June 3rd, not simply dividing the audience, but driving many of them out of the room. Journalist Richard Grabel, observing events for the *NME*, reported, 'At both shows, the set ended with about half as many people in the room as had been there at the start,' although 'those that stayed were entranced.'

The American tour was the first to give the band an idea of the sheer size of the country: from the vantage of a cramped tourbus, long distances, no matter how mythic, quickly lose their magic. One stretch of highway, one expanse of desert, one day in Kansas, all look much the same as another. Beyond the bars that never close and the TV that never shuts up, America can rapidly blur into one long van ride. The opportunity to make a side trip to Reykjavik, then, was never going to be passed up. Especially as the Fall would be joining one of the most select groups of artists there was: they became only the fourth British touring act to set foot on Icelandic soil. The others were the Clash, the Stranglers and, for reasons unknown, Any Trouble.

The visit consisted of four shows, two at the Hotel Borg – where the band themselves were enlisted to help erect the stage – a third at the Austerbae Javara nightclub, and a farewell at a converted cinema, playing a matinee for all the kids who couldn't stay up for the other shows. 'BRITISH RAW ROCKERS ARRIVE IN ICELAND' announced the local paper the following morning, although the warm reception predictably cooled somewhat when the natives were actually exposed to the band.

With the exception of a handful of local talents – of which the first night's support act, the sometimes topless-female-fronted C4U, were among the more uncompromising – live music was at a premium in Reykjavik. The 'Sold Out' signs were posted on the Borg door long before the show began. But, as Colin Irwin, documenting the trip for *Melody Maker*, recalled, 'they start leaving halfway through the second number. It sounds as if Mark Smith is singing through a megaphone, the band are tense and tame, and the audience becomes increasingly possessed by a demon madness...' At one point in the show, somebody leapt onstage to demand of Smith, 'Icelanders are happy. Why aren't you?' Smith did not reply.

He was certainly happy at the Austerba Javara. The previous day, the Fall were introduced to the music and, perhaps more importantly, the legend of Megas Jonsson, a character widely regarded as the father of Icelandic rock, and an iconoclast of almost supernatural status. Universally banned while his career was underway, unheard on radio and scarcely even permitted to play live in his homeland, Megas finally announced his retirement in 1979, bowing out with the grandiose double album *Plans For Suicide*.

Then he disappeared from the radar, leaving behind only a library of records unknown to anybody outside the island, but venerated by a handful of loyal supporters. When he turned up at the show to introduce himself to Smith and the Fall, it was one of his first public appearances since his departure. Evidently, he was now working on the docks, his music a long-forgotten lifetime ago.

Stopping by a Reykjavik studio the following day, a 16-track set-up carved into a wall of lava, Smith ad-libbed his own impressions of the meeting to a piece of improvised music whose only stipulation, Marc Riley later said, was that it needed to be Dylanish. Alongside 'Hip Priest', recorded that same session (and destined, years later, for an atmospheric place in the movie *Silence Of The Lambs*), 'Iceland' would appear on the following year's *Hex Enduction Hour*.

A third Iceland song, 'Look, Know', would follow on 45; it also proved a funky highlight of the band's next – fifth – Peel session, recorded on August 26th. Earlier in the year, on the eve of *Slates*' release, the Fall's fourth session had sounded oddly unconvincing: the version of 'Middlemass' was effortlessly surpassed by its vinyl counterpart, 'Hip Priest' sounded unformed and 'C'n'C-Hassle Schmuk' was more or less a mess. Only 'Lie Dream of a Casino Soul', earmarked for the band's next single, stood out. This time around, though, the band was in electrifying form, slipping through a magnificent 'Winter', a dramatic 'Deep Park' and a brittle 'Who Makes The Nazis?', before 'Look, Know' simply exploded any last hope of predicting where the Fall were headed next.

Draped in a characteristically grotesque Savage Pencil sleeve, the 'Lie Dream of a Casino Soul' single followed in November, the Fall's first release for Kamera, a newly-formed independent whose releases so far included a live set by folkie Tim Hardin, and jazz rock bassist Jack Lancaster's *Skinningrove Bay*. (Palais Schaumberg, the Dancing Did, the Au Pairs and Charge would subsequently be lured to the label, while staffer Saul Galpern would go on to found the Nude label.)

The UK tour that November introduced an entire new dimension to the band's sound, as Smith, unable to choose between the two drummers now at his disposal, opted to retain them both. 'Karl gave a different angle on the new material. It would have been a shame to let him go at the end of the tour, so Paul came back in and now we have both of them. It's a bit confusing on stage, but it's good.'

Not since the heyday of Gary Glitter – if you discount Adam and the Ants – had a rock band used two drummers. Smith admitted he enjoyed joining that exclusive club: 'I was really into Gary Glitter, and I used to get bad-mouthed for it. It was like, "You've got to be into David Bowie or Yes – Gary Glitter's just tripe". And I was going, "It's fuckin' great. It's avant-garde." Two drummers and all that – it was really percussive. It was the only decent thing around. But Karl's really there for the balance. He's a very high-tech musician and he could play in a technical band easy, [while] Paul's a self-taught drummer.' The ensuing collision would prove as capable of chaos and cacophony as creation. But that, of course, was the point.

This latest sequence of gigs swiftly proved among the most successful the Fall had ever played, a non-stop celebration that climaxed with what Smith, in the guise of his alter-ego Roman Totale XVII, celebrated in the liner notes to *Hex Enduction Hour*: 'Never knew had so many friends till Venue [the London date on December 7th]. In awe. The fans were awed And cowered. Still needing the HEXAN school. Still bowing to: Mythical Thingy, and the fresh stool, at 'Venue' No decision equals 'consultation'. One True Sentence. On Morning Of It: Saw Flabby Wings and Ran cross frosty crusting of Plate glass, from the SKRIKKING KIDS, NOT FIT FOR: HEX END. the Big P.'

(MUSICIANS)

LINE-UP #10 (Jan-May) MARK E SMITH (vocals), MARC RILEY (guitar, keyboards), CRAIG SCANLON (guitar), STEVE HANLEY (bass), PAUL HANLEY (drums)

LINE-UP #11 (US tour May-July) MARK E SMITH (vocals), MARC RILEY (guitar, keyboards), CRAIG SCANLON (guitar), STEVE HANLEY (bass), KARL BURNS (drums)

LINE-UP #12 (remainder) MARK E SMITH (vocals), MARC RILEY (guitar, keyboards), CRAIG SCANLON (guitar), STEVE HANLEY (bass), PAUL HANLEY (drums), KARL BURNS (drums)

(LIVE) Queen Mary Union, London, February 5th 1981
    UNR Your Heart Out
    UNR Totally Wired
    UNR Leave the Capitol
    UNR An Older Lover
    UNR New Face in Hell
    UNR Middle Mass
    UNR C'n'C-S'Mithering – Crap Rap #19
    UNR Fiery Jack
    UNR Jawbone and the Air Rifle
    UNR Slates, Slags, etc.
    UNR Fit and Working Again
    UNR Prole Art Threat
    UNR Impression of J. Temperance
    UNR Container Drivers
    ORIGINAL RELEASE: Proposed 1998 2 CD set with Derby Hall, Bury April 27th 1982 show.

(BBC SESSION) 31 March, 1981
    8101. C'n'C – Hassle Schmuck
    8102. Middle Mass
    ORIGINAL RELEASE: 8101 'Kimble' single (1993), 8102 *The Peel Sessions* (1998)
    COMMENTS: see appendix I/BBC sessions

(SINGLE) *Slates, etc*

8103. Middle Mass
8104. An Older Lover etc.
8105. Prole Art Threat
8106. Fit and Working Again
8107. Slates, Slags etc.
8108. Leave the Capitol
ORIGINAL RELEASE: Rough Trade RT071 (10") April 1981
REISSUE (1): Dojo LOMA CD 10 (CD) 1992 (with *A Part Of America Therein*)
REISSUE (2): Essential ESMCD 637 (CD) 1998 (with *A Part Of America Therein*)
UK INDIE CHART PEAK: #3
COMMENTS: Often overlooked because of its brevity, *Slates etc* offers a clutch of songs which had already been shaped onstage, then were restructured here in what could be called their ultimate state. 'Fit and Working Again', a rockabilly rhythm punctuated by a peek-a-boo guitar line, is a stand-out, while the muddy blurge and dissolute vocalizing of 'Leave The Capitol' has a compulsive edginess that borders, at times, on quirky.

Best of all, though, is the tumultuous 'Middle Mass', a raw Smith rant imposed on an anthemic soundscape which 'cut through' Marc Riley every time he played it. The guitarist told *Debris*, ''Middle Mass' [was] about me and some of the people I was hanging around with at the time. It's a great song, but... I went up to him one day in the studio and said, "It's about me, this song, isn't it?" And he started fumbling and said, "Oh no, it's about somebody else called Marc." My respect for him went right down. I always stand by what I write. The biggest cop-out about Mark is that he never stands by his words. When he made a personal attack on somebody, he never stood by what he said. Having said all that, Smith is one of the best lyricists that I've ever encountered.'

'Prole Art Threat' [*aka* 'Pink Press'], meanwhile, provided the flashpoint that finally sundered Smith's contentious working relationship with Rough Trade. Originally written as a play in which a city commuter becomes obsessed by leftist politicking, the song was intended to be humorous. According to Smith, however, Rough Trade missed the joke entirely. 'They'd go, "This song sounds a bit fascist to us." I told them that was what I was gettin' at, that fascism doesn't have to be the men in suits. If they'd been a big label and gave me 50,000 pounds, then I might've let them have a say.' They hadn't, so he didn't.

Disputes also arose over the band's planned marketing ploy for the EP. For all its socialist pretensions, Rough Trade lived and died by its presence on – some might say domination of – the alternative/independent charts, a roost that the Fall themselves ruled since 'Fiery Jack' went to #4 in early 1980.

Smith, however, was sick of dancing to that particular tune, so manager Carroll suggested releasing *Slates* as a 10-incher, with a retail price that rendered it inappropriate for either the singles or LPs chart. In the event, *Slates* qualified for the former listings regardless, and only narrowly missed the top spot. But a stand was taken. Now only animosity could be certain of breeding.

(LIVE) June/July 1981, US tour (Chicago?)
8109. The N.W.R.A.
8110. Hip Priest
8111. Totally Wired
8112. Lie Dream of a Casino Soul

8113. Cash 'n' Carry
8114. An Older Lover, Etc
8115. Deer Park
8116. Winter (Hostel Maxi)
ORIGINAL RELEASE: as *A Part Of America Therein, 1981*, Rough Trade Cottage LP1 – 1982.
REISSUE (1): Dojo LOMA CD 10 (CD) 1992 (with *Slates, etc.*)
REISSUE (2): Essential ESMCD 637 (CD) 1998 (with *Slates, etc.*)
UK INDIE CHART PEAK: #9
COMMENTS: As the MC says at the start of the show, 'from the riot-torn streets of Manchester, England, to the scenic sewers of Chicago…' In the summer of 1981, inner city Britain was tearing itself apart: Manchester's Moss Side only one of several areas to implode as the mean season wore on. The Fall, making their second visit to the United States, noticed how things had changed since their first visit at the end of 1979. Back then, audiences were drawn as much by their high profile in imported music papers as by any familiarity with the band's *oeuvre* – the poor attendances at some of the shows spoke volumes for the Americans' lack of curiosity. This time around, even the poseurs were thin on the ground. This didn't stop Smith from reinventing 'Totally Wired' to lash out at the handful that did turn up to see him – often braying their discontent that the Fall weren't 'real' Punks.

An excellent recording is marred only by some light distortion, but benefits from the lifelike mix of scheduled performances and deviating asides. Smith was, by all accounts, in fine verbal form throughout this tour. Americans buying the album as a souvenir of the live show would probably have felt cheated if it had excluded his introductions. Equally, there's a sense of the band working to put on a representative show, unlike some of the more obtuse offerings to which homeland crowds had become accustomed. 'Totally Wired' aside, there is little deviation from the regular versions of the songs, lyrically or musically, while the roar of two guitars (Craig Scanlon and Marc Riley) occasionally permits the band to sound like a rock group. Occasionally.

(BBC SESSION) September 15, 1981
8117. Winter (Hostel Maxi)
ORIGINAL RELEASE: *The Peel Sessions* (1998)
COMMENTS: see appendix I/BBC sessions

(SINGLE) Lie Dream of a Casino Soul
8118. Lie Dream of a Casino Soul
8119. Fantastic Life
ORIGINAL RELEASE: Kamera ERA001 (7-inch) November 1981
UK INDIE CHART PEAK: #5
COMMENTS: 'Lie Dream of a Casino Soul' was a jagged, pointed single, haunted by splorrocky guitar and cheap keyboard jingle. Its mocking tones acquired increased resonance, Smith told *NME* two years later, when word went around that the song was attacking one of northern England's proudest musical accomplishments, the Northern Soul underground.

'That song actually did create quite a bit of resentment in the North because people thought it was being snobby and horrible about the old soul boys, which it was never about anyway, because I was brought up with people that were into

Northern Soul five years before anybody down [south] had even heard about it. But they've all grown out of it, which is what the song is about. It wasn't putting them down at all. If anything, it was glorifying them.'

In fact, 'Lie Dream Of A Casino Soul' could be said to be the Fall's concise answer to the Who's *Quadrophenia*, an invocation of a Mod-ish existence at a time when that was considered neither an insult nor an anachronism. Lyrically chasing similar age-related demons to 'Fiery Jack' but with tongue less firmly in cheek, the opening drum rhythm is straight of a Motown-y classic, while the handclap beat chases the dance floor all the way round the block.

'Fantastic Life' retains the most-favoured tinkling keyboard sound together with a riffing rhythm that nags familiarly at the ears – of course! It is 'Lie Dream' again, lightly revised and slightly removed, then grafted to a lyric that is pure James Bond. If he was played by a Buzzcock.

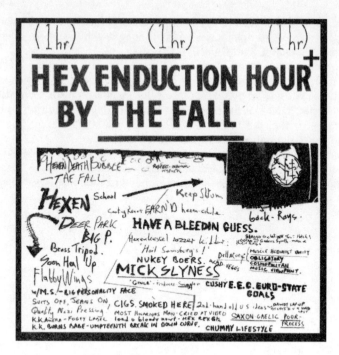

1982

The fourth best group in the 1981 *NME* readers poll released their latest album, *Hex Enduction Hour*, in March 1982, to coincide with their latest tours of Britain and the Low Countries. In the UK, they were supported by Icelandic art Punks Purkurr Pilnikk, who they'd met on the previous year's visit to Reykjavik. (Future Kukl/Sugarcubes trumpeter Einar Orn Bendiktsson was a member of the group.)

The response to the new album, possibly their best-received LP yet, shocked Smith. '*Hex* was a huge sort of kiss-off to, like, everything. Like *Slates*, a similar attitude towards the aim of – this is the one, sort out the wheat from the chaff. I was genuinely surprised that people found *Hex* accessible. I wouldn't have thought that it was more approachable than *Grotesque*, which was, like, a bit old-fashioned y'know.'

Similar plaudits greeted 'Look, Know', from the Icelandic sessions, when it was released as a single in April. It suddenly seemed as if the Fall were becoming accessible. Naturally, Smith would have something to say about that, later in the year.

The British and European dates over, summer brought the next step in the group's world tour by instalments: visits to Australia and New Zealand. The tour was the brainchild of a pair of Australian promoters whose past triumphs included organising regional tours for the Birthday Party and Residents associate Snakefinger, a hardy resumé that convinced Kay Carroll that the tour was a possibility. The fact that the New Zealand leg of the tour would skirt traditional rock venues and arenas also intrigued her: apart from the biggest names, few bands ever bothered adding New Zealand to their itinerary; fewer still stepped off the beaten track. As with the Icelandic dates the previous summer, the Fall were moving into uncharted territory.

It was an under-strength line-up that arrived in Australia. Karl Burns' passport had been stolen while in the USA the previous summer: he'd no sooner obtained a replacement than it was eaten by a dog! Delays in issuing a second replacement meant he followed a few days behind the rest of the band, leaving them to play the first shows as a five piece.

Response to the gigs was generally good. (Meaning: the band enjoyed themselves.) The most frequent complaint they heard from audiences was that the material was unfamiliar. In Britain, that complaint had long since been abandoned: the band's penchant for trying out new songs on stage, long before they made it onto record, was an essential part of their appeal. Down Under, however, where Fall records were generally available only as high-ticket imports – if at all – the assumption, as Smith told the NZ magazine *Rip It Up*, was that they were being wilfully obscure.

'People are thinkin' the new stuff's on records you can't get here. [But] I'm approaching this as if playing in England. I'm not goin' to come over here and go back two years just because you think you're behind. It's amazing how many people come up and [ask for] "Totally fuckin' Wired", y'know? We haven't done it in England for a year and a half. Why should I patronise New Zealanders? Are they some fuckin' sub-breed? Australia was the same: "Oh, 'Totally Wired', that's the only one we can get out here." So fuckin' what? I live in Manchester and you can't get any of our records there. What we played… would be new stuff to the biggest Fall fan that had every fuckin' record… it was six-tenths new stuff.'

The Christchurch, New Zealand, gig brought with it another new experience. Through the Fall's years as a support act, they had perforce grown accustomed to abuse from the headliners' fans. To see it happening to their own support band – a line-up of Dunedin legends, the Clean, specially reformed for the occasion – was a total eye-opener. 'They got a very hard time,' Smith reflected. 'All these thugs in the front row started throwing bottles 'n' 'that.' The Clean's response disappointed him, though. 'They just walked off. They should've really got into it, probably would've been better…'

Back home, he reflected that the entire tour was 'dead weird. We went to Sydney, for instance, and it's like some sort of surrogate 'Frisco. They'd expected us to be somewhere in the UB40/Jam category, not being able to get our records and that. It was incredible seeing their faces when we started to play. We did six gigs there, the first night 1,200 people came, the last we counted two hundred! But that's one of the reasons I wanted to play there, an old fashioned pioneer, like they were Rip Van Winkle and I was waking them up!'

Not everybody enjoyed being roused, however. One Marie Ryan, writing in Australia's *RAM* magazine summed up her impressions with a terse 'Mark Smith is a cynical, bitter critic of English Society. He's also a rude and sarcastic man… I disliked him intensely.'

Returning from Australia, the band stopped off for their first-ever performance in Greece, headlining the second night of a three-day festival staged in an Athens basketball stadium. The Birthday Party and New Order topped the first and third evenings. Smith was unusually magnanimous towards at least the first-named. Nick

Cave's men were joined onstage by Jim 'Foetus' Thirlwell, who added saxophone to a tumultuous version of the Stooges' 'Fun House'. 'At the end of the gig,' Thirlwell recalled, 'I remember Mark E Smith saying that he liked my saxophone because it was so minimal.'

Smith himself told *Masterbag* magazine's Helen Fitzgerald that the Birthday Party were 'one band I really like and I would say we have similar vibes. What they played in Athens was real bluesy stuff, which I really liked. When I saw them at the Venue [in August 1982], I went home and wrote a couple of songs the same night... mostly about the audience though, not the band!'

Smith's affection for the Birthday Party was reciprocated. Following the group's relocation to Berlin (immediately after that Venue gig), guitarist Rowland Howard admitted, 'for the first time since we left Australia we felt part of some sort of "scene." There was nothing like that in England. The Fall were the only group we felt any affinity with.'

The two bands came close to an even firmer link after Kay Carroll and Birthday Party publicist Chris Carr began discussing trying to attract major label interest in their charges with a so-called Gods of Indie package deal – the Go-Betweens and the Moodists were among other bands considered for inclusion. Nothing came of the scheme, however, and slowly the parties drifted apart: the Birthday Party to Mute, the Go-Betweens to Sire. The Fall remained with Kamera.

The band's return from their travels coincided with the release of the mini-album, *Room To Live*, a seven-track affair that Smith insisted marked a return to the basics that once fired the Fall. With strange serendipity, however, it also precipitated the kind of crisis that hallmarked those early days. The record had barely reached the streets before it was announced that both Marc Riley and manager Kay Carroll were departing (the former sacked, the latter leaving for a new life in the US). These ruptures shocked the band's followers as much as any of the new record's contents. Sudden splits were nothing new to the Fall but the seeming stability of the band's recent line-up had inured many to the possibility that the Fall could ever be sundered again.

Smith refused to allow sentimentality to obscure his vision. 'Half the reason that Marc Riley had to leave,' he explained, '[was] because he kept on saying, "Ah, it's not as good as this or that we did a year ago," and that is just not the point of The Fall at all. If we've ever had any videos done, I've tried to keep the lads from watching, so that we're always looking towards the future and never towards the past.'

(MUSICIANS)

LINE-UP #12 (Jan-Nov) MARK E SMITH (vocals), MARC RILEY (guitar, keyboards), CRAIG SCANLON (guitar), STEVE HANLEY (bass), PAUL HANLEY (drums), KARL BURNS (drums)

LINE-UP #13 (remainder) MARK E SMITH (vocals), CRAIG SCANLON (guitar), STEVE HANLEY (bass), PAUL HANLEY (drums), KARL BURNS (drums)

(ALBUM) *Hex Enduction Hour*
8201. The Classical

8202. Jawbone and the Air-Rifle
8203. Hip Priest
8204. Fortress-Deer Park
8205. Mere Pseud Mag. Ed.
8206. Winter (Hostel Maxi) (Hostel-Maxi)
8207. Winter 2
8208. Just Step S'ways
8209. Who Makes the Nazis?
8210. Iceland
8211. And This Day
(*) BONUS TRACKS
8220. Look, Know
8221. I'm Into C.B.
ORIGINAL RELEASE Kamera KAM005 March 1982 (LP)
REISSUE (1): Line LICD 9.00126 (CD), (white vinyl LP) 1986
REISSUE (2): Cog Sinister COGVP119CD (CD) 1999
REISSUE (3): Cog Sinister COGVP141CD (CD) 2002 with bonus tracks (*)
UK CHART PEAK: #71
UK INDIE CHART PEAK: #2
COMMENTS: Looking back on *Hex Enduction Hour* with a few months'
distance, Smith described it as the Fall's most violent album, deliberately recorded
in some of the world's most rugged surroundings – the studio in Iceland where the
self-explanatory 'Iceland' and the keening dirge 'Hip Priest' were cut, was hewn
from the lava of a past volcanic eruption. Titles such as 'Who Makes The Nazis?'
(inspired by visits to the American south during their last US tour) and 'Jawbone
and the Air Rifle', too, posited a querulous air of danger and destruction, yet it was
the less pregnant numbers that really established the album's agenda.

The opening percussive ricochet of the angrily mumbled 'The Classical' – with
its famous refrain of 'hey there, fuck face!' – puts one in mind of the Cure's near-
simultaneous *Pornography*, an album that has also been described by its maker as
the sound of violence (or, at least, the inability to be truly violent). From there, *Hex
Enduction Hour* slides through a variety of tensions, with the EuroDisco pulse of
'Fortress – Deer Park' (yes, that is the disembodied spirit of Trio's 'Da Da Da'
tinkling over the intro) and the slowly-percolating motorik plunge of 'Winter
(Hostel Maxi)' the poles around which the album revolves. The closing 'And This
Day', meanwhile, wraps ten minutes of clunky, Glitter-esque drums around the
listener's skull with such a relentless energy that Smith's own contribution to the
proceedings is all but lost in the tumult.

It is a fabulous record, one half, with the year-end's *Room To Live* mini-album,
of the Fall's most potent delivery yet. Whereas media response to the latter was torn
between muted disapproval and downright loathing, *Hex Enduction Hour* could not
have been made more welcome: '60 minutes of The Fall with all their previous
incarnations toughened to a bitterly frightening degree,' proclaimed the *New
Musical Express*. With *Hex Enduction Hour*, the Fall had created 'their masterpiece
to date.'

(LIVE) Derby Hall, Bury, April 27, 1982 (release states Manchester, May 1982)
8212. Look, Know
8213. Tempo House

8214. I'm into C.B.
8215. Mere Pseudo Mag. Ed.
UNR Who Makes The Nazis
UNR Solicitor In The Studio
8216. Draygo's Guilt
8217. Joker Hysterical Face
8218. Lie Dream of a Casino Soul
8219. Hexen Definitive Strife Knot
UNR Backdrop
UNR Container Drivers
UNR And This Day

ORIGINAL RELEASE: 8212-8215 included with CD reissue of *In: Palace Of Swords Reversed*; 8216-8219 included with CD reissue of *Room to Live (Undiluteable Slang Truth)*. These releases appeared following the scrapping of a proposed 2 CD set comprising the entire concert, coupled with a second performance taped the previous year at the Queen Mary Union, London (see above, Feb 5th 1981).

COMMENTS: A rough but undeniably powerful performance suffering only from its dissection. All concerned are in irrepressible form, performing to what – at whichever venue it was actually taped – amounts to a hometown crowd, and rewarding them with one of the strongest sets of the entire tour. The versions of 'I'm Into C.B.' and 'Joker Hysterical Face' are especially electrifying.

Noted above are the tracks unreleased from this particular show. As various circulating live tapes demonstrate, Fall shows around this time were a prickly minefield of verbal and musical tripwires – 'Middle Mass' seemed to feature a new diatribe every day, while the band also experimented with some interesting medleys ('C'n'C' and 'Gramme Friday' is a long-standing fan favourite). Most fascinating of all, however, are the songs that have never yet appeared on any official release.

'Session Musician' was a live regular for around a year (spring 1981-spring 1982), its closing refrain 'Jingles! Cabaret! Merseybeat!' ranking among Smith's most infectious chants.

Other numbers known only from underground tapes are 'Don't Like Maggie', an anti-Thatcher improvisation from the band's March 1982 Hammersmith Palais show, and a piece titled (whether by Smith or an enterprising taper) 'Stars on 45 Lines', a play on the *Stars On 45* pop/Disco medleys that were so popular at the time. While Smith performs the lyrics to 'I'm Into C.B.' (appropriate because that was exactly the sort of person who bought those records), the band lurch through riffs and hooks from whichever Fall songs came to mind.

(SINGLE) Look, Know
8220. Look, Know
8221. I'm Into C.B.
ORIGINAL RELEASE: Kamera ERA 004 (7-inch) April 1982
UK INDIE CHART PEAK: #4
COMMENTS: One of the songs that clearly shows the Fall's spiritual links to the Birthday Party, 'Look, Know' – recorded in Iceland the previous summer – marries a clattered drum and bass (as opposed to drum'n'bass) to an almost drunken, definitely idiosyncratic, lambasting of modern club-hoppers. Voiced more coherently, it might have provided a generation of impressionable youngsters with

the strength to set themselves apart from the celebrity squares that queued outside the Hacienda, *et al*. Smith's tone and diction are as venomous as the lyric, making 'Look, Know' a poison pen letter many of its recipients wouldn't bother to read.

'I'm Into C.B.' is equally hostile, the story of Happy Harry Plank and a salutary lesson in the perils of operating that most fashionable of early 80s automobile accessories, an unlicensed Citizen's Band radio. Dimly perceiving unfettered access to the airwaves as an open invitation to crime and pirate radio broadcast, the government cracked down hard on unlicensed CB operators. Perhaps, if the government had left them alone, cell-phones wouldn't seem so exciting. Today, Happy Harry probably has one in every pocket.

(LIVE) Aug 2 1982, Prince of Wales Hotel, Melbourne, Australia

8222. I Feel Voxish
8223. Tempo House
8224. Hard Life In Country
8225. I'm Into C.B.
8226. Lie Dream Of A
   Casino Soul
8227. Solicitor In Studio
8228. Marquis Cha-Cha
8229. Room to Live
8230. Hexen Definitive-Strife
   Knot
8231. Deer Park
8232. Totally Twisted
   (Totally Wired)
8233. Joker Hysterical Face
8234. Hip Priest
ORIGINAL RELEASE: as
Live to Air in Melbourne, Cog
Sinister COGVP108CD (CD) 1998. Tracks 8232-34 are not listed on the CD sleeve, and appear on an unlisted second CD within the package.

COMMENTS: Filed alongside the 1997 release of *Fall In A Hole*, which was recorded in New Zealand less than three weeks after this show, the collector can now experience the band's 1982 Australasian tour from two dramatic high points. Originally broadcast on local radio, this particular recording appears to have been taped straight off the air – although its greatest fault is the occasional fluctuation in recording levels. It's a little boomy in places but *Live To Air* is extremely rewarding, a thoughtful set list highlighting both the rancour and the romance of Smith's best work. Even he seems to have a lump in his throat as the melancholy 'Hard Life in the Country' inches along. Tingling emotional goosepimples are soon forgotten as 'Solicitor in Studio' explodes with the kind of fury that people always associate with the Velvet Underground (but which you'll be hard-pressed to find on their records). 'Lie Dream of a Casino Soul' captures the manic spontaneity of the Fall in full flow. Smith's ad-libbed rampage through the lyric is a slice of genuinely memorable mayhem.

(LIVE) 21 Aug 1982, Auckland, New Zealand
8235. Impression of J. Temperance

8236. Man whose Head Expanded
8237. Room to Live
8238. Hip Priest
8239. Lie Dream of a Casino Soul
8240. Prole Art Threat
8241. Hard Life in Country
8242. The Classical
8243. Mere Pseud Mag Ed
8244. Marquis Cha-cha
8245. Backdrop
8246. Fantastic Life
8247. English Scheme
8248. Joker Hysterical Face
8249. No Xmas for John Quays
8250. Solicitor in Studio
ORIGINAL RELEASE: as *Fall In a Hole*, Flying Nun (NZ) MARK1/2 (LP) 1983
REISSUE (1): bootleg – details unknown
REISSUE (2): Cog Sinister COGVP 102 (CD) 1997
REISSUE (3): Cog Sinister COGVP 137 (CD) 2002
COMMENTS: A super-rare release on New Zealand's Flying Nun label which was reissued as an only marginally less-scarce German bootleg and which merits every last plaudit it has ever won – in terms of the performance, at any rate. Sonically, it's quite another matter.

Despite being recorded just months after the Manchester show preserved on the *Room To Live/In: Palace* bonus discs, the set has undergone a complete overhaul. Just three songs are repeated from that earlier gig ('Mere Pseudo Mag. Ed.', 'Joker Hysterical Face' and 'Lie Dream of a Casino Soul') and the freshness of the material certainly seems to drive Smith's performance up a notch. That said, 'No Xmas for John Quays' is as dramatic as any available performance, while the presence of the seldom-heard 'Backdrop' and 'Solicitor in Studio' also gives the album a certain cachet.

Unfortunately, only the original Flying Nun release alone is worth spending time with. The German bootleg was evidently sourced from a less than pristine copy of the Flying Nun release. Cog Sinister simply took a well-worn copy of the boot for its source, heedless even of sundry skips and clicks. It's a major disappointment that did much to undo the goodwill that the label's pledge to unearth further live rarities had generated.

(ALBUM) *Room to Live (Undiluteable Slang Truth)*
8251. Joker Hysterical Face
8252. Marquis Cha Cha (LP version)
8253. Hard Life in Country
8254. Room to Live
8255. Detective Instinct
8256. Solicitor in Studio
8257. Papal Visit
(*) BONUS TRACKS
8118. Lie Dream of a Casino Soul

8119. Fantastic Life
(**) BONUS CD
8216. Draygo's Guilt
8217. Joker Hysterical Face
8218. Lie Dream of a Casino Soul
8219. Hexen Definitive Strife Knot
ORIGINAL RELEASE Kamera KAM011 (LP) October 1982
REISSUE (1): Line LILP4.00109 (LP) 1983 with bonus tracks (*)
REISSUE (2): Cog Sinister COGVP105CD (CD) 1998 with bonus tracks (*) +
bonus CD (**)
REISSUE (3): Cog Sinister COGVP139CD (CD) 2002 with bonus tracks (*)
UK INDIE CHART PEAK: #4
COMMENTS: The most contentious Fall release in a while, largely because it
was the most overtly topical. Released with very little fanfare, the EP prompted
reviewers – lulled by the more straightforward production of recent Fall releases –
to slam it for sounding rough, unpolished, unconsidered. Which, of course, was the
point: *Room To Live* offers an introduction to the soul of the Fall which even their
live recordings rarely match, the sound of the band at its most spontaneous, the
sound of Smith at his most inchoate. As Julian Cope observed, 'all the uncool
thoughts you'd have, he'd say.'

Inspired, according to Smith, by the tumult of the previous spring, as the
jingoistic fervour surrounding Britain's war in the Falklands offered a dramatic
counterpoint to the nationwide outbreak of piety prompted by the Pope's visit.
Smith summed it up as 'me going off on a tangent... most of the songs are about
Britain as I see it on a wider scale, having been abroad a lot.'

Even so, the songs were not solely concerned with the so-called 'wider picture'
of British life. 'Joker Hysterical Face,' for example, was inspired by 'a couple who
live downstairs from us, where we were living, and they used to play Abba and that
stuff, they always used to have it on full blast. She was a divorcee, and it's not very
far from the feminist movement. Like the man is the main thing to blame.'

The sessions that begat *Room To Live* were originally intended only to produce a
one-off single of 'Marquis Cha-Cha'. They quickly gathered momentum. The entire
mini-album was written, recorded and released within a fortnight. 'The songs are an
overflow,' Smith explained. 'I decided to put down this other material I had, the
songs all went together, and I wanted to do something instantaneous... to get back
to the old Fall way of recording songs straight off the top of our heads! I thought we
were getting a bit restricted by *Hex*, it was so "thought out", planned, and...
intensive.'

Room To Live, on the other hand, was... if not quite thrown together, certainly
uninhibited. Individual band members were omitted from some songs – 'all of the
Fall are on the record, but not all of them on every track' – while other songs were
recorded cold. Totally unrehearsed. Some featured passing guests Arthur Cadman
(guitar) and Adrian Niman (sax). Smith recalled, 'We just went in and did them
which is how we always operated in the good old days!'

Of course, the backlash against the album was assisted by Smith's unusual
willingness to discuss the songs in depth. In the past, he'd preferred to dismiss
analysis of his lyrics with fervent denials. This time around, he exposed the thoughts
and beliefs that lay at the heart of every song, with the most heated discussion
cantering around 'Papal Visit'.

Inspired by the arrival of Pope John Paul II, the first Pope to visit Britain in 450 years, critics interpreted the song as being anti-Catholic, even though Smith insisted it was merely anti-Pope. He told *Masterbag*, 'This Polish boy he really frightens – no – *disgusts* me. I mean, he's reeking of socialist dictatorship man, he's propagating populist myths. "The people's Pope" – but he's really quite insidious. The guy stinks.'

Smith's opinions were not popular. His apparent support for the Falklands war challenged the unthinking opposition of the liberal left, which coloured the record's reception. The often scratchy sound simply offered a fresh quiver of arrows to the album's citics. ("Right crap" – Amrik Rai, *NME*.)

In musical terms, however, it was that very roughness which ensured the collection's longevity. Removed from contemporary concerns, *Room To Live* has an immediacy that few of its peers can match. Certainly the directness of Smith's lyrics has a private spluttering diary feel that reveals the 'angry poetry' of others as the overwrought precocity it usually was. Neither could that fact be undermined by Smith's later insistence that, 'I don't want [to write] anything that will date fast because that would destroy everything The Fall have ever stood for. If I wrote a song about trade unions, it would be irrelevant in six months 'cos they would have changed by then.' Yet that was precisely what he had done and, in so doing, he'd proven himself utterly wrong. While it's true that a single record can never really recapture a true sense of the era in which it was made, *Room To Live* comes close.

(SINGLE) Marquis Cha-Cha
  8252a. Marquis Cha-Cha (7-inch version)
  8254. Room to Live
  ORIGINAL RELEASE: Kamera ERA014 (7-inch) October 1982 – WITHDRAWN
  COMMENTS: The furious percussive assault that sets the scene puts one vaguely in mind of Killing Joke. The whistling that underpins the song, on the other hand, makes it plain that it shouldn't, long before Smith's barked command sends the sound of the band dropping back several notches, to content itself with a loose tinkling and a circuitous bass line. As singles go, Smith's invocation of a Falklands-flavoured equivalent to the English-born Nazi propagandist Lord Haw Haw, was an odd choice – the song worked much better within the context of *Room To Live*. Few tears were shed when the release was shelved before issue. According to the *Backdrop* liner notes, approximately 800 copies of the single eventually hit the streets in November 1983.

(LIVE) date and location unknown
  8258. Who Makes The Nazis?
  8259. Just Step S'ways
  8260. Jawbone And The Air-Rifle
  8261. And This Day
  ORIGINAL RELEASE: bonus tracks on CD reissue of *Hip Priests And Kamerads*
  COMMENTS: Muddy and distorted, but scintillating in its intensity, a short burst of primal live Fall is topped by an unbeatable 15-minute version of 'And This Day.'

1983

One of the most dramatic years in the Fall's career opened, unfussily, with business as usual: a string of live shows throughout the UK, Switzerland and the Netherlands, a John Peel session in March (the sixth in as many years) and the release of a live album taped during the summer 1981 American tour, the aptly titled *A Piece of America Therein*. The latter accompanied the launch of the Fall's next US outing, a month-long excursion that, once again, preceded a flying visit to Iceland.

Still operating as a somewhat ungainly quintet with two drummers, but only one guitarist, the Fall nevertheless created a stunning mood – indeed, they made a virtue of the imbalance, one which *NME*'s Don Watson encapsulated when he caught the band in Brixton in July, at the end of their global wanderings. 'Not since the paradoxical peaks of the Birthday Party has a live performance caused such an increase in the collective heart rate, or a music blended so brilliantly the maverick dynamics of jazz and the cut gut thrill of rock.'

News that Smith had recently married 20-year-old American Laura Elise – 'Brix' to her friends – barely effected on the Fall's public persona. Nor was it expected to. Only when September brought the announcement that she would be joining the band, at least partially filling the melodic void created by Marc Riley's departure, did cynics nod knowingly, muttering about Linda McCartney. Boy, did they mutter.

In fact, the very opposite was true. McCartney found a wife, then left his band. Mark E Smith was seriously considering leaving his band before he found a wife. Five years of slogging the circuit to the same uncomprehending gaze and unquestioning praise every time had finally taken their toll. Brix brought more than companionship and love. She also brought new reason for the Fall to continue.

The couple met in April at Chicago's Cabaret Metro, just a few weeks after one of Brix's friends, Lisa, prompted her to listen to *Slates* for the first time. Armed with the fake IDs that are standard gig-going equipment for Americans aged under 21, the pair went along to the show – only for Brix to suddenly find herself alone on the dancefloor after Lisa disappeared. For want of anything better to do, Brix made her way downstairs to the Smart Bar, stopped to talk with a friend and found herself next to Mark E Smith.

Interviewed on Radio 1, Brix recalled, 'We were just sitting there talking and he just said out of the blue, "Can I kiss you? I know, it's really cheeky, I know it's shocking." And I said, "No way. I don't know you, you're a stranger, no way." And he was like, "All right then," and we kept on talking about music and stuff and I was saying I was in a band and blah blah blah, and then he just reached over and grabbed me and he started kissing me and I just pulled back and I said, "You're a bastard." That's what I said to him, I was really shocked and my eyes began to spin around in my head and everything and then we went to a party the rest of the night. And that was it. And we were together ever since. The word 'marriage' came up the next day after that party.'

The couple originally hoped to wed while the Fall toured Europe – Copenhagen was a favourite choice. Unfortunately, they were never stayed in any one city long enough to meet even the most relaxed licensing regulations and the marriage finally took place at Bury registry office.

Brix's induction into the Fall was somewhat slower – the initial plan was to launch her as a solo artist, with Smith producing. Then, as Smith's thoughts turned towards the group's next album, he earmarked one of Brix's compositions, 'Everything For The Record', for inclusion, and invited her to guest on that one recording.

As the sessions developed, it became apparent that the material the band had been playing live for months needed re-arrangement, needed heavier artillery. Brix would help provide both. She explained later, 'I thought I could be a good contrast for the band,' she remarked. 'I give it a lot of drive as well as adding some glamour.' Which was something, even her husband admitted, that nobody ever expected to hear from a member of the Fall.

Joining Smith in interviews, Brix acknowledged that, both within and without the Fall's immediate circle, her recruitment remained surprising to some, anathema to others. 'Everyone was watching me very critically to start with. [But] after I proved myself, there was a spark that stimulated the band, a new way of looking at things. I feel I just brought out what was needed. I wasn't calculating in any way – I just did what come naturally to me, and fitted in where I could. When I came in it was like an already-painted canvas, so I just added light and shadow where I could. I didn't force it in any way. I was asked to do what I did.' And, again, she injected some glamour. 'From the image point of view, Brix is almost incongruous,' Smith continued, 'which is great. She's beautiful y'know, so she's stuck at the end of a bunch of paddies and me!'

Close to a decade later, following the dissolution of their relationship, Smith remained wholly enamoured with the music that the Fall created with Brix. 'She could sing and play guitar, whereas we couldn't! It was a good period. Her contribution was amazing. She took the band by the neck and fucking organised it. What I hated with the Brix thing was they blamed it all on her lust because she's a bloody woman, but it was my decision. I rule The Fall.'

Buoyed by the release of a brace of new singles, the post-anorak nightmare warning of 'The Man Whose Head Expanded', and the turbulent, football violence-themed 'Kicker Conspiracy', the new-look Fall hit the road in September, ahead of the release of the next album, *Perverted By Language*.

Somewhat cautiously, the group had returned to Rough Trade. Kamera had fizzled out during the year, leaving Smith to mourn years later, 'we had to leave Kamera because we knew it was going down. It broke my heart. Kamera were like, "Here y'are mate, what you're saying is fantastic. *Hex Enduction Hour* is brilliant, you're brilliant, here's a cheque." You play *Hex* to them, they go, "Fuckin' brilliant, mate! Uriah Heep at its best!" Only label I was upset to leave.'

Returning to Rough Trade, on the other hand, 'was a bastard. Because it was

Rough Trade, they put us in some fucking crap studio for like four days. Some of the tapes were actually recorded too slow, things kept breaking down.' At the time, however, Smith made the best of the situation, telling *Zig Zag*, 'There's a lot more beauty on this new LP. Some of the new songs aim straight at the heart. It's still aggressive. [But it's] a lot funnier as well. We craft everything much better these days. Seriousness and humour are blended together more now.'

(MUSICIANS)
LINE-UP #13 (Jan-Sept) MARK E SMITH (vocals), CRAIG SCANLON (guitar), STEVE HANLEY (bass), PAUL HANLEY (drums), KARL BURNS (drums)

LINE-UP #14 (remainder) MARK E SMITH (vocals), CRAIG SCANLON (guitar), BRIX SMITH (guitar, vocals), STEVE HANLEY (bass), PAUL HANLEY (keyboards, drums), KARL BURNS (bass, drums)

(LIVE) March 21, 1983, Victoria Venue, London
  8301. Plaster On The Hands
  UNR. Mere Pseud Mag Ed
  UNR. Words of Expectation
  UNR. Ludd Gang
  UNR. Wings
  UNR. Kicker Conspiracy
  UNR. Tempo House
  UNR. Hexen Definitive-Strife Knot
  UNR. The Man Whose Head Expanded
  UNR. Smile
  UNR. Garden
  UNR. Room to Live
  UNR. Eat Y'self Fitter
  UNR. Middlemass
  ORIGINAL RELEASE: on compilation *Backdrop* (Pseudo Indie 1994)
  COMMENTS: 'Plaster on the Hands' (*aka* 'Pilsner Trail') presents the view from a mike at the back of the bathroom – a raw live recording that pushes Smith's vocals to the front of your head, while the band buzzes angrily in the background. Not an essential recording, but certainly a representative one.
(BBC SESSION) March 23, 1983
  8302. Eat Y'self Fitter
  8303. Smile
  ORIGINAL RELEASE: 8302 on *Manchester: So Much To Answer For* (Strange Fruit SFRCD 202, 1993), 8303 on *The Peel Sessions* (1998)

(LIVE) May 4 1983, White Columns, New York
  8304. Smile
  8305. Tempo House
  UNR. Hexen Definitive-Strife Knot
  UNR. I Feel Voxish
  UNR. The Man Whose Head Expanded

UNR. Kicker Conspiracy
UNR. Look, Know
UNR. Ludd Gang
UNR. Wings
UNR. The Classical
UNR. Backdrop
ORIGINAL RELEASE: various artists live album *Speed Trials*, Homestead (US) HMS011 (LP) 1984
REISSUE (1): Homestead 011 (CD) 1995
COMMENTS: Looking ever-so-slightly out of place, the Fall line up alongside such formative giants of noise as Sonic Youth, the Swans, Live Skull, Lydia Lunch and the pre-rap Beastie Boys.

(LIVE) May 6 1983, Austurbae Jarbio, Reykjavik, Iceland
8306. Tempo House
8307. The Classical
8308. Eat Y'self Fitter
8309. Hexen Definitive
8310. I Feel Voxish
8311. The Man Whose Head Expanded
8312. Garden
8313. Kicker Conspiracy
8314. Look, Know
8315. Backdrop
ORIGINAL RELEASE: as *Austurbae Jarbio*, Cog Sinister COGVP125CD (CD) 2001
COMMENTS: A Fall line-up built around Smith, twin drummers Karl Burns and Paul Hanley, guitarist Craig Scanlon and bassist Steve Hanley touches down to offer a preview of material that would ultimately comprise the *Perverted By Language* album – as it stood before Brix Smith moved into their lives.

It's a rough-and-ready performance, a point that becomes a positive virtue as an excellent stereo soundboard recording unfolds. The new songs sound new all over again, while older ones are given startlingly fresh lives to live. From the then-current *Hex Enduction Hour*, 'The Classical' is a revelation, while 12 minutes of 'Backdrop' close the show with breathless majesty. For that, and for the glimpse of the alternative reality therein, *Austurbae Jarbio* joins the select band of essential Fall albums, no argument.

(SINGLE) The Man Whose Head Expanded
8316. The Man Whose Head Expanded
8317. Ludd Gang
ORIGINAL RELEASE: Rough Trade RT133, June 1983
UK INDIE CHART PEAK: #3
COMMENTS: Opening with lightly tinkling keyboard lick (is that Depeche Mode's 'Just Can't Get Enough' dancing therein?), the anorak-analysis of 'The Man Whose Head Expanded' is one of Smith's most compelling songs, the haunting repetition of the vocal leaving the listener utterly unprepared for either the snatches of guitar, piano, bass and electronics-fuelled discordance that trace through the first couple of minutes, or for the deliberate slackening of the tempo that threatens, at times, to reduce the entire thing to a grinding halt.

The stop-start 'Ludd Gang' is somewhat less enthralling. Despite the connotations of its title, this duet for Nuremberg chant and Morse code bass has less in common with destroying the machines than it does simply gnawing at the status quo. However, an explosion of anger against Shakin' Stevens for 'the massacre of "Blue Christmas' slashes almost at random out of the lyric, and has become one of Smith's most oft-quoted sentiments.

(SINGLE) Kicker Conspiracy
    8318. Kicker Conspiracy
    8319. Wings
    8010. The Container Drivers
    8011. New Puritan
    ORIGINAL RELEASE: Rough Trade RT143, October 1983 (2 x 7" gatefold sleeve)
    UK INDIE CHART PEAK: #5
    COMMENTS: When 'Kicker Conspiracy' came out in 1983, Smith reflected a decade later, 'no bugger wanted to know about soccer songs.' The game itself was in turmoil, beset by hooliganism, assaulted by the government, and on a collision course with some kind of disaster, even before the triple blows of Heysel, Hillsborough and Valley Parade served to damage the game's reputation beyond redemption. Tailor-made, it was sniped, for the Casual hordes who swaggered round the stadium in matching shirts and Stanley knives, 'Kicker Conspiracy' was… uncool, uncouth, un-everything that a right-minded mid-80s pop star should be thinking about.
    Since that time – or, at least, since New Order's 'World In Motion' – soccer songs, like soccer itself, had become a national obsession, while 'Kicker Conspiracy''s own subtext of institutionalised hooliganism has enjoyed its own nostalgic revival, the subject of a thousand (it seemed) identi-thug memoirs of riots and rumbles past. (The institutional stupidity, on the other hand, never went away.) The irony would not be lost on Smith.
    As much a sequence of linked tirades (including an excellent, and still pertinent, parody of television football-reporting) as a song, 'Kicker Conspiracy' is addresses what, even today, seems the guiding principle of the game's governors, the crushing of individual flair in favour of workmanlike doggedness. But, of course, that's not unique to football.
    The exercise in taut dynamics continues on the b-side. The uncompromisingly mixed 'Wings' is an extraordinary song, a homeless man explaining how time travel caused his present predicament.
    Two final songs in the package, exploring the loneliness of the long distance lorry driver and the lovelessness of political correctness, were drawn from the Fall's September 1980 John Peel session. With cryptic incompetence, the 2002 *Rough Trade Singles Box* reissue replaced these cuts with their (inferior) counterparts from the regular LPs.

(STUDIO) out-takes
    8319a. Wings (alternate version)
    8320. Medical Acceptance Gate
    8321. Pilsner Trail
    8322. Pilsner Trail (live)

8328a. I Feel Voxish (alternate version – 4 mins, 23 secs)
8328b. I Feel Voxish (alternate version – 4 mins, 13 secs)
8323a. Eat Y'self Fitter (alternate version)
ORIGINAL RELEASE: 8320 on *The Collection* (1990), 8321 on *Perverted By Language* (1998 reissue), 8322 on *Levitation* bonus disc, 8328a on *Totally Wired* (2002), remainder see Receiver label comps (appendix II)
COMMENTS: 'Pilsner Trail' is a revised studio version of the live track 'Plaster On The Hands'.
NOTE: The so-called '1983 session' version of 'Strychnine' included on the *Backdrop* compilation was, in fact, taken from the Fall's 1993 John Peel session.

(ALBUM) *Perverted By Language*
8323. Eat Y'self Fitter
8324. Neighbourhood of Infinity
8325. Garden
8326. Hotel Blôedel
8327. Smile
8328. I Feel Voxish
8329. Tempo House
8330. Hexen Definitive-Strife Knot
(*) BONUS TRACKS
8316. The Man Whose Head Expanded
8317. Ludd Gang
8318. Kicker Conspiracy
8319. Wings
8321. Pilsner Trail
ORIGINAL RELEASE Rough Trade ROUGH62 – December 1983 (LP)
REISSUE (1): Line LICD 9.00006 (LP, CD) 1986
REISUE (2): Castle CD CLACD392 (CD) 1993
REISSUE (3): Cog Sinister COGVP104CD (CD) 1998
REMIXED REISSUE (4): Castle/Essential ESMCD639 (CD) 1998, with bonus tracks (*)
UK INDIE CHART PEAK: #1
COMMENTS: Though hindsight certainly makes it seem that way, the advent of Brix Smith's 60s pop inflections did not immediately send the Fall lurching off in a new, more pop-friendly direction; nor did it in any way quell the acerbic atonality that was the band's chosen form of delivery. Rather, any number of factors influenced the slow shift towards less purposefully obtuse arenas, including – though his words forever fell on deaf ears – Smith's own disgust with the constant analysis to which his lyrics were subjected by fans and critics.

He told *Zig Zag*, 'I sometimes dislike the fact that everything I write has to be picked apart, though I usually play up to it straightaway. Some songs are just poetic exercises or something. There's too much of this sort of disease – people wanting to tamper with everything to see how it works. It's just that I've never had that particular disease and it's never fascinated me. Things can be tampered with too much, y'know.'

He was not a spokesman for the downtrodden northerner, he was not the repository for revolutionary game plans, he was not interested in any of the other guises and disguises up for grabs in the rock and pop changing room. Those jobs were already taken, anyway. The only stance that was truly the Fall's by choice was one of remaining true to their own opinions and observations. 'And if people don't like it, tough.'

Concert recordings from earlier in the year demonstrate just how radically different the album might have been. Much of the record's content was already in the live set, with a recording of the Reykjavik gig back in August a virtual dry run for the recording sessions – five of the album's eight tracks were featured. The difference was Brix.

Perverted By Language was not tough, and was likeable – this despite Smith's promise, to *Melody Maker*, that the last months of the Marc Riley era suffered from 'too much melody. I'm going to erase it and get down to a very biased one channel of noise that I've been after for years.' The slow-moving tension of 'Smile', the live and lucid 'Tempo House' and the strangely delivered 'Hexen Definitive', with its vocal line apparently phoned in from another room, all snarled defiantly at the Fall's past reputation, with racket replaced by reinstated repetition, mayhem by near-mantra.

Brix's scratchy vocal showcase, 'Hotel Blôedel', meanwhile, celebrated its contrasts by impressing at least one listener as perhaps the most Fall-like track on the album – high praise indeed when ranked alongside the racked rockabilly of 'Eat Y'self Fitter', an almost numbing six-plus minute guitar and bass blurge that is characterised by one of the most hauntingly nonsensical hooklines you'll ever hear.

1984

The Fall returned to the John Peel show on January 3rd 1984, with the broadcast of a session recorded three weeks earlier. As usual, they performed four songs; as usual, all four were new and, at that time, unreleased: versions of 'c.r.e.e.p.' and 'Pat Trip Dispenser' would make it out as a single in August; '2x4' was destined for their next album; 'Words of Expectation' remains unissued.

A little more than two months later, the band were back at the BBC to record a session for the early-evening David Jensen show: 'Oh Brother' and 'God Box' (previewing another forthcoming 45), 'Lay of the Land' and a reprise of 'c.r.e.e.p.' Before the year was out, they would venture twice more onto the airwaves, for Janice Long and *Saturday Live*.

Tours of Holland, Germany, Norway and the UK devoured the first half of the year. But, behind the welter of activity consuming the Fall, Smith was locked in a furious dilemma. Relations with Rough Trade soured once again and the band soon found itself back on the street.

This second severance was acrimonious, as Smith recalled: 'Rough Trade were soft, boring hippies. They'd go, "Er, the tea boy doesn't like the fact that you've slagged off Wah! Heat on this number." And fuckin'... "the girl who cooks the fuckin' rice in the canteen doesn't like the fact that you've used the word 'slags'." They had a whole meeting over the fact that we mentioned guns in one song. Y'know? "It is not the policy of Rough Trade to be supporting fuckin'..." And I'd go, "What the fuck has it got to do with you? Just fuckin' sell the record, you fuckin' hippy." I'd rather retire than work with them again.'

Label head Geoff Travis saw a more prosaic reason for Smith's angry departure. That spring saw the label – like the UK media in general – adopt a whole new Mancunian cause, in the form of the Smiths. Travis reflected, 'When the Smiths were successful, that immediately alienated Mark E Smith. I don't think [he] was thrilled to see these upstarts pass him by and I can understand why he felt like that.'

The two bands could scarcely have been further removed from one another – although they shared a loathing for anything existing beyond the insulating wall of the Pennines. Indeed, vocalist Morrissey had long since shown sympathy to the Fall's cause, when he predicted, via the *Kid's Stuff* fanzine in 1978, that they were one of just four local bands likely to advance further than they'd already come (the others were the Worst, the Drones and Warsaw: two out of four ain't bad). *Dragnet* producer and sound engineer Grant 'Showbiz' Cunliffe was now a key member of the Smiths' entourage. (By the end of the year another former member of the Fall's road crew, Oz McCormick would join him.)

The two bands had played together, as well: days after of the release of their debut single, 'Hand in Glove', the Smiths opened for the Fall at London's Electric Ballroom on May 21st 1983. Whether the Fall felt threatened by this latest claim on their crown as Kings of the Indie scene is a question that exercised many minds at the time. But, when one re-reads contemporary media insistence that a mantle-of-sorts was being passed (the coincidence of the name Smith escaped nobody), you can understand why the Fall were unhappy. Whether they admitted it or not.

Both their status and their safety were at stake – *not*, perhaps, in the game of eternal one-upmanship that the media liked to imagine, but certainly within the realms of Rough Trade. A small label thinks small – the Fall had experienced that on more than one occasion. If the Smiths really did escape the cult status of the label's other acts, who would be the first to suffer, as all hands leapt to the superstars' cause? Everybody that wasn't the Smiths!

The first label to take interest in the Fall's newfound free agency was, unlikely as it sounds, Motown. 'It was hilarious,' Smith recalled. 'They gave me this LP from Rare Earth, this ecology group, first white group on Motown, and were going on about how we were going to be the second. I just thought it was so funny. They did us a favour really, because loads of companies started chasing us when they heard Motown were interested.' In fact, Motown's interest was very short-lived – rumour insisted it collapsed when the label's American paymasters chanced across the lyrics to 'The Classical': 'Where are the obligatory niggers? Hey there, fuckface!' Suspend Political Correctness and simply look at the Fall from the standpoint of a Tamla traditionalist. It was all a very long way from 'Baby Love'. Or even Rare Earth.

The Fall ended up with Beggars Banquet, another scion of the early post-Punk era, catapulted to major status by its success with, first, Gary Numan's Tubeway Army, then by its farsighted patronage of the manifold extremes of the formative Goth scene. Bauhaus, the Birthday Party, Gene Loves Jezebel and the Cult: all called the little office on Battersea's Alma Road home. If the Fall's presence among them jarred more than it ever did at Rough Trade, then so much the better. At least they would never get lost in anyone else's backwash. 'We must be the only ones on the label who get good reviews,' Smith reflected the following year. 'I like it because they're straights. The other labels we've been on, you get the bleedin' teaboy interfering in the cover design. Everybody thinks they've got the right to say something to yer, but Beggars just want to have hit singles.'

Indeed they did – and they were rather good at getting them. The Fall were leaving a label whose sights were set on the independent charts for one well-versed in gnawing at the national listings, a poll the Fall had visited just once, when their first Kamera album scratched #71. In the six years that the Fall spent with Beggars Banquet, they placed each of their LPs in the UK chart. They also amassed seven hit singles, while 1984 alone saw them appear on both *The Tube* (where they were introduced by John Peel) and *the Old Grey Whistle Test*, mainstream TV rock programming that had never even glanced in their direction in the past.

June's 'Oh! Brother' single debuted the Fall on their new label; 'c.r.e.e.p.' followed in August; incredibly, a third 45, the *Call For Escape Route* EP, arrived in October, on the tail of the band's next album, the widely-proclaimed as accurately titled *The Wonderful and Frightening World of the Fall*.

'Oh! Brother' passed more or less unnoticed upon release. No longer eligible for the independent chart, but not yet ready for the nationals, it became the band's first release since 'It's The New Thing' not to make an impression on one listing or other. 'c.r.e.e.p.' didn't trouble the pollsters, either, but it received its fair share of attention all the same, as various parties raced to ascertain precisely who the c.r.e.e.p. might be. Smith wasn't saying.

A full touring itinerary, naturally, accompanied *The Wonderful & Frightening World of the Fall*. Of more than passing interest were a pair of events that attracted very little notice at the time, the first in Paris and then, over October 26/27, at the Royal Northern College of Music's Opera Theatre in Manchester. Ballet Rambert graduate Michael Clark, the latest *enfant terrible* of the *Observer*-reading arts scene, was presenting *New Puritans*, a ballet duet with Ellen van Schuylenburch that was schemed around the music of the Fall.

Clark had already used some Fall music in an earlier production with the Scottish Ballet Company, *Hail The Classical*, but, still... the pairing was bizarre. The Fall's former mentor from the Manchester Musicians Collective, Dick Witts, writing in Manchester's *City Life* magazine, called it the combination of 'Michael, star of *Vogue* and idol of the gay sado-masochist set (amongst other); Mark, a concentration-camp Bernard Manning for the giro generation.'

Smith himself was neither shocked nor concerned. 'I like his piece – I was pleasantly surprised. He's going to do some more with us, which is fine. I know he's taking three songs from [*The Wonderful & Frightening World Of*] to do something with...' Plans for a full-scale collaboration between Smith and Clark were already underway; had, in fact, been scheduled for a year hence. For now, as *Muze* remarked, 'one of the year's most hilarious occupations has been the study of *Times* and *Guardian* Arts Reviewers attempting to come to terms with "New Face In Hell," or whatever.' The magazine sympathised with their plight – 'this music is hardly danceable, it being so utterly discordant.' So, it transpired, did Smith.

'That's why he picked it, I think. He had to build a routine around the uncoordinated tempos. It furthered his art. He is a tremendous hard worker who is completely dedicated. He had to live ballet twenty fours hours a day. I have great admiration for people like that. He was so brave to break away from the traditional expected route of ballet and create his own style and following. He is immensely popular and is, in fact, changing the course of modern dance.'

Plans were afoot, too, to launch Brix Smith's own adjacent career, fronting her own band, the Adult Net. Named from a lyric in the latest Fall album's 'Craigness', the Adult Net's repertoire raced from Brix's own, distinctly Garage-pop flavoured originals, through the Strawberry Alarm Clock classic 'Incense and Peppermints' and on to what she ingenuously described as 'one of the best songs ever written – I knew it from way back – then one day Mark was playing [his] old records and I went mad! "*You* wrote this?"' The Adult Net's version of 'Rebellious Jukebox', retitled 'Searching For The Now', partnered 'Incense and Peppermints' on the band's first single in 1985, a sparkling reinvention that confirmed the startling promise that the band ultimately spread across four singles over the next two years. A much-anticipated album, *Spin The Web*, would never appear, however, scrapped when Brix decided it was not up to standard, and the original incarnation of the Adult Net collapsed in mid-1986 – although not without leaving their own mark on the Fall.

(MUSICIANS)
LINE-UP #14 MARK E SMITH (vocals), CRAIG SCANLON (guitar), BRIX SMITH (guitar, vocals), STEVE HANLEY (bass), PAUL HANLEY (keyboards, drums), KARL BURNS (bass, drums)

(BBC SESSION) January 3, 1984
    8401. Words Of Expectation
    8402. 2 x 4
    ORIGINAL RELEASE: 8401 on 'Kimble' single (1993), 8402 on *The Peel Sessions* (1998)
    COMMENTS: see appendix I/BBC sessions

(LIVE) 4 Apr 1984, Munich, Germany
    8403. Lay Of The Land
    8404. Ludd Gang
    8405. Kicker Conspiracy
    8406. Smile
    8407. 2 x 4
    8408. C.R.E.E.P
    8409. Neighbourhood Of Infinity
    8410. Copped It
    8411. Garden
    ORIGINAL RELEASE: as *C.R.E.E.P. SHOW*, Schlick Yarbles Revisited F101 (bootleg LP) 1984. Ltd ed. 200 copies.
    COMMENTS: The only Fall title noted in the *Hot Wacks* bible of bootlegs – and the sound quality is better than many of the Fall's official releases.
    Though there a handful of lyrical ad libs ('Is the fungus damp in the cellar? It smells like Holland' – 'Smile'), Smith's between-song conversation has been edited out. In fact, the album itself fades in with a slightly truncated 'Lay Of The Land' (and ends abruptly on the last stroke of 'Garden'), the consequence of its original 43+ minute broadcast on German radio.
    The album is at its best with newer material: 'Kicker Conspiracy' is no more than perfunctory, despite Brix's best efforts on backing 'ah's, but 'Smile' is magnificent, echo ricocheting round the concert hall, while the band simply churns through a scalding 'Neighbourhood Of Infinity' and the newly revised 1977-era 'Copped It'.

(LIVE) spring? 1984 – unknown date/venue
   8412. Neighbourhood Of Infinity
   ORIGINAL RELEASE: on *in: Palace Of Swords Revisited* compilation.

(SINGLE) Oh! Brother
   8413. Oh! Brother
   8414. God-Box
   8415. O! Brother (12-inch only)
   ORIGINAL RELEASE: Beggars Banquet BEG 110/T (7/12-inch) June 1984
   COMMENTS: 'Oh! Brother' is one of the oldest songs in the Fall's entire repertoire. An early version turns up on *Live 77*, performed to what Smith described as a Bo Diddley beat. Rewritten 'at least a dozen times' since then, it finally emerges in somewhat more leisurely style, but retains its growling Garage spirit, fed through a punchy whirl that was just a shade reminiscent of Joy Division.

Signing to Beggars Banquet was, in many outsiders' eyes, the Fall's acknowledgement that it was finally time they started selling records – and the band would not disagree. But anybody seeking to ascertain how Smith himself would deal with mass popularity needed only translate the pidgin German that echoes through 'Oh! Brother': 'I hate the crowd, the impotent crowd, the pliable crowd… who, tomorrow, will rip my heart out.'

The dark, near-Gothic insistence of 'God Box', on the other hand, dated from the Fall's American experiences, and the effects wrought on the mind by falling asleep while watching one of the religious TV channels. According to the accompanying press release, it also marked Brix's full-time debut as a member of the Fall – that's her speaking in the snatch of studio chat that opens the song.

(SINGLE) c.r.e.e.p
   8416. c.r.e.e.p.
   8417. Pat-Trip Dispenser
   8418. C.R.E.E.P (12-inch only)
   ORIGINAL RELEASE: Beggars Banquet BEG 116/T (7/12-inch) August 1984
   COMMENTS: With a dashingly sunny rhythm and Brix's 'la la' backings, even her husband's half-mumbled/half Elvis vocals cannot distract from the very real possibility that 'c.r.e.e.p.' would have made a great Adult Net backing track. Quite possibly the most fun anyone could ever expect to find on a Fall single, the song's ingenuous gleefulness nevertheless disguised one of Smith's most debated lyrics, as Brix explained:

'Everyone always thinks that Fall songs are about themselves and that was especially so with "c.r.e.e.p." Some people thought it was about Morrissey, which it wasn't. Marc Riley, our old guitarist, thought it was about him, which it wasn't. In fact, it's about every creep in the world.'

'I'm so proud of "c.r.e.e.p.",' Smith continued. 'It's got good words in it and that throws people off – their brains are so degenerate now. I always thought it would appeal to children and it does. A lot of very young kids (seven or eight) seem to like it. I never thought, though, that the creep was the guy who smelt bad at school; it was always the most popular guy in the class, 'cos you knew damn well he wouldn't do well in life, the sort who'd cry when the exam results came out.'

(BBC SESSION) Sept 17, 1984
    8419. Stephen Song
    8420. No Bulbs
    ORIGINAL RELEASE: Bootleg single/white label, 1984
    COMMENTS: see appendix I/BBC sessions

(ALBUM) *The Wonderful and Frightening World of...*
    8421. Lay of the Land
    8422. 2 x 4
    8423. Copped It
    8424. Elves
    8425. Slang King
    8426. Bug Day
    8427. Stephen Song
    8428. Craigness
    8429. Disney's Dream Debased
    CD/CASSETTE ONLY BONUS TRACKS
    8413. Oh! Brother
    8414. God-Box
    8417. Pat-trip Dispenser
    8418. C.R.E.E.P.
    8430. No Bulbs
    8431. Draygo's Guilt
    8432. Clear Off
    ORIGINAL RELEASE Beggars Banquet BEGA58 (LP, CD, cass) October 1984
    UK CHART PEAK: #62
    COMMENTS: If any one song captures the ugly contradiction and hypocrisy of the landscape arrayed before Mark E Smith's eyes, it is 'Disney's Dream Debased'. It was based, Brix said, on an incident she and Mark witnessed during a visit to Disneyland: a woman fell from one car into the path of another on the Matterhorn roller coaster ride, and was decapitated. Yet, even as the medics raced to remove the grisly remains from the horrified gaze of the onlookers, Mickey and Pluto and Goofy were still laughing, and celebrating the wonderful world in which they lived.

Produced by John Leckie, whose past projects have taken in some of the most inventive (Doctors of Madness, Adverts, XTC) and galling (Simple Minds, anyone?) of modern rock icons, *The Wonderful And Frightening World* ranks high in any poll of the band's finest albums. From lyrical inception to final delivery, it caught the band operating so far above their previous levels as to represent, if not an entire new concept, then at least a brand new outlook. For the martial mutant funk autobiography of 'Slang King', Smith even admitted he tried to persuade Burns to play drums like 70s Disco faves the Moments (of …And Whatnauts fame). 'And I had this organ tune and this ongoing fable about this historical character. Worked dead well, didn't it?' The historical character might well have been Smith himself, with his attributes machine-gunned out with music paper copy-writer finesse.

Despite media assumptions, Brix herself was not overtly responsible for ringing the musical changes. She took straight co-writing credit on just three of the original vinyl's nine tracks, with one of those, 'Elves', wholly deconstructing its central rhythm and keyboard from a minimalist reinterpretation of the Stooges 'I Wanna Be Your Dog', an early example of the magpie midwifery that would soon become one of the Fall's most potent weapons. She lay a hand, too, on the disconcerting 'Lay of the Land', a middle-eastern Punkoid rampage launched out of an eerie chant lifted from the Traveller scenes in Nigel Kneale's sci fi television drama, *The Quatermass Conclusion*.

Nevertheless, the first album to be conceived in its entirety following the Smiths' meeting and marriage rejoiced not in the convulsions and lurches of 'traditional' Fall, but in a commitment to melody which survived even when everything else went into overdrive. Even the addition of Virgin Prune Gavin Friday to layer yowling echo over 'Stephen Song' and the 77-era resuscitation, 'Copped It' (plus the b-side 'Clear Off'), could not dislodge the sense that here, at last, was a Fall album that even Fall-haters could get into.

(SINGLE) *Call For Escape Route* EP
    8433. No Bulbs 3
    8431. Draygo's Guilt
    8434. Slang King 2
    8432. Clear Off
    8430. No Bulbs
  O R I G I N A L RELEASE: Beggars Banquet BEG120/E (7-inch + bonus disc, 12-inch) October 1984

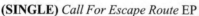

COMMENTS: The insistent cacophony of one of the Fall's least single-like singles yet, 'No Bulbs' is best experienced across the eight-minute 12-inch mix, where the driving rhythm and chanted vocals have room to spread out, before merging into an instrumental passage that quickly becomes compulsive. The thought that 'Sister Ray' might have featured on the Smiths' stereo recently is encouraged by the threat of a keyboard solo around the five-minute mark. The return of the vocal shortly thereafter packs a remarkably dynamic punch.

'Clear Off' is less intense, although it's amusing to remember the first time one heard it, in 1984, wondering whether the first notes of guitar were going to loop cheekily into those other Smiths' 'This Charming Man'. In fact, it becomes a slowly loping melody that may or may not benefit from Gavin Friday's yelping presence.

(LIVE/STUDIO) out-takes
    8422a. Fiend With A Violin (*aka* 2 x 4)
    8422b. Fiend With A Violin (vox)
    8435. 2 x 4 (live)
    ORIGINAL RELEASE: see Receiver compilations (appendix II)
    COMMENTS: Of the many drawbacks in the material that Smith handed over to Receiver for their various collections during the mid-1990s, perhaps the most galling is the fact that, after sorting through however many tapes he sorted through, he never selected the year's one burning legend, the occasional in-concert favourite 'Hey! Marc Riley'. Musically, of course, it's nothing to write home about, just a rockabilly ramble with Smith throwing out remarks at his erstwhile guitar picker. But closing the show, as it did at Heaven in June 1984 (the Swans supported: how graceless they were!), it sent a veritable fleet of night bus travellers home chanting and grinning.

1985

The Fall returned to action in early 1985 with a handful of British gigs warming up for their next American outing, opening at Hammersmith Town Hall on March 7 with a gig that even Smith recalled as somewhat hard-going. 'We were lucky to get out of that alive, really. [John] Leckie's mixing! He bust all the sound meters on the PA, everything full up like in a studio. A lot of people liked it, a lot thought it was the worst gig they'd seen. Leckie did us once in Essex and we were deaf for days.'

Nevertheless, it offered a fair indication of the repertoire that the Fall would be taking to the US a fortnight later. Spread over two weeks in late March/early April, the tour was a well-received outing, if not the all-round sell-out that might have been expected – audiences at the Hollywood Palace and Washington's 9.30 Club, both strong Fall territoriy, fell somewhat short of capacity.

Plans to follow through with an Italian tour, meanwhile, were cancelled when the promoter neglected to send the band their return air tickets – always ominous. In this instance, however, he was doing them a favour. While the band stayed at home in Manchester, Turin – where they'd been scheduled to play – exploded in anti-English rioting, as the locals protested the deaths of 39 of their compatriots at the Heysel Stadium disaster. 'Best thing that ever happened to us,' a relieved Smith told the *NME*. 'Imagine being in a Turin hotel, in dorms, with no locks on the doors, and they're burning flags on the fuckin' street!"

The band did play a handful of European dates during this year, supported on some by former Purkurr Pillnikk trumpeter Einar Orn's latest band, the Bjorkpowered Kukl. Their *The Eye* debut album was over a year old, but Kukl were challenging and overwhelming audiences with some of the most dramatic, amazing, music of the age. One sincerely hopes that audiences who caught them sharing the bill with the Fall appreciated their good luck.

Back home, the Fall previewed their next single, 'Couldn't Get Ahead', with a new John Peel session, taking the opportunity, also, to introduce a wholly revised rhythm section. Paul Hanley quit, while classically trained bassist and keyboard player Simon Rogers moved over from sessions with Brix's Adult Net to deputize for Steve Hanley as he set off on what was officially described as his summer holidays. Rogers brought with him the band's first-ever synthesizer, an advanced replacement for the familiar old Snoopy electric piano and one that Smith initially regarded with some suspicion. Nevertheless, it stayed, bringing new musical dimension to the band's sound – even if it wasn't necessarily apparent from 'Couldn't Get Ahead'.

With Steve Hanley back on board, a new album, *This Nation's Saving Grace*, followed in September, bringing with it yet another Peel session, and full tours of Germany and the UK.

(MUSICIANS)
LINE-UP #14 (Jan-June) MARK E SMITH (vocals), CRAIG SCANLON (guitar), BRIX SMITH (guitar, vocals), STEVE HANLEY (bass), PAUL HANLEY (keyboards, drums), KARL BURNS (bass, drums)

LINE-UP #15 (remainder) MARK E SMITH (vocals), CRAIG SCANLON (guitar), BRIX SMITH (guitar, vocals), STEVE HANLEY (bass), SIMON ROGERS (keyboards, bass), KARL BURNS (bass, drums) [Hanley absent for some summertime shows/recording]

(LIVE) Apr 6 1985, Peppermint Lounge, New York
 8501. Wings
 UNR. No Bulbs
 UNR. God Box
 UNR. Clear Off
 UNR. Couldn't Get Ahead
 UNR. Elves

UNR. 2 x 4
UNR. Hexen Definitive-Strife Knot
UNR. The Classical
UNR. Petty Thief Lout
UNR. Lay of the Land
UNR. Copped It
ORIGINAL RELEASE: Various artists album *Bugs on the Wire*, Leghorn
SAW399 (LP) 1987 (LP)
COMMENTS: The haunting 'Wings' was an odd, but intriguing, addition to the
band's live set, all the more when it was restyled as a partial duet between the
Smiths and punctuated by a desperately ragged mouth organ. The sound quality here
is a little scratchy, but the interplay between metronomic drums and swirling fuzzed
guitar is hypnotic. And Mark E Smith is in powerful voice.
(BBC SESSION) June 3, 1985
  8502. Spoilt Victorian Child
  8503. Gut of the Quantifier
  8504. Cruiser's Creek
ORIGINAL RELEASE: 8502-3 'Kimble' single (1993), 8504 *The Peel
Sessions* (1998)
COMMENTS: see appendix I/BBC sessions

(SINGLE) Couldn't Get Ahead
  8505. Couldn't Get Ahead
  8506. Rollin' Dany
  8507. Petty (Thief) Lout (12-inch only)
ORIGINAL RELEASE: Beggars Banquet BEG134/T (7/12-inch) June 1985

(SINGLE) *By Grace Are Ye Saved*
  8505. Couldn't Get Ahead
  8506. Rollin' Dany
  8507. Petty (Thief) Lout
  8508. Vixen
  8509. Barmy
ORIGINAL RELEASE: PVC PVC5909 (US) (12-inch) June 1985
COMMENTS: Smith's masterpiece of under-achieving apology, 'Couldn't Get
Ahead', was backed by the first non-original ever to enter the Fall's recorded
vocabulary, the semi-obscure Gene Vincent chestnut 'Rollin' Dany.' It would not
be the last. (Of previous assaults on other artists' material, the best known is
probably Deep Purple's 'Black Night', performed during the 1982 Australian tour.)
  Elsewhere on the various permutations of the release, the home thoughts from
exiled-abroad 'Barmy', catchily borrowing its riff from a distorted stab at the
Stones' 'Satisfaction', packs an adrenal punch, but it's 'Petty (Thief) Lout' that
most impresses, a relaxed lope telling tales on a record-collecting cat burglar, and
swinging between whispered Philip Marlowe intrigue and bellowed rockabilly
revision.
NOTE: the American *By Grace Are Ye Saved* EP plays all five songs on both
sides.

(ALBUM) *This Nation's Saving Grace*

8510. Mansion
8511. Bombast
8509. Barmy
8512. What You Need
8513. Spoilt Victorian Child
8514. L.A.
8515. Gut of the Quantifier
8516. My New House
8517. Paintwork
8518. I am Damo Suzuki
8519. To Nk Roachment: Yarbles
CD BONUS TRACKS
8508. Vixen
8505. Couldn't Get Ahead
8507. Petty (Thief) Lout
8506. Rollin' Dany
8521. Cruiser's Creek
ORIGINAL RELEASE Beggars Banquet BEGA67 (LP, CD) September 1985
UK CHART PEAK: #54
COMMENTS: Retaining John Leckie as the most dynamic producer the Fall
have ever employed, *This Nation's Saving Grace* was the slap in the face for
everyone who feared the band might be easing their foot from the pedal – an
aggressive record company and the first signs of commercial success can have that
effect.

A brief glimpse into some parallel world where the Deviants were a surf band,
Brix Smith's brief 'Mansion' rides the psychedelic warlords' 'Billy The Monster'
riff to open (and close) the show, a magnificently atmospheric curtain raiser to
'Bombast' – as spiky a statement of perceived intent as Mark E Smith has ever
wrapped his bellow around. Or maybe that would better describe the abrasive
clunky 'My New House.' It was, Smith shrugged, about his new house.

'What You Need', a slurred lullaby rhythm beneath a murmured rumble; the
hyper-active 'Spoilt Victorian Child' and the exhaustive conversation of 'Gut of the
Quantifier', riding another of Brix's semi-Stooges guitar lines ('Sick Of You'),
would all move to the fore of the band's live repertoire, but the true mark of *This
Nation's Saving Grace* lies in those numbers that either predicted directions the
band would be taking later, or gazed back at imagery that informed their earliest
movements.

The haunting, warming 'I Am Damo Suzuki' was titled for the enigmatic former
vocalist with Kraut Rock pioneers Can, rooted in a melody at least lightly based on
the German band's own 'Oh Yeah'. Smith told *The Wire*, 'He's a good mate of mine
now. If we play Cologne or Essen or somewhere, he comes to see us play. He's one
of the heroes of mine who've actually lived up to expectations.'

Can (and, maybe, countrymen Faust)'s influence is also apparent in the
meandering, rather lovely 'Paintwork', a semi-acoustic dreamscape whose
experimental tendencies were either confirmed or created when Smith erased a few
seconds of sound while playing the tape at home. Anybody else would have wrung
their hands in dismay, then recut the track. Smith, however, liked the accident – and,
as usual, he was right. Still, even he later remarked, 'I thought it was amusing to
read that *Nation's Saving Grace* was supposed to be accessible.'

(BBC SESSION) October 7, 1985
  8520. What You Need
  ORIGINAL RELEASE: *The Peel Sessions* (1998)
  COMMENTS: see appendix I/BBC sessions

(SINGLE) Cruiser's Creek
  8521. Cruiser's Creek
  8514. L.A.
  8508. Vixen
  ORIGINAL RELEASE: Beggars Banquet BEG 150/T (7/12-inch) October
1985
  COMMENTS: If the B52s hadn't come out with 'Love Shack', you'd probably
never have guessed they listened to the Fall, although there's a lot more going on
down at Cruiser's Creek than Cindy, Fred and co would ever have let on. An
exuberant party is highlighted by everything from a gas mains explosion to a
prohibition on Frankie Goes To Hollywood, while some glorious ramshackle
backing vocals and a half-quirky guitar riff gnaw at the senses long after the record
ends. A classic Fall 45.
  On the other side, the album track 'L.A.' weds minimal lyric to mocking
harmonies and the teetering promise of a killer melody, chiming over a bubble that
beats any other dance record of the month feet down. The Smith'n'Smith 'Vixen'
duet, drawn from the American 'Rollin' Dany' 12-inch to take the edge off a gnarly
import market, only proved that it hadn't really been worth calling for in the first
place.

(LIVE/STUDIO) out-takes etc
  8505a. Couldn't Get Ahead (alternate)
  8507a. Petty (Thief) Lout (alternate)
  8512a. What You Need (alternate)
  8513a. Spoilt Victorian Child (alternate)
  8515a. Gut of the Quantifier (alternate)
  8522. Bombast (live – 4 mins, 4 secs)
  8523. Bombast (live – 3 mins, 41 secs)
  8524. L.A. (live)
  ORIGINAL RELEASE: see Receiver label comps (appendix II)

THE FALL.

BEND SINISTER

1986

For the first time in a long time, Mark E Smith could concentrate on the music. He didn't know if he was going to enjoy it, but the decision, in January 1986, to take on John Lennard as the Fall's first full-time manager since the departure of Kay Carroll certainly possessed some appealing qualities. The Fall had endured three or four short-lived managers, Smith explained, before he finally realised what was happening. 'I was training them what to do, they'd get good at it, and then leave.

'So I said fuck it. I'll do it myself. I really enjoyed it, but I became more of a clerk than... [a songwriter]. Two days a week was for filling in tax forms and shit. Which was really enjoyable... that's why these last two albums have been particularly good. Before that, I was a very violent person – the early days of the Fall are very, very violent. Aggressive, real, didn't give a fuck. I had loads of time to be the moody writer thing, which I despised in myself. It's not good for your work. I found by throwing myself into taxman and accountant, it teaches you a few things. You realize that you're not that important. The strange thing about it was that then, the writing came real easy. I was doing it for pleasure. And it made me think, when I started the band that's what I used to do. I used to write my songs during the dinner hour on the typewriter.'

It was a role, inevitably, to which he would be returning. But, for now, such weights lay on other shoulders and Smith was free to pursue other avenues of thought, like wondering what happened to the *Miami Vice* production team member who made an appointment to meet the band in Los Angeles, ostensibly about using their music in the TV show. The unsuspecting listener watched the gig and was never heard from again. Crockett and Tubbs found something else to run around to.

Once again, the year opened with a short string of UK shows, warming up for a longer US/Canada outing in the early spring (a second visit, highlighted by a couple of stadium shows with New Order, followed in October).

Of the British gigs, the most memorable was the *From Manchester With Love* benefit on February 8, at Liverpool Royal Court. There, the Fall joined New Order, John Cooper Clarke and the Smiths to raise funds for 49 Liverpool Labour councillors, led by Derek Hatton, who were being taken to court by the government as a dispute over a newly imposed system of rates (the predecessor of the Poll Tax) got ugly.

In North America, meanwhile, packed houses in New York, Washington DC and Toronto, among others, more than compensated for the handful of shows where either the audience or the band – or both – left something to be desired. Indeed, an appearance at the Anthrax Club in Connecticut was later enshrined in Fall folklore as, according to Brix, the worst gig she ever experienced, whether as a musician or an onlooker.

Returning home, the 'Living Too Late' single prefaced the next round of line-up changes, as Karl Burns departed 'amid rumours,' according to the *NME*, 'of debilitating personal problems and a growing, violent antagonism between him and Smith.'

For a moment, the band hung drummerless. Paul Hanley stepped back in for a while, and Smith briefly contemplated abandoning human drummers altogether. He told *One Two Testing*: 'I'm thinking of using Paul when he's available and using other things, like a DX7 rhythm section. We've proved how good we are with drums and I'm sure I could do it just as well on a machine.'

In the event, Smith poached former early-Smiths/Colourfield drummer Simon Wolstencroft from the Weeds, the Fall's support band on their last UK tour. Wolstencroft made his live debut at Leas Cliff Hall in Folkestone on June 5th, before being thrown into the band's latest (tenth) Peel session in July, and their appearance at the Factory label's 10th Anniversary of Punk celebration, the Festival Of The Tenth Summer.

Featuring art exhibitions, fashion shows, several concerts, alongside film and video shows, the event wrapped up with an all-day concert at Manchester G-Mex, spotlighting a veritable history of local rock – attractions included New Order, OMD, the Smiths, Sandie Shaw, Wayne Fontana and the Mindbenders, Pete Shelley, A Certain Ratio and the specially reformed Worst. But it was the Fall who hogged the headlines the next day, as they were joined onstage for 'Prole Art Threat' by Derek Hatton and London councillor (and future Mayor) Ken Livingstone.

Scheduled, but ultimately cancelled, another major show would have billed the Fall alongside the Smiths at an Anti-Apartheid benefit at the Royal Albert Hall in November. Unfortunately, the headliners' Johnny Marr was seriously injured in a car accident three days beforehand and, when the gig was rescheduled, for December 12th, it was without the Fall. (That performance, at Brixton Academy, was to prove the Smiths' final UK concert.)

Accompanied by an excellent Smith-directed video, September brought a new single, a lucid blast through a cover of American Garage band the Other Half's 'Mr Pharmacist', unusually pulled from the next album, the pseudo-heraldically titled

Bend Sinister. December then delivered 'Hey Luciani' – the band's next single and Mark E Smith's first stageplay, launched at Hammersmith's Riverside Theatre, with a cast that included Michael Clark, Trevor Stewart as the Pope, Lucy Burgess as the Pope's right hand girl, and mid-1980s Disco celebrity and costume designer Leigh Bowery (star of the 'Mr Pharmacist' video) as the head of accounts at The Vatican.

Comprising both fresh material and highlights from *Bend Sinister*, *Hey Luciani* – as Smith told American journalist Michael Azerrad in the spring – 'was very direct, not like the stuff we usually do. It's about murder and Israeli commandos and Pope John' – to which could also be added demonic possession, Italian fascists, ex-Nazis and a Scottish communist. 'It's a musical.'

In fact, the play centred around the rumours, outlined in author David Yallop's *In God's Name*, that claimed Pope John Paul I – born Albino Luciani – was murdered after just a month in power by Vatican forces fearful of the newcomer's planned reforms of the Catholic church's business practises. (Interestingly, similar ruminations fired much of Stiv Bator's writing for both the early Lords of the New Church and the preceding Wanderers.)

The 100-minute opus was, Smith insisted, a cross between Shakespeare and *The Prisoner*. He told *NME*, 'The play is a simulation of the conspiracy theory in the book, the middle bit splits up other things – South America and Britain, for instance. No way is it a factual indictment of Catholicism or even the Vatican. People think, when they hear it's about the Pope, that it must either be a "rock musical" or anti-religious statement or something. Which is a sad reflection on the way the theatre is viewed in this country. I chose the setting because the characters appealed to me and hopefully it makes good drama.'

But to what purpose? *Hey Luciani* was neither filmed nor recorded (not officially, anyway), and the best of its music was given no grander release than a few b-sides and isolated album tracks – the reggaefied 'Sleep Debt Snatches' and 'Haf Found Bormann', for example, turned up as b-sides to the following year's 'There's A Ghost In My House'.

Nor were the press overly indulgent, as *Melody Maker*'s Stud Brothers made clear in their review: 'After an hour and a half of false moustaches, occasional Fall songs, inexplicable typing-pools, unnecessary costume changes, Leigh Bowery's inadequate clowning and dismally poor acting, we ceased to care about the fate of Smiley, ceased to be impressed by Smith's linguistic perversity, and called for an immediate and bloody end to Arts Council funding.' Not to be undone, *NME*'s Len Brown added: 'the play wot Mark E Smith has wrote is a heap of shite.'

The Fall, however, remained unbowed. In fact, even before the play opened, Smith was adamant, 'we financed it and we're not going to make any money off it. But it's a good little thing to do, [and it] alleviates the tedium.'

(MUSICIANS)

LINE-UP #15 (Jan-May) MARK E SMITH (vocals), CRAIG SCANLON (guitar), BRIX SMITH (guitar, vocals), STEVE HANLEY (bass), SIMON ROGERS (keyboards), KARL BURNS (drums)

LINE-UP #16 (May/June) MARK E SMITH (vocals), CRAIG SCANLON (guitar), BRIX SMITH (guitar, vocals), STEVE HANLEY (bass), SIMON ROGERS (keyboards), PAUL HANLEY (drums)

LINE-UP #17 (remainder) MARK E SMITH (vocals), CRAIG SCANLON (guitar), BRIX SMITH (guitar, vocals), STEVE HANLEY (bass), SIMON ROGERS (keyboards), SIMON WOLSTENCROFT (drums) + MARCIA SCHOFIELD (keyboards, some shows)

(SINGLE) White Night (Stars Say Go) by ADULT NET
    8601. Naughty But Nice
    ORIGINAL RELEASE: Beggars Banquet BEG 164 (7-inch) June 1986
    COMMENTS: Mark E Smith contributes vocals to the b-side of the third Adult Net 45.

(SINGLE) Living Too Late
    8602. Living Too Late
    8603. Hot Aftershave Bop
    8604. Living Too Long (12-inch only)
    ORIGINAL RELEASE: Beggars Banquet BEG 165/T (7/12-inch) July 1986
    COMMENTS: A sombre single – did anyone imagine it would be a hit? Smith's thoughts on aging make this one of his most immediately sensitive numbers, an unquestioned successor to Brel's 'Old Folks' and a precursor of Pulp's 'Help The Aged', a slow, careworn rumination noting the physical and emotional ravages of the calendar. Unexpected splinters into semi-cacophony by way of a chorus disrupt the mood considerably, but they are necessary, a relief from the relentless passage of years marked by Steve Hanley's ticking time-bomb bass. As one would expect, the 12-inch 'Living Too Long' is even more remorseless, adding a couple of extra verses and the especially crucial line, 'I'm super sad sweet sad' to define nostalgia in a nutshell.

(LIVE) Sept 7 1986, Albany Empire, Deptford
    8605. L.A.
    UNR. Copped It
    UNR. City Hobgoblins
    UNR. US 80's-90's
    UNR. Terry Waite Sez
    UNR. Gross Chapel-GB Grenadiers
    UNR. Mr. Pharmacist
    UNR. R.O.D.
    UNR. Living Too Late
    UNR. Gut of the Quantifier
    UNR. Bournemouth Runner
    UNR. Lucifer over Lancashire
    UNR. Bombast
    UNR. My New House
    ORIGINAL RELEASE: various artists album *Fruitcakes and Furry Collars*, mail order LP available from *Record Mirror* 1986
    Fruitcakes and Furry Collars
    COMMENTS: A tight live version, subsequently delivered from obscurity by the *Backdrop* compilation.

(SINGLE) Mr. Pharmacist

8606. Mr Pharmacist
8607. Lucifer Over Lancashire
8608. Auto Tech Pilot (12-inch only)
ORIGINAL RELEASE: Beggars Banquet BEG168/T (7/12-inch) Sept 1986
UK CHART PEAK: #75
COMMENTS: After the introspective oasis of 'Living Too Late', 'Mr Pharmacist' was a Garage rock monster, the kind of sonic savage epiphany that used to make American Garage Rock collecting such fun – you never knew when you were going to stumble across the next undiscovered gem. Today, the record shops overflow with boxed sets of the stuff and they'll never sound the same way again. But 'Mr Pharmacist', a 1968 snarl that brought future Blue Cheer noisemeister's Randy Holden's The Other Half their two-and-one-half minutes of nuggety glory, never surrenders its bombastic swagger. Indeed, in the thrall of the Fall, it is even louder and lewder, Smith stripping the coy tone from the original vocal and all but gargling on Mr Pharmacist's wares. A masterpiece!

The frenetic 'Lucifer Over Lancashire' works a lot better live than on vinyl but, wrapping up the 12-inch on a high, the bass blurge 'Auto Tech Pilot' opens and closes with almost Gothic intent, but in between times explodes into raw verse matching the rise of high-tech surveillance equipment to the corresponding increase in low-tech crime.

(SINGLE) *Vinyl Conflict*
8607a. Lucifer Over Lancashire
ORIGINAL RELEASE: EP free with *Melody Maker*, 1986
COMMENTS: Alternate version from the *Bend Sinister* sessions.

(LIVE) summer?, 1986
8609. The Man Whose Head Expanded
ORIGINAL RELEASE: various artists album *Bang Zoom cassette fanzine #7*, 1986
COMMENTS: An unexpectedly powerful, five-minute live recording, subsequently reprised for *Backdrop*.

(ALBUM) *Bend Sinister – Domesday Pay-Off*
8610. R.O.D.
8611. Dktr. Faustus
8612. Shoulder Pads #1
8606. Mr Pharmacist
8613. Gross Chapel – British Grenadiers
8614. U.S. 80's-90's
8615. Terry Waite Sez
8616. Bournemouth Runner
8617. Riddler!
8618. Shoulder Pads #2
CD BONUS TRACKS
8602. Living Too Late
8608. Auto-Tech Pilot
ADDITIONAL CASSETTE BONUS TRACK
8619. Town and Country Hobgoblins

ORIGINAL RELEASE: Beggars Banquet BEGA75 October 1986
UK CHART PEAK: #36
COMMENTS: You have to chuckle when you re-read the reviews of the Fall's third Beggars Banquet album, the third to be recorded with John Leckie at the helm. Accusations like 'down beat,' 'dark' and 'sounds a bit like Joy Division' have all been levelled at *Bend Sinister*, usually after just a few moments exposure to the guitar line that chimes through the locomotive opener, 'R.O.D.' But hold on 'til 'Dktr. Faustus', a not-quite-duet between the two Smiths first tried (as 'Faust Banana') at the October 1985 Peel session, and the mood shifts remarkably.

Metronomic in places, icy in others, draped in the gothic overtones of the Faustus tale itself, the song is surprising because neither the discipline of Goethe nor the intensity of Mann hangs most heavily over the piece. What predominates, rather, is the freedom of Diermaier, Peron and Sossner, the German Kraut Rockers whose own band's energies were so frequently compared to the Fall that you can readily imagine Smith's quizzical response: 'Faust? Us?' As for Brix's starring role alongside his own vocals, Smith remarked, 'I don't really like working with other voices, but "Faustus" is okay because the mix is fucked up. The backing vocals are at the level the lead vocals should be. It works because it sounds like hell straining to break through.'

It was that same impression of *something* straining to break through that left a handful of songs hanging like demos of an unrealised dream – an effective and disconcerting device. Another common comment was that the Fall didn't bite your leg like they used to, but the distinctly Velvets-flavoured guitar and rhythm base that flows beneath the two parts of the apparently autobiographical 'Shoulder Pads' reminds us that teeth don't have to be sharp to make an impression.

'U.S. 80's – 90's', a beat box-driven acknowledgement (if not necessarily endorsement) of rap, has an insistent funk base that drapes comfortably over a lyric that would rather smoke and drink its way to an early grave than live clean-lunged and sober to die of senility and boredom. Also guaranteed to sit uncomfortably with the liberal lights of the day, 'Terry Waite Sez' is a none too complimentary examination of the Archbishop of Canterbury's Special Envoy (pre-kidnap crisis), again set to contagiously repetitive motion.

It's not all great. With a lyric based around a backdrop-purloining Fall fan who did, indeed, do a runner in Bournemouth, 'Bournemouth Runner' outstays its welcome no matter how evocative the keyboard line, and 'Gross Chapel – British Grenadiers', frankly, drags. But the deliciously dense and atmospheric 'Riddler' more than compensates, in terms of intent if not meaning. The song, Smith unhelpfully revealed, was based on a childhood memory, of when 'we used to shout "Riddler" when we were kids in Salford.' Unfortunately, 'I can't remember what for.'

(LIVE)/(STUDIO) out-takes etc
8611a. Dktr. Faustus
8614a. U.S. 80's-90's
ORIGINAL RELEASE: see Receiver label comps (appendix II)

(STUDIO) out-take
8620. Hey! Luciani! (original version)
ORIGINAL RELEASE: on EP *Sounds Showcase 1*, Beggars Banquet SHOW

1 (7-inch) free with *Sounds*
May 1987
COMMENTS: One of
several *Hey! Luciani* tracks cut
with producer John Leckie
during the *Bend Sinister*
sessions, 'Hey Luciani' itself
was ultimately abandoned in
favour of the more sparkling
vision put across by Lightnin'
Seed Ian Broudie.

Leckie's departure from the
Fall camp was – for Smith, at
least – characteristically
confrontational. In 1999,
Leckie told *Melody Maker*,
'The last straw was a
mastering session for *Bend
Sinister*. We'd mixed it,

everyone was happy and we ran some cassette copies off but, when it came to
cutting it, after side one he said, "What are you fucking playing at? Do you think
I'm some kind of twat? That's not the mix we decided on. You've done another
one." And insisted I listen to his Dolby chrome cassette, which was running at
slightly the wrong speed. So the whole album was cut from his cassette. We haven't
spoken since.'

The original *Melody Maker* EP also includes 'Spin The Web', the title track of
what was then scheduled to be the Adult Web's debut album, similarly produced by
Broudie. With the album eventually scrapped, this remains its only release.

(SINGLE) Hey! Luciani
    8621. Hey! Luciani
    8622. Shoulder Pads #1B
    8623. Entitled (12-inch only)
    ORIGINAL RELEASE: Beggars Banquet BEG176/T (7/12-inch) Dec 1986
    UK CHART PEAK: #59
    COMMENTS: There's an almost eastern tinge to the treated guitars that open
the vivacious 'Hey! Luciani', a rapid-fire blistering that sets out the basic premise
of the play of the same name – the life and, more pertinently, the death – of John
Paul I, 'Pope of three days.' A shimmering Ian Broudie production and archetypal
Brix backing harmonies complete a stunning single and the best-ever advertisement
for the stage show.

Overleaf, 'Entitled' revisits the musical pastures mapped out by 'Auto Tech
Pilot', nudging into New Order parody – a mischievous notion that Smith's
purposefully lackadaisical (and deliberately under-sung) vocal only heightens.
'Shoulder Pads #1b,' meanwhile, extends *Bend Sinister*'s 'Shoulder Pads #1b' to
almost double its length.

The Fall

1987

The massive tours of Germany, the Netherlands and the UK that devoured the first quarter of 1987 testified to the pulling power that the Fall now had. The arrival, in April, of their first Top 30 hit simply confirmed what should not have been ignored for so long. At ten years of age, the Fall were the grand statesmen of the generation that grew out of Punk without having quite belonged there in the first place. And now it was time to have some fun.

Single of the week in *NME*, 'There's A Ghost In My House' was a cover of an old R Dean Taylor number and, of course, it raised a frown or two, as pursed-lipped fans tutted disapprovingly and wished the band could have made it with their own song, on their own terms. Mark Smith simply ignored them. These were their own terms.

Neither, as the remainder of the year dropped increasingly more positive reviews into the Fall's scrapbook, did he give any credence to another oft-asked question: namely, had the world finally caught up with the Fall? 'To say that, would suggest that the Fall has always been wilfully obscure. Either that, or that the group hasn't developed over the years. It hasn't, and it has.'

The early-year departure of Simon Rogers was remedied by the full-time recruitment of New Yorker Marcia Schofield, a former member of the agit-Punk pop combo Khmer Rouge and, more recently, the Adult Net. Originally drafted into the group the previous October for a short Austrian tour, her first live performance (a warm-up in Ipswich) was a nerve-wracking event, walking onto the stage with her notes scattered across a heap of paper scraps. The soundcheck was the first time she ever played with the band; the encore threw her in at the deep end, when Smith unveiled two songs she'd never even heard. Afterwards, once she'd settled into the band, Smith constantly referred back to that debut. He called it the best gig she'd ever played with the band.

Initially, Schofield added little that Rogers had not already blueprinted. But fears that the Fall were simply turning into a new Adult Net were dispelled by the knowledge that Rogers, too, once performed with that band.

Summer brought the festival season, opening with the Fall's recruitment to U2's mammoth July 1st bash at Elland Road, Leeds. Weeks later, a second-on-the-bill spot at Finsbury Park placed them behind the Banshees, but ahead of Wire, at the post-Punk equivalent of the highschool reunion dance. The chance to match the Fall against surviving contemporaries was one that the music press relished, but the band was indifferent and the show bore little in common with the sunshine. Smith, as the *NME* put it, 'is still the Pope of post-Punk pre-grebo abstract expressionism.' And the Banshees were still art students.

In August, a Hamburg show played beneath the Kings Of Independence banner, placed the Fall alongside with Nick Cave, the Swans and Butthole Surfers. This time, it was the Fall's turn to suffer the slings and arrows of disrespectful upstarts. Smith found it interesting, he said, 'seeing them still making the same mistakes we used to make and thinking they were great for it. Like, we were the only ones to ask for a separate dressing room and they were calling us "pop stars" for it. They were giving us this shit and Thommo, our tour manager, turned to them and says, "Look, it's nothing to do with being fucking pop stars, it's to do with being fucking professional which is something fucking Butthole Surfers will never be!"'

In fact, the Knopf Music Hall show was less memorable for the music than for the utter carnage that took place outside when 1,000 fans discovered that the event was completely oversold and responded by catching fire to everything within reach of the venue, including a neighbouring petrol station.

The group wrapped up the summer by stepping out at the Reading festival, one of the precious few oases of even vaguely contemporary relevance holding back the sandstorm of reborn metal and rehashed Punk acts on display that year (headliners: Status Quo and the Stranglers). But the meanness of the season did at least afford the band one unaccustomed luxury – sufficient income to spend the rest of 1987 off the road, the Fall's longest gig-free period ever.

The band played just two shows, in Salford and Stafford, between the end of August and December, while plans for a new album were placed on hold until the New Year. Nevertheless, October brought a new single, the hip-hop flavoured 'Hit The North' – commissioned, said Smith, by the Lancashire Tourist Board. Dismissed by radio as being 'too clubby' for airplay, it peaked at #57, familiar territory for the Fall of old, of course, but their lives had changed.

'The hit record did make things easier for us,' Smith told *Underground* magazine. 'Since then it's been better for us when we play.' Locally, around the band's stubbornly retained Prestwich homebase, you could sense the difference. 'It is weird round here. The people are dead proud of the Fall. They are genuinely pleased for us, which surprised me because, just prior to "Ghost", I was dreading it. We do get kids standing outside the house, which I've always had to some extent, but now it's nine or ten year-olds...'

The time off also allowed Smith to fulfil an ambition of his own, launching his own Cog Sinister label to try to address the welter of unreleased and/or unavailable material that trailed behind the band – over which, almost uniquely, Smith had retained full control. No matter that this control ensured the Fall had been broke since their inception, Smith resolutely refused to sign away either his publishing or recording rights, simply tearing up contracts when they were offered, preferring control to cash.

It was an heroic, if not insane, stance, based upon the not-even-vaguely likely premise that, somewhere down the historical road, the noises the Fall were making would still be in demand. The fact that he'd been proven correct afforded Smith no end of satisfaction. On the eve of releasing *in: Palace Of Swords Reversed*, a digest of the Fall's Rough Trade era, he reflected, 'it was worth starving the band for.'

(MUSICIANS)

LINE-UP #18 (Jan-May) MARK E SMITH (vocals), CRAIG SCANLON (guitar), BRIX SMITH (guitar, keyboards, vocals), STEVE HANLEY (bass), SIMON WOLSTENCROFT (drums)

LINE-UP #19 (remainder) MARK E SMITH (vocals), CRAIG SCANLON (guitar), BRIX SMITH (guitar, vocals), STEVE HANLEY (bass), MARCIA SCHOFIELD (keyboards), SIMON WOLSTENCROFT (drums)

(LIVE) Feb 14 1987, HFT Mensa, Bremen, Germany
8701. U.S. 80's-90's
UNR. Terry Waite Sez
UNR. Living Too Late
UNR. c.r.e.e.p.
UNR. Lucifer over Lancashire
UNR. Haf Found Bormann
UNR. Mr. Pharmacist
UNR. Hey Luciani
UNR. I Am Damo Suzuki
UNR. There's A Ghost in My House
UNR. Bournemouth Runner
UNR. R.O.D.
UNR. Hot Aftershave Bop
ORIGINAL RELEASE: various artists album *Head Over Ears – A Debris compilation*, Play Hard DEC7 (LP) December 1987 (includes a copy of *Debris* magazine)
COMMENTS: One of the all-time great live interpretations, as frenzied electronics bleep, whoosh and percolate around relentless bass and dramatically delivered vocals. Subsequently salvaged for *Backdrop*.

(SINGLE) There's A Ghost In My House
8702. There's A Ghost In My House
8703. Haf Found Bormann
8704. Sleep Debt Snatches(12-inch only)
8705. Mark'll Sink Us (12-inch only)
ORIGINAL RELEASE: Beggars Banquet BEG187/T (7/12-inch) April 1987

UK CHART PEAK: #30
COMMENTS: '"There's A Ghost In My House" was our old press officer, Karen Ehlers', idea,' Smith acknowledged. 'She sent us a tape and suggested maybe us or Brix should do it, and I thought "Fucking hell!" Because when I was at youth clubs when I was 13 that was the record I was getting beaten up to, and I thought we should do it.'

The original version of 'There's A Ghost In My House', by Motown second divisioner R Dean Taylor, made #3 back in 1974. A spectral lost love song that the Fall toyed with, but never quite deconstructed, it rode now on a mighty fuzz guitar line but strip that away and the rhythm is quintessential Motown – proving that those long ago overtures from America's premier soul label may not have been quite so misplaced as some thought.

The song rose to the nosebleed peaks of #30. The Fall was a decade old at that point: did it ever get dispiriting, waiting to score a real hit record? 'No,' says Smith, 'because we weren't waiting. We never expected a hit, and we never *not* expected one.'

On the b-side, the mood-enhanced 'Mark'll Sink Us' and the playful industrial motorik of 'Sleep Debt Snatches' offer little more than some extra music for the 12-inch buyer. But the miasmic electronica of 'Haf Found Bormann', one of the very best of the *Hey! Luciani* numbers, more than compensates. With Schofield and Brix taking the lead vocals (or, at least, speech) in the guise of the Israeli girl commandos who unearth the Nazi fugitive, 'Haf Found Bormann' loses much of its meaning when divorced from its natural surroundings – *ie*: the plot of the play – but its impact remains the same.

(BBC SESSION) May 11, 1987
8706. Athlete Cured
ORIGINAL RELEASE: *The Peel Sessions* (1998)
COMMENTS: see appendix I/BBC sessions

(LIVE) May 25 1987, Rock City, Nottingham
8707. Australians In Europe
8708. Shoulder Pads
8709. There's A Ghost In My House
8710. Hey! Luciani
8711. Terry Waite Sez
8712. Fiery Jack
8713. Lucifer Over Lancashire
UNR. remainder of set unknown
ORIGINAL RELEASE: as *BBC Radio 1 Live In Concert*, Windsong International WINCD038 (CD) 1993
COMMENTS: An incomplete (34-minute) segment from what sounds like a truly classic Fall show, as aired by the BBC in May 1987. Unfamiliar to all but the doughtiest acolytes, the unreleased 'Australians In Europe' provided an epic opener, one which came close to touching eight minutes, but was mercifully enacted at a considerably less manic pace than its b-side counterpart would be.

Journalist Mark Paytress' liner notes serve up a few pithy observations, including the reminder that the band's reputation for shambolic noise-making was taking a serious drubbing, as Brix weighed in to invest the band with the friendliest sound it would ever have. Of course, nothing can detract from the turbulence of 'Terry Waite Sez' or 'Lucifer Over Lancashire', nor the disquieting frolics of 'Fiery Jack' and 'Shoulder Pads'. Even so, Paytress is correct, all the more so since most casual listeners' attention was probably reserved for 'There's A Ghost In My House', the R Dean Taylor classic which allowed the band to celebrate their tenth anniversary with their first Top 30 hit. This is one of the best sounding live documents that the Fall have ever had. One only regrets that it's so short.

(SINGLE) Hit The North
   8714. Hit The North Part 1
   8715. Hit The North Part 2 (7-inch only)
   8716. Hit The North Part 3 (12-inch only)
   8717. Hit The North Part 4 (ltd 12-inch only, cass only)
   8718. Hit The North Part 5 (ltd 12-inch only)
   8714a. Hit The North (Double Six Mix) (cassette only)
   8719. Australians in Europe (12-inch, cass only)
   8720. Northerns in Europ (12-inch only)
   ORIGINAL RELEASE: Beggars Banquet BEG200 T/TR/C (7-inch, 12-inch, ltd 12-inch, cass) October 1987 (cassette)
   UK CHART PEAK: #57
   8714b. Hit the North (Zeus B. Held Remix)
   8714c. Hit the North (Extended Version)
   8714d. Hit the North (Dub Version)
   ORIGINAL RELEASE: Beggars Banquet SOVX2410 1987 (12")
   COMMENTS: 'Hit The North' is another of the Fall's all-time greats, a thumping dance number powered by horns, chant and echo. Even in its 'original' Part One format, it feels like a club mix, an electrifying stomp that defies identification even after you know who's responsible. It becomes even more frenzied across the five further remixes and remodels to which it was subjected. Best of these are Part Two, with Smith delightedly playing up his vocal intonations, and Part Five, a near skeletal electro-dub; the worst is the Double Six Mix, which cuts phrases and riffs to ribbons, then reassembles them in what must have been deliberately annoying fashion.
   Somewhat peculiarly, Cure bassist Simon Gallup reviewed 'Hit The North' for the *NME* and described it as sounding like Van Der Graaf Generator. The teenaged Smith would have been thrilled.
   The Punkoid 'Australians In Europe' and its super-tinny, and much-interrupted 'Northerns In Europ' counterpart follow in the recent tradition of Fall b-sides that are 'interesting,' rather than fulfilling.

(LIVE/STUDIO) out-takes etc
   8721. Mark'll Sink Us (live)
   8714e. Hit The North (alternate)
   ORIGINAL RELEASE: 8721 free single with *The Frenz Experiment* (1988), 8714e on *Cheetham Hill* (1997)

1988

Another year, another hit single. No sooner had the Stranglers raided the Kinks' kabinet of 60s klassiks for a chart-busting rendition of 'All Day And All Of The Night', than the Fall were shopping the same shelves, in search of a similar fillip. They found it in 1970's 'Victoria' and promptly marched to #35, lowly by top pop standards, of course, but a triumph for a band like the Fall's ... and a triumph for 'Victoria' herself. The Kinks' original only climbed two places higher.

Of course, it was also a shrewd lure for anybody considering buying their next album. As *The Listener* put it, 'tame commercial singles... act as trailers for Smith's persistently egocentric, dark satanic albums.'

The latest of these, *The Frenz Experiment*, was released in March, at the outset of the band's next tour, a campaign that took in Britain, Europe and the United States, and kept the band on the road for almost four months. That over, it was on to rehearsals for the Fall's next act of cross-cultural terrorism, linking up with dancer Michael Clark for *I Am Kurious Oranj*, the long-promised, or threatened, Fall ballet.

I Am Kurious, Oranj was based (loosely) on the life of the Dutch Prince William of Orange, the 17th century Protestant kingmakers' last hope of ending the dynastic quirk that placed the Papist James II on the throne of England.

The performance itself had little in common with the traditional elements of the history; nevertheless, it premiered in Amsterdam on June 11, as part of the city's own celebrations of the Tercentenary of William's accession to the English throne

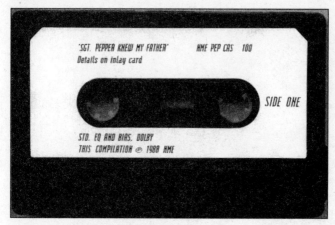

'SGT. PEPPER KNEW MY FATHER'   NME PEP CAS   100
Details on inlay card

SIDE ONE

STD. EQ AND BIAS. DOLBY
THIS COMPILATION ℗ 1988 NME

in 1687, before opening at the Edinburgh Festival in August, then moving down to the Sadlers' Wells Opera House, London, in late September.

Designed, as Smith put it, to pursue modern attitudes back through history and find how much (or how little) the relations between Protestants and Catholics have changed in three centuries, *I Am Kurious, Oranj* was darkly surreal – 'chock-full of nonsensical and funny images,' as journalist Caren Myers reported. 'A huge green telephone hurried across the stage, never to reappear, a carton of McDonald's fries lowered gently from the roof, and spilling its contents over the dancers who fall down dead, an execution where a plaster head goes flying, Brix getting wheeled in on a giant Big Mac and, incredibly, Mark E Smith looking downright dapper.'

Smith excused such liberties by admitting to the *NME*, 'Until I got into doing this, it was a period that I knew sod all about. I'm pretty well up on the period before and after but, apart from the obvious stuff, I didn't know much about William of Orange. So I guessed a lot of it. And it was weird 'cos a lot of it turned out to be true. Like he couldn't stand music, apparently. Typical Dutch. When he came to court, he got rid of all [predecessor King James II]'s musicians. I didn't know this, but I'd already written the thing about "Can't dance, can't sing/Cursed forever is William of Orange".'

The plot, such as it was, was developed while the Fall were on tour. Smith penned much of it in dressing rooms around the world, then mailed his thoughts to Clark for his input and, just as importantly, some indication of where in the ballet each song should be placed. 'That's important for the dancers. Like we couldn't have started with "Bremen Nacht", for instance, 'cos the dancers would have just been knackered straight away and wouldn't have been able to do the rest!'

Unsurprisingly, audience response tended towards the extremes. Fall fans, naturally, applauded the music, even if the dancing left them a little bewildered. Clark's admirers, on the other hand, took the opposite tack. Smith recalled, 'Apparently some of them have said, "Oh, the dancing is wonderful but the music's a nightmare."' Even more damning – as Smith delightedly recounted later, was the conversation he overheard in a nearby café one day. 'This bloke came in with about eight girls. He must have been a dance teacher or something and he sat about a yard away from me and rambled on about how this ballet had been ruined by some bloke called Mark Smith, who had his hand in his pocket and couldn't sing.'

Other commentators, however, entered into the ludic spirit of the things – *NME*'s Sean O'Hagan, for one. 'I abandoned my notes somewhere between the bomb blast that ended the Celtic/Rangers fannydancer's cup final and the attack of the giant French fries. Thus liberated from the constraints of a theoretical analysis, I abandoned myself to the chaos on stage. Zen-like, I merged into a state of complete oneness with the noise, the movement and the sight of Leigh Bowery dressed as a tin of Heinz Beans.'

Neither would this exercise suffer the obscure fate that awaited *Hey! Luciani*. Great swathes of the music appeared as the Fall's next album, *I Am Kurious Oranj*, in October, accompanied by their latest single, a Top 60 take on the hymn 'Jerusalem', updated to show William Blake precisely what had befallen his precious green and pleasant land.

(MUSICIANS)
LINE-UP #19 (all) MARK E SMITH (vocals), CRAIG SCANLON (guitar), BRIX SMITH (guitar, vocals), STEVE HANLEY (bass), MARCIA SCHOFIELD (keyboards), SIMON WOLSTENCROFT (drums)

(SINGLE) Victoria
    8801. Victoria
    8802. Tuff Life Boogie
    8803. Guest Informant (12-inch, cassette only)
    8804. Twister (12-inch, cassette only)
ORIGINAL RELEASE: Beggars Banquet BEG206/T/C (7/12-inch/cass) January 1988
UK CHART PEAK: #35
COMMENTS: Describe the Fall's hit recording of the Kinks' 'Victoria' as a mere cover version and Mark E Smith will be the first to disagree: 'It isn't a cover version. [It's]… an Original Interpretation. The original was brilliant, all 70s British boogie, but we tried to cut it to bits. We wanted to do something extreme to it, almost like early Can. We wanted it really shrill and fuzzy, which is why you can't really hear what Marcia's organ is doing… she played "Land Of Hope And Glory".' Whereas the Kinks' original oozed nostalgia for a Britain buried with the old Queen of the same name, the Fall's version was, as Smith put it, more descriptive of Britain in the late 1980s, paradoxically poised between the Victorian moralities of Margaret Thatcher and a yearning for older, simpler, times, when government found better things to do than pickpocket the electorate at every opportunity.

That said, it's as faithful a make-over as the Kinks could hope for, the lyric as wry ('I was born… lucky me') as Ray Davies ever emoted, and the chorus as air-punchingly celebratory. Only Smith's attempt at swallowed scat singing in the bridge hints that something (or someone) very sinister lurks beneath the surface.

On the b-side, 'Guest Informant' uses Gary Glitter drums and a chant – which informed ears insist cries 'Baghdad, space cog, analyst' – to set the scene of a spy drama set in a Scottish hotel that 'resembled a Genesis or Marillion 1973 LP cover.' Calmer, 'Tuff Life Boogie' could be a warped Echo and the Bunnymen number, punctured by the delighted reiteration of such rocking clichés as 'give it to me baby, one more time' and, of course, the title. 'Twister' reverts back to the Fall's early 80s fascination with rockabilly, all twanging guitars and wildebeest drums.

(ALBUM) *The Frenz Experiment*
    8805. Frenz
    8806. Carry Bag Man

8807. Get a Hotel
8801. Victoria
8808. Athlete Cured
8809. In these Times
8810. The Steak Place
8811. Guest Informant (excerpt)
8812. Oswald Defence Lawyer

CD/cassette bonus tracks
8813. Bremen Nacht (cass only)
8803. Guest Informant
8802. Tuff Life Booogie
8804. Twister
8702. There's A Ghost In My House (CD only)
8714. Hit The North part 1 (CD only)
ORIGINAL RELEASE: Beggars Banquet BEGA 96, March 1988
UK CHART PEAK: #19
COMMENTS: The crashing, crushing percussive tricks of recent (and future) singles were no accident. Reclaiming the 'expected' sound of the Fall after the electronic adventures of *Bend Sinister et al*, *The Frenz Experiment* sounds strangely friendless all the same. Smith stripped back the effects and went it alone. His vocals are louder than on all but the most unbalanced live bootlegs, while the prominence of the drums overwhelms anyone else's chance of shining.

Headache time? Not quite. Reviving the visceral power of the old two-drummer Fall line-up was bound to find favour with the faithful, all the more so since Smith was looking back to his professed love of hard rock (its impact, if not its delivery). 'Athlete Cured' even glanced towards the hit movie *Spinal Tap* in search of its guitar riff, while the bombast of the hit single 'Victoria' was certainly amplified within the confines of the album. As for the experimental 'Frenz', the skewed dynamic that gave the album its title: 'When we laid that down I was very excited about that. When we were playing it live, I thought it would be quite interesting and a bit out of the ordinary for the Fall.'

However, Smith was well aware that he was delivering an album that utterly confounded predictions and, possibly, hopes. He told American journalist Dave Segal, 'With this LP, we were supposed to do a very commercial one because we had had two (UK) top 40 singles. So, everybody expected a commercial album, which was the last thing I wanted to do.' Even the chance to record at Abbey Road didn't persuade him to pursue more accessible sounds: 'It was the first time in our career we'd been able to use a top-class studio. I thought it would be a shame if we came out with a load of glossed product. I'm very adamant in the studio. I don't like anything being polished up and shit.'

(SINGLE) Bremen Nacht Run Out
8814. Bremen Nacht Run Out
8721. Mark'll Sink Us
ORIGINAL RELEASE: Beggars Banquet FALL1 (7-inch free with *Frenz Experiment* LP)
COMMENTS: Staccato and brusque, pidgin German gleefully goose-stepping around the studio, 'Bremen Nacht Run Out' is a dry run for *I Am Kurious, Oranj*

and thoroughly compelling. The live 'Mark'll Sink Us', unlike the rough and sketchy versions that proliferate elsewhere, is stronger and certainly more atmospheric, built around a descending minor-chord riff that reminds one of the Cure's 'Carnage Visors' – except when the chorus kicks into mood-shattering atonality.

(LIVE)/(STUDIO) out-takes etc
    8803a. Guest Informant
    8805a. Frenz
    8807a. Get a Hotel
    8812a. Oswald Defence Lawyer
    8813a. Bremen Nacht
    8872a. Big New Prinz
    ORIGINAL RELEASE: as *Oswald Defence Lawyer*, Receiver Records RRCD 213, 1996

(LIVE) March 18, 1988 Hammersmith Odeon
    8815. Lucifer Over Lancashire
    UNR. U.S. 80's-90's
    UNR. Cab It Up
    UNR. 2 x 4
    UNR. Get A Hotel
    UNR. Hit The North
    UNR. Shoulder Pads
    UNR. Bremen Nacht
    UNR. Frenz
    UNR. Pay Your Rates
    UNR. Oswald Defence Lawyer
    UNR. L.A.
    UNR. Carry Bag Man
    UNR. Victoria
    UNR. Tuff Life Boogie
    UNR. Mr Pharmacist
    UNR. Guest Informant
    UNR. Bombast
    ORIGINAL RELEASE: a-side of bootleg single, 1989?

(LIVE) March 19, 1988 Cambridge Corn Exchange
    8816. Shoulder Pads
    8817. 2 x 4
    8818. Get a Hotel
    8819. Cab it Up
    8820. Hit the North
    8821. Bremen Nacht
    8822. Frenz
    8823. Pay Your Rates
    8824. Hey! Luciani
    8825. Oswald Defence Lawyer
    8826. L.A.

8827. Carry Bag Man
8828. Victoria
8829. Mr. Pharmacist – U.S. 80's-90's
8830. Lucifer over Lancashire

ORIGINAL RELEASE: as *Live in Cambridge 1988*, Cog Sinister COGVP115CD – 2000

COMMENTS: *Live in Cambridge 1988* was recorded on the final night of the Fall's latest UK tour, undertaken just as their reinvention of the Kinks' 'Victoria' approached its chart peak of #35 – no prizes for guessing which song gets the biggest roar of the evening. One wonders what it was like back then, catching the Fall for the first time on the back of two big hits ('There's A Ghost In My House' was less than a year old), only to be confronted by the likes of '2 x 4', 'Lucifer Over Lancashire' and 'Bremen Nacht'? A blessed epiphany? Or a sense-shattering shock?

This performance seems intent on winning the former response. Contemporary reactions culled from the band's print archive centre around a passing resemblance to New Order. There *is* a poppy, dancey edge to the performance – largely thanks to Marcia Schofield's keyboards, but apparent elsewhere too. What is the chorus of 'Oswald Defence Lawyer', after all, if not a dramatic jingle, as memorable as a nursery rhyme, as catchy as a fishnet? The medley of 'Mr. Pharmacist' and 'U.S. 80's-90's', too, hinges on the two songs' most obsessive elements, while 'Victoria' is performed with such guilelessness that one could almost believe that the Fall enjoyed being pop stars.

Great sound quality is marred only by the sort of points that should concern hard-nosed pedants alone – a couple of songs cut off abruptly, and the show's opening number, 'Athlete Cured', is nowhere to be heard.

(LIVE) Apr 15 1988, Fritz Club, Vienna, Austria
  8831. Guest Informant
  8832. Carry Bag Man
  8833. Yes, Oh Yes
  8834. U.S. 80's-90's
  UNR. Cab It Up
  UNR. Get a Hotel
  UNR. Hit The North
  UNR. Frenz
  UNR. In These Times
  UNR. Pay Your Rates
  UNR. Oswald Defence Lawyer
  UNR. L.A.
  UNR. Victoria
  UNR. Bad News Girl
  UNR. Bremen Nacht
  UNR. Mr Pharmacist
  UNR. 2 x 4

ORIGINAL RELEASE: 8831 on various artists EP *Sniffin' Rock* SR006A7 – free with *Sniffin Rock* magazine June 1989/issue 9; remainder on *Live Various Years* (1998)

COMMENTS: An excitable live recording, adding some serious turbulence to the familiar studio version. 'Guest Informant' was subsequently included on

Backdrop. In addition to the released tracks, several numbers from this show were broadcast live on local radio.

(ALBUM) various artists: *Sgt. Pepper Knew my Father*
  8835. A Day in the Life
  ORIGINAL RELEASE Youth NMEDEPLP100 1988 (LP)
I read the news today – ho ho. Wrapping up the *NME*-sponsored *Sgt Pepper Knew My Father* charity tribute to the Beatles' most overrated album, the Fall's 'A Day In The Life' emerges out of Three Wize Men's electro-hellish reinterpretation of the title track as, perhaps, the most faithful translation on the entire album. Smartly blending a Xeroxed rendition of the Beatles' arrangement with some unavoidably Fall-like trademarks (Smith's cracking voice on the high notes, for example), Smith adds a minor lyrical rearrangement that makes sense of the end of the mid-section dream sequence, then takes the original's cacophonous climax to shattering lengths.

Elsewhere, of course, it was Wet Wet Wet's damp damp damp 'With A Little Help From My Friends' that drew the plaudits. In truth, you could dispense with the entire album, so long as you kept the Fall track.

(LIVE) August 17 1988, Edinburgh Festival, King's Theatre
  8836. Dog Is Life
  8837. Jerusalem
  8838. Kurious Oranj
  8840. Yes, Oh Yes
  8841. Big New Prinz
  8842. Wrong Place Right Time
  8843. Acid Priest 2088
  8844. Frenz
  8845. Bad News Girl
  8846. Dead Beat Descendant
  8847. Van Plague
  8848. Cab It Up!
  8849. Bremen Nacht
  ORIGINAL RELEASE: as *I Am Pure As Oranj*, Burning Airlines PILOT 61 – 2000
  COMMENTS: As 'Tempo House' warned all those years

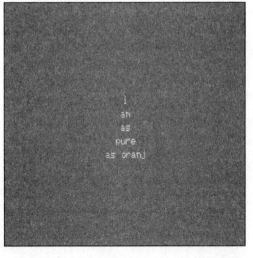

before, 'the Dutch are waiting... in four languages, at least!' And this was what they were waiting for. A clean recording of the opening night of the Fall's so-remarkable balletic collaboration, captured with all the stunned silence and awed anger of the audience intact. One can only imagine, for example, the effect that the opening scatology of 'Dog Is Life' had on anybody expecting something more conventional from the production, while the impressive bass-led intro to William Blake's updated 'Jerusalem' is merely the prelude to an aural assault that didn't require Smith's presence to send the tolerance needles soaring into overload.

It is remarkable how well the soundtrack works alone. The tight choreography that was part and parcel of the production caused the band to dispense with all but the spirit of their customary tightrope walking, with even Smith's impromptu rants and rampages forced to take a back seat. But moments that the show's admirers recall as transcendent – the seven-plus minute 'Hip Priest', six minutes more of 'Jerusalem' and 'Kurious Oranj' itself – retain their magic and their momentum, while the jerking 'Dead Beat Descendant' has a percussive electricity and verbal immediacy that the following year's studio recreation couldn't match. Several of the performances here easily outstrip their vinyl counterparts, a throbbing 'Van Plague' and an assertive 'Wrong Place Right Time' among them.

Well packaged with a colour booklet that readily complements that accompanying the regular *I Am Kurious, Oranj* LP, *I Am As Pure As Oranj* was prepared for release by bassist Steve Hanley and therefore lacks the 'official' stamp that Mark E Smith's own releases enjoy among Fall cognoscenti. But it is a mistake to write it off it among the flood of Receiver/Rialto/Castle label collections released on either side. Rather, *I Am As Pure As Oranj* reasserts the earlier album's claim that this event transcended the artistic boundaries customarily associated with Rock and ballet. Transcended them, and then rebuilt them around its own requirements.

(ALBUM) *I am Kurious, Oranj*
   8850. New Big Prinz
   8851. Overture from 'I am Kurious Oranj'
   8852. Dog is Life-Jerusalem
   8853. Kurious Oranj
   8854. Wrong Place, Right Time
   8855. C.D. Win Fall 2088 AD
   8856. Yes, Oh Yes
   8857. Van Plague
   8858. Bad News Girl
   8859. Cab It Up!
   CD BONUS TRACKS
   8860. Guide Me Soft
   8861. Last Nacht
   8862. Big New Prinz
   ORIGINAL RELEASE: Beggars Banquet BEGA96 October 1988
   UK CHART PEAK: #54
   COMMENTS: One of the Fall's most divisive albums, the Ian Broudie-produced *I Am Kurious, Oranj* combines music from the ballet score with a mishmash of material either drawn from, or available elsewhere: 'New Big Prinz' and the CD/cassette bonus track 'Big New Priest' simply Glitterize *Hex Enduction Hour*'s 'Hip Priest'; 'Last Nacht' is a messily invasive electronic rendering of 'Bremen Nacht'; and 'CD Win Fall 2088' is essentially a cut-up-and-keep distillation of much of the rest of the album.

When it's good, however, it is excellent, from the widescreen guitars that herald the 'Overture from *I Am Kurious, Oranj*' to the muttered speech that introduces 'Jerusalem' and steals the hymn back from whichever past indignities have been dealt it in the name of rock'n'roll; from the near-detuned acoustics that guide in the tipsy mumbling of 'Guide Me Soft' to the mischief-making bass line that plays around 'Yes, O Yes' and on to 'Bad News Girl' (which tracks abruptly from profound sobriety to teasing silliness, and has been construed as a comment on the state of the Smiths' crumbling marriage). Brix herself later admitted that she thought the song was about her. 'He wrote it when we were going through our break-up. I used to hate playing it. It drove me crazy.'

Powerful, too, was the closing 'Cab It Up!', built around a rhythmic resemblance to the Stooges' 'TV Eye' but more intent on pursuing an infectious keyboard pattern uptown than leaving the cab in Garageland.

Not the Fall's most cohesive album, nor an especially accurate document of the play itself, *I Am Kurious, Oranj* is nevertheless a dramatic reminder of one of the most audacious moves made by any band of the era – and, critics be damned, one of the most successful.

(BBC SESSION) October 31, 1988
    8863. Dead Beat Descendant
    ORIGINAL RELEASE: *The Peel Sessions* (1998)
    COMMENTS: see appendix I/BBC sessions

(SINGLE) Jerusalem
    8862. Big New Prinz
    8864. Wrong Place, Right Time 2
    ORIGINAL RELEASE: Beggars Banquet FALL4, November 1988 (7-inch)
    UK CHART PEAK: #59
    8852a. Jerusalem
    8865. Acid Priest 2088
    8862. Big New Prinz
    8864. Wrong Place, Right Time 2
    ORIGINAL RELEASE: Beggars Banquet FALL2-3 / CD (Ltd, numbered box inc 2 45s/CDs + postcard – FALL2B) November 1988
    COMMENTS: A reworking of four tracks drawn from *I Am Kurious, Oranj* peaks by snubbing the precocious club culture that was burgeoning all around. 'Acid Priest 2088' is another of the Fall's experiments with cut-up electronics and eerily floating voices, while 'Wrong Place, Right Time #2' and the revised 'Hip Priest', 'Big New Prinz' (another Glitter-drum extravaganza), look to simple percussion and repetition for their energies. Bright and joyful, they make ideal companions for the heart-attack redevelopment of Blake's 'Jerusalem', re-recorded with dance producer CJ. Sliced away from the album's spoken word 'Dog Is Life' prelude, this new version retains only a few lines of the 'it was the fault of government' mid-section. But that was still sufficient to make the point.

(LIVE) unknown date/venue
    8866. Squid Law
    8867. Kurious Oranj
    8868. Hit the North
    8869. 2 x 4
    8870. Elf Prefix
    8871. L.A.
    8872. Victoria
    8873. Pay Your Rates
    8874. Introduction
    8875. Cruiser's Creek
    8876. Frenz
    8877. In These Times
    8878. Victoria

8879. Bad News Girl
8880. Carry Bag Man
ORIGINAL RELEASE: 8866 b-side of 'Lucifer Over Lancashire' bootleg single, 1989; 8867-68 on 'Cab It Up!' single; 8878-80 on *Oswald Defence Lawyer*; remainder on *Seminal Live* LP 1989

(STUDIO) out-takes
8881. Dead Beat Descendent
8882. Pinball Machine
8883. HOW
8884. Squid Law
8885. Mollusc In Tyrol
ORIGINAL RELEASE: *Seminal Live* LP 1989

THE FALL
Backdrop

1989

If any single event dominated the world of the Fall in 1989, it was the departure of Brix, first from the marriage in January, then from the band that summer. Her last album with the group, the largely-live *Seminal Live*, was also the Fall's final release for Beggar's Banquet. It was the end of an era in every way.

Smith told *Sounds*, 'Beggars are alright for money, but not quite enough. The singles we were bringing out – it was like, we were getting into the *Guinness Book Of Records* for singles going in at number 30 or something and then going straight out again. We were just flogging ourselves to death and not seeing anything for it. Last year we played like three times a week. I don't mind it, but...' It was exhausting. '*Seminal Live*? We could've called it *Half Dead*.'

Now the bastard sons of Indie were finally shrugging off their parentage. After a dozen years scaling the ladder, the Fall were signing to their first major label, Phonogram's recently revitalised Fontana imprint. The label had already picked up Adult Net, as Brix – still a member of the Fall at that time – reconfigured the group around an axis of ex-Smiths guitarist Craig Gannon, Blondie drummer Clem Burke and bassist James Eller; now the Fall would follow them.

From the moment their Beggars Banquet contract expired, the Fall had been approached by a number of labels, with Arista proving especially tenacious. Smith, however, was difficult to impress. 'We must have had about 25 offers from Arista. They must have been interested for the last ten years without doing anything. Then they send some 17-year-old brat down who says, "Oh, send me a tape!" And I think,

"Will I fuck send you a tape!" A lot of these people wouldn't get jobs as window cleaners now. And that's an insult to window cleaners. They know fuckin' nowt. But the A&R people at Phonogram are brilliant. Really on the ball.'

Examples: 'I had this song that I wanted to do that's like Gershwin, y'know, a bit avant garde with the oboes and shit. I said to them, "Well, the only person I know who can produce this is Craig Leon, who did Brix's stuff," and they said, "OK, yeah." Then they said, "What about doing some more stuff with Adrian Sherwood?" So it's good. What's great is, they're being enthusiastic about it. Most record companies, they just send you a tape with all the different producers who are cheap.'

It was a pair of UK gigs in late June that introduced the Fall-without-Brix to the public at large, *NME*'s review of the Cambridge Corn Exchange show sounding quite shocked as 'the Smith story takes a new twist when Brix fails to emerge on stage. Her non-appearance – whether it be for musical or marital reasons – seems to lend the evening a feeling of despondency, but maybe that's my romantic imagination playing tricks on me.'

She was replaced, with unimpeachably circular logic, by Martin Bramah, the band's first guitarist. Bramah and Smith had, in fact, reignited their songwriting partnership around a month before Brix announced her departure – when that day came, he promptly agreed to take her place.

As for the sundering of his marriage, however, Smith politely – and firmly – made it plain that some subjects were not up for discussion. 'I don't think anyone wants to know about our private life and I wouldn't be arrogant enough to impose it upon people.' But he did pause to admit, 'personally I've had a bad year, my dad going, and a car crash. It was like one thing after another.'

Brix was a little more forthcoming. Back in Chicago in November, she told the local *Illinois Entertainer*, 'basically, Adult Net began to take up more and more of my time and I began to feel really torn about which way to go musically. I gave the Fall 100% of my abilities for six consecutive years. But I just felt something inside me, something strong, which made me want to compose and play and sing my own music, in my own way. And, to put it bluntly, the music I wanted to play was very, very opposite from what the Fall were doing. It just wasn't fair for me to keep playing with them. It wasn't fair to the other band members because suddenly my heart just wasn't in it. I also think a lot of these problems started to wade into my relationship with Mark, because it was all so inextricably and dramatically bound together, you know – the music, the marriage, the British media exaggerations, and of course, the Fall.'

It would be five years before she was prepared to go deeper into the break-up, by which time – though no reconciliation was in sight – she herself was back in the Fall. 'I left Mark because I needed to find my own identity outside the Fall. I was 20 when I married. I moved from my mum's to Mark Smith. I'd never been on my own. I was socially retarded. I didn't know how to sign a cheque. I was just this weird cult pop princess and really arrogant bitch. You know that bit in Spinal Tap where the guy goes, "This bread is too small for this meat"? That was me. I was really unhappy, except when I was playing.'

The summer took the new-look Fall to South America for the first time, for a brace of Brazilian festival dates. Back in England at the end of August, the group guested at John Peel's 50th birthday party at Subterrania, wrapping up their set with a tribute to another of their long-time mentor's all-time favourites, Gene Vincent's 'Race With The Devil'.

The bulk of the remainder of the year, however, was spent in the studio, working on what would emerge as the Fall's major-label debut, the new year's *Extricate*, a title that Smith surely selected with a certain irony. Extricated from his marriage, he also removed himself from the entire circumstance of it, abandoning both Manchester and the musical madness that was swirling up there in the footfalls of Stone Roses and Happy Mondays, for a rented flat in Edinburgh, Scotland. He would remain there for the next 18 months – a period he subsequently looked back upon as one of the happiest of his life.

MUSICIANS
LINE-UP #19 (Jan-May) MARK E SMITH (vocals), CRAIG SCANLON (guitar), BRIX SMITH (guitar, vocals), STEVE HANLEY (bass), MARCIA SCHOFIELD (keyboards), SIMON WOLSTENCROFT (drums)

LINE-UP #20 (remainder) MARK E SMITH (vocals), CRAIG SCANLON (guitar), MARTIN BRAMAH (guitar), STEVE HANLEY (bass), MARCIA SCHOFIELD (keyboards), SIMON WOLSTENCROFT (drums)

(SINGLE) Cab It Up!
   8901. Cab It Up!
   8881. Dead Beat Descendant
   8867. Kurious Oranj (12-inch only)
   8868. Hit the North (12-inch only)
   ORIGINAL RELEASE: Beggars Banquet BEG226/T (7/12-inch)
   COMMENTS: Beggars Banquet bade farewell to the Fall by lifting 'Cab It Up' direct from the previous year's *I Am Kurious, Oranj* album – and were rewarded, ironically, with the band's first non-charting single since the sombre 'Living Too Late'. The economy of the band's most recent studio work was summarised by the appearance of just one additional studio track, a sharpened guitar-led 'Dead Beat Descendant' recorded with producer Shan Hira; the accompanying 12-inch single then lifted two tracks from the CD version of *Seminal Live*, 'Kurious Oranj' and a very punchy 'Hit The North', necessarily stripped down from its manifold studio counterparts, to reveal what it might have sounded like without the added club dub convolutions.

(ALBUM) *What's That Noise* by COLDCUT
   8902. (I'm) In Deep
ORIGINAL RELEASE Ahead Of Our Time CCUTLP1, 1989
   COMMENTS: Electro-duo Jonathan More and Matt Black formed Coldcut in the mid-1980s, originally as a pirate radio DJ-ing team. 1987's single 'Say Kids, What Time is it?' – widely acclaimed as the first sample-built record in the UK – brought them to wider attention, establishing them among the key influences on the electronic scene at the end of the 1980s. Their initial approach to Smith came in mid-1989, in the form of a handful of tapes from which he was invited to select one he'd like to join them on. In fact, Smith chose two – the acid house rampage '(I'm) In Deep' and 'My Telephone', a piece that became the basis of 'Telephone Thing', from the Fall's next album.
   Smith's recruitment was generally regarded as something of a shock – albeit

mainly by commentators who'd missed the Fall's own pioneering embrace of electro textures; in fact, the combination was so successful that Smith promptly co-opted the duo to co-produce the Fall's own next album, *Extricate*.

(ALBUM) *Seminal Live*
    8881. Dead Beat Descendent
    8882. Pinball Machine
    8883. HOW
    8884. Squid Law
    8885. Mollusc In Tyrol
    8869. 2 x 4
    8870. Elf Prefix
    8871. L.A.
    8872. Victoria
    8873. Pay Your Rates
    8874. Introduction
    8875. Cruiser's Creek
CD BONUS TRACKS
    8867. Kurious Oranj
    8868. Hit the North
    8876. Frenz
    8877. In These Times
ORIGINAL RELEASE: Beggars Banquet BBL102 (LP) June 1989
UK CHART PEAK: #40
COMMENTS: Wrapping up the Fall's Beggars Banquet years, *Seminal Live* is generally referred to as their 'contractual obligation' album, although the departure of Brix from both band and marriage would surely have precluded a more coherent release, no matter where the band's priorities lay. Besides, it's an awful lot better than most records tarred with that brush

With the exception of the sparkling 'Dead Beat Descendant', the opening five studio tracks are largely disposable. Recorded quickly, and not always with the hiest of fi ('Mollusc' was taped in Smith's front room), they are more notable for their intent than their delivery, a jab at the ongoing late-decade insistence on devoting as much time to getting the drum sound as on recording the other instruments. As an awkward experiment, it works fabulously. As a long-term listening experience, it palls.

The live performance, however, catches the band sounding tight and athletic, not adding much to the studio counterparts ('Pay Your Rates' sounds a little angrier, although that might just be Poll Tax memories talking) but offering enjoyable alternatives all the same. It's not a crucial recording by a long chalk – it presents a friendlier Fall than most people probably care to remember – but a nice album to play to the curious.

(LIVE) August 29 1989, Subterrania
    8903. Race With The Devil
    UNR. Mere Pseud Mag Ed
    UNR. I'm Frank
    UNR. Arms Control Poseur
    UNR. Fiery Jack

UNR. Carry Bag Man
UNR. Mr. Pharmacist,'
ORIGINAL RELEASE: on *Backdrop*, Cog Sinister COGVP 127 CD
COMMENTS: Returning to the scene of former glories – Subterranea was the latest occupant of the late 1970s Acklam Hall – the Fall made a special appearance at a gig arranged to celebrate DJ John Peel's 50th birthday. Their necessarily brief (seven-song) set included Gene Vincent's 'Race With The Devil', a special request from Peel himself. 'We learned this specially,' Smith announces as the band kick into a delightfully loose version of the 1956 rock'n'roll classic – the follow-up to Vincent's seminal 'Be Bop A Lula'.

(SINGLE) 'Lucifer Over Lancashire'
8815. Lucifer Over Lancashire (live)
8866. Squid Law (live)
ORIGINAL RELEASE: Bootleg 45, Fall-In Records 1, 1989
COMMENTS: As with so many 'legendary,' 'rare' and 'collectible' bootlegs, 'Lucifer Over Lancashire' is worth more as an artefact than as a listening experience. 'Lucifer' itself seems to have been taken from one of the poorer quality tapes of the Fall's Hammersmith show the previous year; 'Squid Law' could be from anywhere (except Hammersmith).

THE FALL /
/ EXTRICATE

1990

1990 dawned as 1989 had ended: with Manchester being fêted as the new centre of all that was great in British rock. From the Happy Mondays to the Inspiral Carpets, from the Stone Roses to Primal Scream and on into the deepest recesses of a Scallydelic rave scene, Madmanchester sparked the 24 Hour Party People cult which is the subject of much nostalgic reminiscence today, the cult of Generation Ecstasy which fried brains from here to eternity. Extricate, the Fall's first 'post-Brix' album, wanted nothing to do with it.

Extricate was released in February, hot on the heels of the band's 13th John Peel session, a dynamite preview of three tracks (plus the unbroadcast, unreleased 'Whizz Bang') that also saw the Fall augmented by Kenny Brady's violin. It was greeted – perhaps surprisingly, given the climate of the day – with reviews shamelessly proclaiming it the best new Fall album since... the last best new Fall album.

Buoyed by the enthusiasm, the band launched its first major UK tour in close to two years in March and, four nights in to the outing, marched straight into the lion's den with a gig at the Hacienda, high temple of the local loons.

These UK dates were the prelude to a worldwide outing that kept the Fall on the road until July, and included return visits to Greece, Australia and New Zealand – the latter for the first time since a Fall fan suicide-bombed the foyer of the New Zealand Nuclear Energy centre. According to Smith, 'When they went back to his house, they found his record collection was just Fall albums – nothing else. All over the house. They wanted to make a documentary. I had to put the clampers on the script. Imagine that getting out!'

In early August, however, the line-up responsible for the latest string of triumphs collapsed midway through the Australian leg. Schofield and Bramah were both fired, sent home while the Fall played on as the core quartet of Smith, Scanlon, Hanley and Wolstencroft.

From the outside, the sackings came as a serious shock – not to mention a somewhat ruthless action. Smith himself was utterly unrepentant. He told *Select*, 'Martin was always a fill-in, really, and Marcia is a brilliant keyboards player, great image and all that. But I wanted to change the sound, make it even more sparse than it is already. I think the two of them were really out of sync with us, so I sent 'em home. We've done that six-piece thing now. It's very *de rigueur* at the moment, samplers and everything, but we've already done it. I want to get back to a more fuckin' metal, fuckin' sparse sound. We were ending up like fuckin' Ian Dury And The Blockheads.'

He celebrated the change with a new single, 'White Lightning', and a warm-up for the new line-up in Norwich in October; there were further UK gigs through December (alongside another single, 'High Tension Line') at which the quartet gave some of the Fall's most ruthless performances in a while. Without the frills and flounces which recently departed members had provided, the Fall were closer to the sonic sandblasting of earlier incarnations than many of their 1980s-vintage fans might have dreamed possible – or even imagined.

Not all were impressed. *Melody Maker* hovered on the verge of dismissal by concluding a review of the Norwich gig: 'a floundering "Hit The North" has bassist Hanley grimacing as the subtleties are pummelled out of it, while "White Lightning" has the veins in his neck bulging as he desperately tries to inject some energy into proceedings. Their self-evident frustration,' mourned writer Adam Green, 'sets your teeth on edge.'

(MUSICIANS)

LINE-UP #20 (Jan-Aug) MARK E SMITH (vocals), CRAIG SCANLON (guitar), MARTIN BRAMAH (guitar), STEVE HANLEY (bass), MARCIA SCHOFIELD (keyboards), SIMON WOLSTENCROFT (drums)

LINE-UP #21 (remainder) MARK E SMITH (vocals), CRAIG SCANLON (guitar), STEVE HANLEY (bass), SIMON WOLSTENCROFT (drums)

(BBC SESSION) January 1, 1990
9001. Black Monk Theme
ORIGINAL RELEASE: *The Peel Sessions* (1998)
COMMENTS: see appendix I/BBC sessions

(SINGLE) Telephone Thing
9002. Telephone Thing
9003. British People in Hot Weather
9002a. Telephone Thing (extended) (12-inch, CD only)
9002b. Telephone Dub (12-inch, CD only)
ORIGINAL RELEASE: Cog Sinister SIN/CD 412, Jan 1990 (12-inch/CD)
UK CHART PEAK: #58

COMMENTS: 'Telephone Thing' was based upon Coldcut's 'My Telephone', a collaboration with singer Lisa Stansfield that was included among the tapes the duo sent him when they first broached working together.

Smith loathed the original performance. According to Coldcut's Jonathan Moore, 'he really liked the guitar, bass and drums' and, taking those elements, Smith transmuted the track into 'Telephone Thing', then called in Coldcut to manipulate it for the Fall's next single. The result was a slab of driving electronica slashing at the authorities' increasingly publicised practise of listening in to private phone calls. Solidly excellent, its only drawback was that the extended version is scarcely any different (and certainly no longer) than the regular 7-inch. The dub version, meanwhile, replaces great swathes of vocal with further effects.

In between-times, 'British People In Hot Weather' melds embarrassingly funny (you *know* these people!) lyrics to a tough, horn-driven dance rhythm that maybe laboured just a little too much. Smith's obvious amusement, however, lends the song a delightfully catchy air. Grrr.

(ALBUM) *Extricate*
9004. Sing! Harpy
9005. I'm Frank
9006. Bill is Dead
9007. Black Monk Theme Part I
9008. Popcorn Double Feature
9002. Telephone Thing
9009. Hilary
9010. Chicago, Now!
9011. The Littlest Rebel
9012. And Therein...

CASSETTE/CD BONUS TRACKS
9013. Arms Control Poseur
9014. Black Monk Theme Part II
9003. British People in Hot Weather
9015. Extricate
ORIGINAL RELEASE: Fontana 842.204-1, Feb 1990
REISSUE (1): Cog Sinister COGVP122CD, 1998
UK CHART PEAK: #31
COMMENTS: Taking full advantage of Fontana's magnanimity, the *Extricate* sessions featured collaborations with four separate producers, Craig Leon, Rex Sergeant, Adrian Sherwood and Coldcut, the latter handling both 'Telephone Thing' and the Fall's revision of the Monks' 'I Hate You' ('Black Monk Theme Part I'), a supremely disdainful Garage classic whose American GI makers shocked the Vietnam era by performing in full Buddhist monk garb.

A sense of wounded-in-love bitterness pervades many of the lyrics, naturally prompting as much speculation as any of Smith's past putative whipping posts. 'Sing! Harpy!' with strings like angry insects and the band locked in undisguised tribute to the Stooges' 'Little Doll', stamps like an angry buffalo, but the tale of a girl from a nowhere village who finds fame on *Junior Show Time* is as ambiguous as it can be construed as direct. Ditto 'The Littlest Rebel' ('... and she doesn't kiss and tell'), the tale of a tomboy who is as much Minnie the Minx as anyone else.

Elsewhere, 'I'm Frank' is built around a tribute to Frank Zappa devised by Scanlon. 'Now we can all laugh about this,' Smith said later, 'but that was his attempt to be Frank, therefore I've entitled it "I'm Frank".' In fact, it's difficult to see where the connection lies although that, in itself, is tribute – like the five year old 'I Am Damo Suzuki', the message is in the motive, not the delivery.

The succession of producers does lend the album a somewhat disjointed feel, although not to the detriment of the sound – more the actual mood of the pieces. But the back-to-back presence of two singles ('Telephone Thing' and a version of the Searchers' 'Popcorn Double Feature') does lend a reassuring familiarity to the set. Any latter day fans fearing the post-Brix Fall might fall back to their early 80s impenetrability were sadly mistaken. In the sequence of albums that commenced with *Hex Enduction Hour, Extricate* may not have been the greatest, but it certainly puts on its trousers the same way.

(SINGLE) Popcorn Double Feature
   9008. Popcorn Double Feature
   9016. Butterflies 4 Brains
   9013. Arms Control Poseur (12-inch only)
   9017. Zandra (ltd ed 7-inch/12-inch only)
   9014. Black Monk Theme pt. II (ltd ed 12-inch only)
   ORIGINAL RELEASE: Cog Sinister SIN/R5/12, March 1990
   COMMENTS: After years of hearing Mark E Smith being compared to Lou Reed, how entertaining it was to find out what would happen when he finally addressed those comparisons. Though the song itself dates back to early 1967, and a single by 60s beat survivors the Searchers, 'Popcorn Double Feature' isn't merely delivered with top-notch Lou laconica, it even narrows its focus to his most recent album, 1989's *New York*, a set with which Smith declared himself unimpressed.

Of the b-sides, the cacophonous 'Arms Control Poseur' is a visceral thrill dominated by a wiry guitar, while 'Black Monk Theme Part II', a light-hearted successor to the album's denser Part One, is a jokey pop song that puts one in mind of – it's that man again! – the Velvets of 'Ferryboat Bill' and 'Foggy Notion.'

(LIVE) April 1990, Germany (?)
   9018. Zagreb
   9019. And Therein
   9020. Carry Bag Man
   9021. Sing! Harpy
   9022. I'm Frank
   9023. Telephone Thing
   9024. Hilary
   9025. Hit the North
   9026. Bill Is Dead
   9027. Black Monk Theme Part I
   9028. Tuff Life Boogie (actually Dead Beat Descendant)
   9029. Popcorn Double Feature
   ORIGINAL RELEASE: as *Live in Zagreb*, Cog Sinister COGVP109CD (CD) 2001
   COMMENTS: Cog Sinister's handling of the Fall's live archive has prompted mixed reactions from fans and collectors. On the one hand, it's impossible to fault a series of releases that liberates so many concerts from the murky underground; on

the other, the lack of care, attention and detail that scars the series reduces even the best intentions to the level of mere exploitation – like, we know you're going to buy it regardless, so why should we actually make it look nice?

Any number of examples can be (and frequently are) used to justify this criticism but *Live In Zagreb* is among the most glaring. After all, if Smith himself can't even get the source city right... The smart money reckons it was actually recorded in Germany in May 1990, when *Extricate* was both new in the racks and new in the band's repertoire. Eight of the live shows' 12 tracks hail from that set.

In terms of sound quality, *Live In Zagreb* comes in on the high end of the bootleg norm while the performance is true to the songs, if not to the maverick nature of the Fall at their finest. No big surprises, no little deviations, and not even much in the way of unscheduled onstage banter. Just another night in another city. Buy it and you probably won't play it more than twice.

(SINGLE) Repetition by TACKHEAD
   9030. Repetition
   ORIGINAL RELEASE: SBK-EMI SBK7014, July 1990 (7-inch/ 12"/ cassette/ CD single)
   COMMENTS: Having co-produced *Extricate*, Adrian Sherwood called Mark E Smith in to lend a few lines of scathing dialogue to a fiery meld of scythed guitar, taunting backing vocals and a drum like an elephant's footfall. Not at all aptly titled, 'Repetition' is no relation, incidentally, to the Fall song of the same name.

(SINGLE) *The Dredger*
   9031. White Lightnin'
   9032. Blood Outta Stone
   9033. Zagreb (Movement I) (ltd ed 12-inch, CD only)
   9034. Zagreb (Movement II) (12-inch, ltd ed 12-inch only)
   9035. Zagreb (Movement III) (ltd ed 12-inch, CD only)
   9036. The Funeral Mix (12-inch only)
   9037. Life Just Bounces (ltd ed 12-inch, CD only)
   ORIGINAL RELEASE: Cog Sinister SIN/X 6/12, August 1990)
   UK CHART PEAK: #56
   COMMENTS: Delivered disguised as a close relation to 'Rollin' Dany', 'White Lightnin'' was the rollicking exhumation of an older-than-rock ode to moonshine and alcoholic heroism that had already endured rock'n'roll, blues and country-flavoured assaults. Now it was time, as *Select* put it, to give it 'a severe beating, clubbing the poor thing mercilessly until there's nothing left of it but two chords and an almighty rattle of noise.' Which pretty much sums it up.

The should've-been-an-a-side b-side 'Blood Outta Stone', meanwhile, suggests that Smith was paying more attention to the admittedly hateful Madchester scene than he was willing to admit, as a ferocious barrage of guitar and drums drives him towards one of his most patently 'modern rock' performances ever – no bad thing. It certainly offers a radical counterpoint to the computer-and-drums duet of 'The Funeral Mix'!

The percussive 'Zagreb' looks back towards 'Big New Prinz' for its most obvious reference points: the near-five minute second movement is the principal part, the first and final amounting to little more than a few fractured seconds of intro and a return to 'The Funeral Mix' for the outro. Anyone who spotting elements of 'Zagreb' within Morrissey's later 'Glamorous Glue' may not be too far off the mark.

Lastly, 'Life Just Bounces' does, indeed, bounce, with Smith again donning his Lou Reed hat – 'Sally Can't Dance' era this time.

(SINGLE) High Tension Wire
    9038. High Tension Line
    9039. Xmas With Simon
    9040. Don't Take the Pizza (12-inch only)
    ORIGINAL RELEASE: Cog Sinister SIN712, December 1990 (12-inch)
    COMMENTS: 'In my perfect world,' Smith told *Sounds*, 'The Fall would bring out a single every month.' The Fontana Powers-That-Were considered even one every few months excessive, but Smith was keen to experiment with the new four-piece line-up. While the label fiercely resisted releasing a new single close to Christmas, Smith prevailed. 'Records should still reflect what people think at the time and it's very tense in England at the moment. Everyone's worried about their mortgages and stuff. You know me, I'm a man of the suburbs.'
    The marketing pill was sweetened, Smith continued, by the inclusion of a Christmas song on the b-side, 'Xmas With Simon'. 'Most people record their Christmas singles in January and I thought, "If we're going to force the record company to bring out a single before Christmas, we might as well write a festive song".' Featuring drummer Simon Wolstencroft on cheesy music-hall keyboards, Smith openly confessed to its 'atrocious lyrics. It is a cynical song.' And, just to rub salt into the figgy pudding, he continued, 'I don't like Christmas in England because everywhere closes down for three weeks. It's disgusting. You can't get any bread or milk and that's what the song's about. Christmas is more of a family time... where families can beat each other up.'

(ALBUM) various artists: *Home*
    9041. Theme from ERROR-ORROR!
    ORIGINAL RELEASE: Sheer Joy SHEER001 (LP) 1990
    COMMENTS: Credited to Mark Smith/M Beddington/S. Hanley/S. Wolstencroft, an earthquake drum-and-bass workout beats around a semi-slurred Smith vocal that ultimately threatens more than it delivers. *Home* itself was largely dedicated to lesser-known Manchester area bands, including the then-formative New FADS, Swirl, dtox and World Of Twist, whose 'Storm', incidentally, was engineered by future Fall drummer Spencer Birtwistle.

(STUDIO) out-takes etc
    9002c. Telephone Thing
    9006a. Bill Is Dead
    9007a. Black Monk Theme Part I
    9010a. Chicago, Now!
    9031a. White Lightnin'
    9032a. Blood Outta Stone
    9042. Life Just Bounces (live)
    ORIGINAL RELEASE: see Receiver label comps (appendix II)

1991

A relaxed year gig-wise began with the Fall's 14th Peel session, again designed to preview a new album, *Shiftwork* (plus a forthcoming b-side, 'Everything Hurtz'). The LP arrived at a time when many listeners were still reacquainting themselves with the Fall's last incarnation, via the three disc's worth of *A-Sides* and *B-Sides* unleashed by old label Beggars Banquet just before Christmas 1990. Admirable compilations in as much as they told the story they were sent to tell without fudging, omission or any of the countless other sins that would become familiar Fall comp foibles over the next decade, the pair were received with a critical gusto that reminded one just what a great singles act the Fall had become, without even trying to.

Smith's attitude towards singles had always been gregarious and seemed set to continue on that way, as Fontana's output maintained the quality of its Beggars forebears. But the six-year sampling that *A-Sides* collected was more than a simple gathering of songs. It spoke loudly for the development of British rock through the mid-late 1980s, and left it in considerably better shape than recent history might have insisted. The irony, of course, was that 1991 would pass without a single new Fall 45 whatsoever, as Cog Sinister – from whom Fontana licensed the band's material – found itself financially unable to produce one.

The situation caught Smith totally unawares. 'I get really fucking fed up sometimes,' he told *Select*. 'Basically, I'm in a business of fucking phonies and idiots. I was dead nervous about this LP, and I was serious about it. If this doesn't work, I'm out. I mean that. Like, when you've got huge debts and shit, and there's Manchester groups coming round your house, looking through your windows to see what clothes you've got on... you just think, "What the fuck am I bothering for?"'

Much of the new album was written on the very eve of the recording sessions, as Smith raced to replace the clutch of collaborations that he and Martin Bramah had already completed before the guitarist's departure. Designed with the trimmed-down quartet's leviathan capabilities firmly in mind, the temperature was then turned up further by the upgrading – initially for just a handful of shows but soon on a full time basis – of roadie Dave Bush to fill the role of a keyboard player 'who can't play the keyboards.'

Proudly, Smith pointed out that, 'There's a way of using machines to make a lot of Grunge,' a revelation that surely explains the Fall's presence in the American Industrial book of profound influences. However, he had no time for the letter-writers who, bemoaning the expansion of the basic four-piece Fall, questioned the need for an onstage computer, no matter how much clatter and racket it made. 'These machines,' he told the *NME*, 'I don't regard them. I don't look at them. But there is a way of using them. Like the dance people did before it all got smoothed out. Machines can sound harsher than any guitar, if you look at it. It's just keeping that balance between not lettin' 'em take over.'

Smith's original plan was to title the Fall's latest album for the song 'The War Against Intelligence'. He backed off after the U.S. led the world's hungriest oil consumers into the Gulf War in January, not necessarily because of the way he felt about the conflict, but because he didn't want people assuming that that was all he was talking about. 'There is a war on intelligence going on at the moment. I do genuinely think that, and it's not because I'm particularly intelligent, I just think there is. Intelligence is actively discouraged in all walks of life, the media and all of it. You talk to somebody, a bricklayer for instance. They're simply told to build badly, as opposed to making a fucking proper job out of it. And the blokes that they tell these things to either have to do it or they're out of work. Same with groups, same with everything.'

Of course, the album's eventual title itself tapped into another of Smith's supposed hobby-horses, the daily drudge of the working man. Only now the comparisons flew not in the direction of the socialist po-faces who plighted the conscience of '80s youth to the hideously flailing wreckage of the Labour Party, but towards the Kinks, perhaps the only other band of recent British memory who'd been able to maintain both their political and national identity, no matter how unfashionable it may have appeared; no matter how many changes they put themselves through.

Melody Maker's Andrew Mueller – an Australian – put the comparison to Smith during 1991, having first painted his own interpretations in mile-high neon. '[English]... What better adjective to encapsulate [Smith's] bleakly absurd sense of humour, his legendarily corduroy notions about image, his occasional wistful longing for other countries, his frequently expressed affectionate contempt for these drizzle-kissed isles and the patent fact that he'll complain, scorn and mock until the cows come home but will rarely show any inclination to actually do anything about it. You're as English as mushy peas and abandoned cricket matches, mate.'

Smith initially responded with total silence, but opened up slowly. Comparisons to Ray Davies, he admitted, 'I find... a big compliment. But I think Davies was much more up front about it. The thing with the Kinks was that they didn't really appeal to the English. The English don't like being told things like that.' Rather, they like to find them out for themselves, and then build their complaints from there – one reason, perhaps, for Smith's refusal ever to plant a lyric sheet in an album. If people know in advance what he's talking about, then why would they listen, and how would they learn?

(MUSICIANS)

LINE-UP #21 (Jan-Aug) MARK E SMITH (vocals), CRAIG SCANLON (guitar), STEVE HANLEY (bass), SIMON WOLSTENCROFT (drums)

LINE-UP #22 (remainder) MARK E SMITH (vocals), CRAIG SCANLON (guitar), STEVE HANLEY (bass), DAVE BUSH (keyboards), SIMON WOLSTENCROFT (drums)

(BBC SESSION) March 23, 1991
  9101. Idiot Joy Showland
  ORIGINAL RELEASE: *The Peel Sessions* (1998)
  COMMENTS: see appendix I/BBC sessions

(ALBUM) *ShiftWork*
  9102. So What About It?
  9103. Idiot Joy Showland
  9104. Edinburgh Man
  9105. Pittsville Direkt
  9106. The Book of Lies
  9107. The War Against Intelligence
  9108. Shift-work
  9109. You Haven't Found It Yet
  9110. The Mixer
  9111. A Lot of Wind
  9112. Rose
  9113. Sinister Waltz
  CD BONUS TRACKS
  9038. High Tension Line
  9031. White Lightnin'
  CD REISSUE BONUS TRACKS
  9032. Blood Outta Stone
  9039. Xmas With Simon
  ORIGINAL RELEASE: Fontana 848.594-1 April 1991
  REISSUE (1): Cog Sinister COGVP134CD, 2002 with bonus tracks
  UK CHART PEAK: #17
  COMMENTS: Produced by the returning Craig Leon and Grant Showbiz (Robert Gordon took on two tracks, the folky alt-rock shuffle 'The Mixer' and 'So What About It'), in sessions that extended over little more than a fortnight, *Shift-work* was the album Smith was dreaming of ever since he felled the six piece Fall. The quartet, he said, 'is working brilliant. It's a lot more improvisational. Also, Craig was so modest and he's a fucking genius. There is no guitarist like Craig Scanlon in the world. He needs to be brought out and the only way I could do it was

to strip the band down. I'm in a state of shock at the moment that it's a fucking good LP, and it didn't sound like a replica of *Extricate*.'

In fact, the album was not created by the quartet alone. Dave Bush's aggressive machines were joined by Kenny Brady's violin and Cassell Webb's backing vocals, elements that brought further textures into play. There was also, a reminder of what had been lost when Martin Bramah departed, as his jangling guitar chimed through the gentle 'Rose' – a song that might well be mourning a departed band member. 'Hear that wah-wah going? Remember you started it.' In fact, 'Rose' was one of a virtual album's worth of material prepared by Smith and Bramah, but (understandably) abandoned when the guitarist was dismissed.

Divided into two side long (but not necessarily linked) halves, *Earth's Impossible Day* and the self-explanatory *Notebooks Out Plagiarists,* the dozen tracks on the original LP (the CD appended the 1990 singles 'High Tension Line' and 'White Lightnin'') were dominated by 'Idiot Joy Showland,' Smith's long-anticipated response to the past year or so's deification of all-things Scallydelic. Smith told *Q*, '[Simon Wolstencroft] was doing all these Madchester beats so I thought, "Let's go the whole hog!"

'But the song's about attitudes that go beyond Manchester too. Competition, again, a promoter said to me recently. They're just a bunch of fuckin' little girls nowadays. It's true. All they talk about is clothes and chart positions. It started about 1987, I can't figure it out, but it fits in with the sampling stuff. Young bands come into the studio when you're mixing and they'll ask – they're blatant about it – "Oh, what BPM's that in?" I go, "What the fuck's it got to do with you! Get out!"'

The labour and industry connotations of the album's title were open to most ears, but the title track itself packed another subtext, albeit one that Smith was swift to dismiss. It concerned the break-up of a marriage, exacerbated by the man's working hours and, while Smith was adamant that it was not about his own broken relationship, he acknowledged that 'other songs on the LP are.' More than two years after the break-up, Smith told *Select*, 'I still get people coming up to me in pubs in Manchester going, "Aah, Mark, know how you must feel mate," and I'm going, "Hang on a sec, I left *her*."' Perhaps the album's most noticeable attribute, however, was the embrace of conventional musical structures – crotch-kickingly apparent on the insistent anti-gasbaggery of 'A Lot Of Wind', and painstakingly sorrowful on the homesick 'Edinburgh Man', a malice and irony-free reflection on the 18 months Smith spent living in the Scottish capital. But the new mood was visible elsewhere, too. Without ever quite exploring the 'verse-chorus-verse' format of popular contempt, certainly there was a sense of dynamic and variety to the songs that was a long way from the tug of war between repetition and shock that was the band's earlier hallmark. In that respect, the addition of the marvellous 'Blood Outta Stone' b-side to the 2002 Cog Sinister reissue should have been done 11 years earlier.

(SINGLE) So What About It?
   9102a. So What About It? (remix 1)
   9102b. So What About It? (remix 2)
   9102c. So What About It? (remix 3)
   ORIGINAL RELEASE: Cog Sinister (12-inch) April 1991
   COMMENTS: A promo-only 12-inch. All three remixes would eventually appear on the *Listening In* compilation.

(STUDIO/LIVE) out-takes etc
  9103a. Idiot Joy Showland
  9104a. Edinburgh Man
  9114. You Haven't Found It Yet (live)
  9111a. A Lot Of Wind
  ORIGINAL RELEASE: see Receiver label comps (appendix II)

And not forgetting…
(SINGLE) *Terry Edwards Salutes The Magic Of The Fall*
  Totally Wired
  Bingo Master's Breakout
  Dice Man
  The Container Drivers
  ORIGINAL RELEASE: STIM 002, 1991
  COMMENTS: Saxophonist Edwards, Mark Bedford and others. The team also
executed similar tributes to the Jesus and Mary Chain and Miles Davis during 1991-
92, before compiling all three onto the album *Plays, Salutes And Executes* (STIM
004) in 1993.

1992

1992 opened with a fresh Peel session (the Fall's fifteenth), a new album, *Code: Selfish*, and, via a rejuvenated Cog Sinister, the 'Free Range' single, all backed up by one of the Fall's longest, strongest and loudest tours in years.

How refreshing it was, as the outing wound on, to see a band of the Fall's vintage still twisting and turning on the spike of audience preconceptions. The early 1990s saw (and, sadly, did not recoil from) more Class Of 77-type reunions than any calendar should ever be forced to contend with and, jokingly, Smith described the reformed hordes of Punk era greats that stretched from the Buzzcocks to X-Ray Spex (not quite A to Z, but close) as 'the competition.'

But even a passing glance into their live show revealed that anybody picking up on the Fall in 1992, in the hope of recapturing the same adrenalined nostalgia jolt they received from the Stiff Little Fingers gig the previous week was in for a painful surprise. Back in 1977, the Fall – and, indeed, almost everybody else who formed and fermented in that momentous year – stood against the deification of the distant past. Now the past was all there was, or so it sometimes seemed.

'When I was 13, the only concerts you could go to were Emerson, Lake and Palmer or fucking Yes. You'd turn on the radio and get Whispering Bob Harris. And that's part of what frightens me, 'cos now, I get back from the pub and switch on the radio and Bob Harris is back! I fought a revolution to get rid of people like him! I had ashtrays thrown at my head by longhairs. And now all these groups are playing Led Zeppelin tunes. That's what groups like the Fall were formed to fight against.'

Smith's assault upon all that the modern pop kids held holy was not confined to the pages of music press. Just three dates into the UK tour, the opening band, shoegazing drone merchants Levitation, were sent packing following an altercation that, apparently, included the words 'a bunch of fucking crusty poofs' being hurled at them by an angry Smith. Smith himself denied such allegations, but did condemn Levitation for luxuriating in 90-minute soundchecks, and drowning the stage in dry ice. They were replaced on the tour by the Garage beat-y Sandmen.

Some of the Fall's own ancient sins, meanwhile, were forgiven, as their longevity and obvious popularity overcame even the most heinous of past indiscretions. On the heels of the 'Ed's Babe' 45, June 27 saw the Fall appear at the Glastonbury Festival, close to a decade after they were banned from ever darkening the esteemed field's gateway. Smith (of course) made a disparaging remark about CND (the Campaign for Nuclear Disarmament), at that time the festival's guiding light, and was promptly rewarded with outlaw status. Now it was revoked, and Glastonbury slotted into the round of festivals that occupied the band through the summer. They then wound up the remainder of the year with a handful of shows at home and abroad – action enough to remove them from the grand clique of artists for whom half the year is a holiday, but time enough, too, to allow them some respite from the public business of the band.

Even in periods of silence, however, the Fall were never far away from Smith's thoughts, as he pointed out the following year. 'I manage the band as well as everything else, so a lot of times people think I'm being an awkward bastard, when really I'm just up to my neck in other things.'

Among Smith's own preoccupations during these months was cementing a deal with the Castle Communications reissue specialists that would restore a clutch of early Fall albums to the shelves – *Totale's Turns (It's Now Or Never)*, *Grotesque (After The Gramme)*, *Perverted By Language* and the US-only *A Part Of America Therein, 1981* live document. Plans to delve even deeper into the archive were also afoot. The public wants to relive the past? Smith was planning an archaeology lecture that they'd never forget.

(MUSICIANS)

LINE-UP #22 (all)
MARK E SMITH (vocals),
CRAIG SCANLON (guitar),
STEVE HANLEY (bass),
DAVE BUSH (keyboards),
SIMON WOLSTENCROFT
(drums)

(BBC SESSION) Feb 15, 1992
  9201. Return
  9202. Kimble
  9203. Free Range
ORIGINAL RELEASE: 9201
on *Radio Daze – The John Peel
Sessions* (1992), 9202 single
(1993), 9203 on *The Peel Sessions*
(1998)

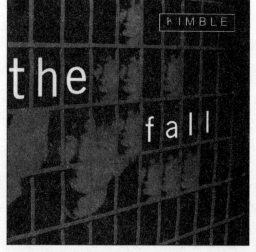

COMMENTS: see appendix I/BBC sessions

(SINGLE) Free Range
  9204. Free Range
  9205. Everything Hurtz
  9206. Return (12-inch, CD only)
  9207. Dangerous (12-inch, CD only)
  ORIGINAL RELEASE: Cog Sinister SIN/CD 8/12, March 1992
  UK CHART PEAK: #40
COMMENTS: One of the Fall's most ferocious latter-day releases, war torn guitars and keyboards cut through with muttered samples, as Smith's chilling vision of a pan-European society regulated according to the Nazi/Nietzsche-ian ideal was borne out by the near-simultaneous eruption of the war in the Balkans. By comparison, 'Return' and 'Dangerous' are little more than moody soundscapes, but 'Everything Hurtz' brags an extraordinarily effective air of Punkoid self-sacrifice, and a litany of losses that somehow manages to predict the gist of Kurt Cobain's journals a full ten years before they were published.

(ALBUM) various artists: *Ruby Trax*
  9208. The Legend of Xanadu
  ORIGINAL RELEASE Forty NME40CD 1992 (Triple CD)
COMMENTS: Dave Dee, Dozy, Beaky, Mick and Tich might have had a daft name and an absurd image, but their pantomime posturing and Howard/Blaikley bubblegum remains a matchless snatch of 60s iconographia. At least, it did until the Fall got hold of it. Recorded, like 'Day In The Life,' for an *NME*-sponsored charity compilation (this time celebrating 40 years of UK chart toppers), the original 'Legend Of Xanadu' was a whip-cracking, back-breaking, knee-jerking jewel – in other words, not the slightest bit like the disinterested drone and featureless fuzz that rattles adenoidally in and out of focus here.

(ALBUM) *Code: Selfish*
  9209. The Birmingham School of Business School
  9204. Free Range
  9206. Return
  9210. Time Enough at Last
  9205. Everything Hurtz
  9211. Immortality
  9212. Two Face!
  9213. Just Waiting
  9214. So-Called Dangerous
  9215. Gentlemen's Agreement
  9216. Married, 2 Kids
  9217. Crew Filth
  (*) BONUS TRACKS
  9234. Ed's Babe
  9237. Free Ranger.
  ORIGINAL RELEASE: Fontana 512.162-1, March 1992
  REISSUE (1): Cog Sinister COGVP133CD, 2002 with bonus tracks (*)
  UK CHART PEAK: #21

COMMENTS: Hands up who rates this among their all-time favourite Fall albums? No, there's not many of you, are there?

Partially self-produced in a converted Glasgow tabernacle after early attempts to rope in a collaborator collapsed, *Code: Selfish* emerged, said Smith, sounding 'like the way I wanna. I'm dead pleased with it. I [was] pleased with the last two LPs, but I wanted to try and get it a bit harder. Something a bit more crunchy because, when it comes down to it, everyone's on rhythm machines and mellowin' out.'

That, he explained, was why the world and its mother was making such a fuss about the Grunge-laden delights of the Seattle sound – Nirvana, Pearl Jam, Soundgarden and co. One loud guitar and everyone loses all sense of proportion.

'Funny thing is, all those American bands, Pearl Jam and Nirvana, are dead into the Fall,' Smith asserted. 'Nirvana tried to get into our bus, Courtney What's-her-name, the actress, tried it and we pushed her off. But they all come from this horrible place called Seattle, which is just like Moss Side on a bad night. And they're nothing more than glorified longhair guitar salesmen, y'know. Fucking idiots playing pub rock. Aye, pub rock, that's what it is. If they were English, you wouldn't put up with it.

'I wanted to get away from that. I wanted to get it really hard like the Fall are live. Really heavy. It's a lot more of a... jack off if you don't like it. We were getting quite melodic on the last couple of LPs and I wanted to get away from it".

Melody, of course, is in the ear of the beholder, but there was certainly a reborn hostility to *Code: Selfish*, one that saw the band's reinvention of techno as a tool for drum and guitar rock explode out of theory and cement itself to the walls of the studio – from whence it dripped down most effectively to the slow-grind of 'Immortality,' with Smith's vocal taking on just a hint of Bernard Sumner inflection to maybe- or maybe-not direct the lyric anywhere particular.

'The Birmingham School of Business School,' on the other hand, left nobody in doubt as to its targets, as Britain's other, umpteenth, second city launched another bid against Manchester to host the Olympic Games ('the jumped up prats... laughing stock of Europe...' – Manchester's own bid would become the skewered subject of *Middle Class Revolt*'s 'City Dweller'). Largely tuneless, purposefully formless, but populated by some odd notions of guitar soloing, 'The Birmingham

School of Business School' is one of those songs that worked better live than in the studio – a sensation that was not necessarily alien to the rest of *Code: Selfish* as well.

(ALBUM) various artists: *Volume 4*

9218. Arid Al's Dream

ORIGINAL RELEASE: *Volume 4* (magazine and CD), August 1992

COMMENTS: With chiming guitars and freakish violin, 'Arid Al's Dream' was sufficiently well-thought of by

Smith to appear on both *Sinister Waltz* and the later *A World Bewitched*.

(LIVE) March 15 1992, Trent Polytechnic, Nottingham
    9219. Time Enough At Last
    9220. Blood Outta Stone
    9221. Idiot Joy Showland
    9222. Free Range
    9223. Immortality
    9224. High Tension Line
    9225. Married, 2 Kids
    9226. New Big Prinz
    9227. Pittsville Direkt
    9228. Return
    9229. Everything Hurtz
    9230. Birmingham School of Business School
    9231. Edinburgh Man
    9232. And Therein...
    9233. The War Against Intelligence
    ORIGINAL RELEASE: as *Nottingham 92*, Cog Sinister COGVP110CD
    COMMENTS: Hey lads, the tapes are rolling. Again. Whatever the provenance of the various Fall live albums to have appeared under the auspices of Cog Sinister, be they surreptitious audience tapes, soundboard recordings or what, the handful that can genuinely claim some historical importance are becoming increasingly outweighed by those that seem to have simply been selected at random from the hundreds percolating underground.

Capturing the opening shot of the band's latest UK tour, a competent and, had you been there, undoubtedly enjoyable performance is strictly for fans of nights that were nothing special – the tour itself would receive a far stronger airing courtesy of the BBC's *Sound City* the following month.

(SINGLE) Ed's Babe
    9234. Ed's Babe
    9235. Pumpkin Head Xscapes
    9236. The Knight the Devil and Death
    9237. Free Ranger
    ORIGINAL RELEASE: Cog Sinister SINCD912 (12-inch, CD) June 1992
    COMMENTS: The EP of many colours. With a refrain of 'D.I.Y.' that refuses to go away, 'Ed's Babe' is a driving rocker riven by delicious harmonies and an insistent eight note keyboard honk that leaves the song impaled on more hooks than many major hit singles. And, talking of which, the rumblesome 'Pumpkin Head Xscapes' is at least a handful of barbs tossed in the direction of 'the senile morons who run KLF,' the hottest techno ambient act of the age… and that was before they torched a million pounds in the name of modern art.

Elsewhere, folky-flavoured prog rock buffs will thrill to 'The Knight, The Devil and Death,' especially with the Fall's involvement wholly disguised by the lack of Smith vocals; while the 'Free Ranger' remix of 'Free Range' ups the original's grungy ante even further. Played loudly, it really can hurt your ears.

(LIVE/STUDIO) out-takes etc
    9204a. Free Range
    9210a. Time Enough At Last
    9215a. Gentlemen's Agreement
    9216a. Married, 2 Kids
    9234a. Ed's Babe
    9235a. Pumpkin Head Xscapes
    9236a. The Knight the Devil and Death
    9238. Birmingham School Of Business School (live)
    9239. Just Waiting (live)
    ORIGINAL RELEASE: see Receiver label comps (appendix II)

1993

After three years with Fontana, 1993 dawned with the Fall's return to semi-Indie-dom, signing in the UK to Permanent, a new label headed up by former (mid-80s era) manager John Lennard, and in America, to Matador. Smith explained, 'when we signed with [Fontana] in 1990, after six years with Beggars Banquet, the deal was that they'd release our albums in the States. It was in our contract that they would do that. Then they decided it would be easier just to give us money instead.'

The albums got over the ocean regardless, picking up readily marketable accolades like 'student LP of the year.' But that wasn't the issue. The five or so years beforehand had seen the Fall's American impetus snowballing in a way few other acts can imagine, not only winning fresh converts, but trawling some mighty megaphones too. The sleeve of the 1992 Fall promotional sampler, *Crash Course 84-92*, was insufflated with a collection of quotes from the band's famous fans – Thurston Moore, Jim Thirlwell, Jonathan Demme, and claiming to own 'more than 25 records by the Fall,' Superchunk's Mac McCaughn.

Henry Rollins was a devoted fan and collector, while an entire tribe of new American bands arose for whom the Fall weren't simply an inspiration, they were a template. Helium's first b-side, 'Pat's Trip Dispenser,' was an unabashed tribute to the Fall song of almost the same name, while Matador labelmates Pavement sounded so true to the sonic source that Smith himself mistook them for a tape of one of the band's old Dutch concerts.

He had long ago grown accustomed to hearing great fillets of the Fall recycled in other band's music, usually a few years after the Fall themselves were soundly condemned for daring to make such a racket in the first place. Touring America that summer, however, brought an entire new dimension to the experience. He told *Melody Maker*, 'People were coming up to me saying "listen to this," and playing me Pavement records on a Walkman, and I just asked, "What live tape is that of ours? Is that from Holland in 1987 or something? That's a fucking drum riff I wrote. The cheek!" They say imitation is the sincerest form of flattery, but I don't hold with that. I feel sorry for them, actually. I don't get mad, I just can't see the point of forming a group if you're imitating someone else, it's like, get a life, man. Get a real job!'

The admiration of such acolytes was all the more frustrating because it simply fed back into the cult confines from which the Fall seemed never likely to escape – at least while Fontana were controlling the promotional budgets. Having sold out their last American tour (again in 1990), the Fall were left looking on in limbo while Uncle Sam opened his arms to a host of lesser Limey lights, including their own labelmates Catherine Wheel, the House Of Love and Ocean Colour Scene. All three received a sizeable push during 1992... and Catherine Wheel even deserved it. But there was no room for the Fall on the new release schedules.

'Then, just before Christmas 1992, [Phonogram] started letting bands go. They sent eight others packing [Julian Cope and Pop Will Eat Itself among them], then told me that we'd be kept on until April '93. We weren't selling enough records.' Smith decided to save them the bother of sacking him, and left under his own steam instead.

It was a smart move. Previewed in the UK by a New Year Peel session, and a hot single invoking the reggae classic 'Why Are People Grudgeful?', *The Infotainment Scan* would become the first new Fall album since *Extricate* to see the business end of an American release. It was also the first to actually do what the band's British fans reckoned should have been done fifteen years back – establish the Fall as a genuine Power In The Land. *The Infotainment Scan* peaked on the U.K. album chart at number 9 and, while both World Party and PJ Harvey debuted higher that same week, that was not the point. The point was, unlike those others, the Fall were not a Hit Record band, the Fall were not a multi-mega-million-dollar bash. The Fall were the Fall were the Fall, and that was all there was to it.

Smith, of course, remained publicly unphased by this sudden taste of success – unphased but not entirely ungrateful, as he readily acknowledged that Permanent's marketing had a lot to do with the band's sudden high profile. Traditionally, a new Fall album was left to sink or swim in the music press alone. Ads for *The Infotainment Scan*, however, leaked into other media as well – there was even a quarter-page ad in the acerbic soccer 'zine *When Saturday Comes*. The seriously raincoated Fall fan was dead. With the spirit of the suddenly rediscovered, and newly rehabilitated 'The Kicker Conspiracy' holding the door wide open, long live the Football-loving Juvenile Renaissance Man .

'We've just come home from a British tour,' Smith mused that summer, 'and I noticed that the audiences really are getting younger. They're not even college age any more, and all the old geezers like me are stuck at the back.' Which, he continued, was exactly how he wanted it. It's all too easy for a band (particularly one 'like us') to settle down in front of its fans, and grow old alongside them; easier still when so many of their contemporaries are already doing precisely that. But, as the Fall moved inexorably towards their 20th anniversary, Smith had no intention of sharing that grisly destiny.

(MUSICIANS)

LINE-UP #23 (all) MARK E SMITH (vocals), CRAIG SCANLON (guitar), STEVE HANLEY (bass), DAVE BUSH (keyboards), SIMON WOLSTENCROFT (drums)

(BBC SESSION) March 13, 1993
    9301. Strychnine
    ORIGINAL RELEASE: on *Backdrop* (1994), *The Peel Sessions* (1998)
    COMMENTS: Anybody recalling Blur's deification of Pavement during their back-to-basics *Blur* album era, should play 'Song 2,' the song singled out by so

many American critics as being most in debt to Steve Malkmus and co, back to back with the Fall's interpretation of the Sonics' 'Strychnine.' Then wonder why Smith sometimes feels that the Fall are rarely accorded their due as an influence.

see appendix I/BBC sessions

(SINGLE) Why Are People Grudgeful?
  9302. Why Are People Grudgeful?
  9303. Glam-Racket
  9304. The Re-Mixer (12-inch, CD only)
  9305. spoken word interlude
  9306. Lost In Music (12-inch, CD only)
  ORIGINAL RELEASE: Permanent 7/12/CD SPERM9, April 1993
  UK CHART PEAK: #43
  COMMENTS: *'The Fall? Aren't they those miserable bastards who play their songs sideways, just in case a tune got in by mistake?' – Alternative Press.*

Not any more, they're not. On an EP that elsewhere tackles Disco, Glam and techno ('The Re-Mixer' dramatically revises *Shift-work*'s 'The Mixer'), then throws in a few moments of spoken computer tech advice in between the two songs on the b-side, the presence of a bona fide reggae classic, delivered with faithful but by no means slavish panache, should not have been a surprise. But it was.

Following on from their reconstruction of Lee Perry's 'Kimble' during their John Peel session the previous year, the Fall returned to the Scratch story for 'Grudgeful?' However, despite the single's own credits assigning the writing to Lee Perry himself, 'Why Are People Grudgeful?' was, more accurately, *about* him. Originally performed by the Pioneers (of 'Long Shot Kickee Bucket' fame), legendary Kingston producer Joe Gibbs composed the song, after Perry departed his Amalgamated label stable in 1968, and hit out at his former employer with the distinctly grudge-laden 'People Funny Boy.'

Exaggerating the original version's own lackadaisical stylings, the Fall's version also switches the lyric from the abstract ('when he was down and out...') to the personal ('when you were down and out...'). But, such considerations are of little concern in the face of such a mixed musical bag. Disco, Glam, techno, reggae... whatever will they think of next?

(ALBUM) *The Infotainment Scan*
  9307. Ladybird (Green Grass)
  9306. Lost in Music
  9303. Glam-Racket
  9308. I'm Going To Spain
  9309. It's a Curse
  9310. Paranoia Man in Cheap Sh*t Room
  9311. Service
  9312. The League Of Bald-Headed Men
  9313. A Past Gone Mad
  9314. Light – Fireworks
  CD BONUS TRACKS
  9302. Why Are People Grudgeful?
  9315. League Moon Monkey Mix
  ORIGINAL RELEASE Permanent PERMLP12, April 1993

REISSUE (1): Artful ARTFULCD22 (CD) 1999
UK CHART PEAK: #9
COMMENTS: *The Infotainment Scan* was recorded at New Order's studios in Rochdale, in the Fall's own time, with the band's own money, and only when it was completed did the group go back to the marketplace, shopping the finished tapes around to labels who couldn't believe their luck.

With its subtle blending of all the disciplines Smith had spent years listening to, *The Infotainment Scam* was as far from any Fall archetype as it was possible to be. How typical, therefore, that it should become the band's biggest ever hit.

The 'Why Are People Grudgeful' single gave out a few broad hints. While Smith's own musical tastes strayed in the direction of the rave scene, the album itself was beholden to no particular noise. There was a nod in the direction of classic Disco, most (but not exclusively) evident in a twisted take on Sister Sledge's Chic-composed 'Lost In Music'; similarly, at a time when the likes of Denim and Suede were spearheading what looked like it might become a full-fledged Glam Rock revival, 'Glam Racket' lambasted its ever-lengthening shadows by slipping straight back to the Gary Glittery flavouring of 'Big New Prinz.'

Of course there were some classic Fall fall-backs. An almost acoustic, getting-away-from-it-all romp through English songwriter Steve Bent's mid-1970s warble 'I'm Going To Spain' re-dignified a song hitherto best remembered for its inclusion on the cult compilation *The World's Worst Record.*

Elsewhere, 15 years spent not reading reviews of his own work finally prompted Smith to retaliate by reviewing his reviews with the clunky 'It's A Curse,' while 'Paranoia Man In Cheap Sh*t Room' and 'The League of Bald-Headed Men' even boasted titles that wouldn't have been out of place a decade earlier... and is that the ghost of Led Zeppelin's 'Misty Mountain Hop' circling around the latter? Smith denied it, claiming he'd never even heard a Led Zeppelin record. But he laughed when he said it, and the jury remains divided.

At least one American review described *The Infotainment Scam* as 'possibly the most complete Fall album in a decade' – then asked, 'but is it complete because of what went into it? Or because of all that was omitted?' That question, too, remains unanswered, but Smith at least lay in one clue as to how he viewed the whole shebang. 'If I ever end up like U2,' he pleaded during the proudly anthemic 'A Past Gone Mad', 'slit my throat with a garden vegetable.'

(SESSION) Mark Goodier session 17 May 1993
   9316. A Past Gone Mad
   ORIGINAL RELEASE: on *The Peel Sessions* (1998)
   COMMENTS: see appendix I/BBC sessions

(LIVE) Sept 17 1993, New York Academy
   9317. Dead Beat Descendant
   9318. Big New Prinz
   UNR. M5
   UNR. Ladybird (Green Grass)
   UNR. High Tension Line
   UNR. Glam Racket
   UNR. Why Are People Grudgeful
   UNR. I'm Going to Spain

UNR. Free Range
UNR. Lost in Music
UNR. A Past Gone Mad
UNR. Idiot Joy Showland
UNR. Strychnine
UNR. War
UNR. The League of Bald-headed Men

(LIVE) Oct 1993, Munich
9319. Why Are People Grudgeful?
9320. Free Range
9321. Shift-work
9322. Strychnine
UNR. remainder of set unknown
ORIGINAL RELEASE: on *Live Various Years* (1998)

(SINGLE) Behind The Counter
9323. Behind The Counter
9324. War
9325. Cab Driver
ORIGINAL RELEASE: Permanent 12/CD SPERMD13 Dec 1993 (12-inch/CD #1)
9326. M5
9327. Happy Holiday
9323a. Behind The Counter (Remix)
ORIGINAL RELEASE: Permanent 12/CD SPERM13 Dec 1993 (12-inch/CD #2)
UK CHART PEAK: #75
COMMENTS: If only for the introduction of Nose Pin and the Punk Piggies, the best unused band name in the history of Manchester, 'Behind The Counter' would merit immortality, as Smith muses (possibly) on the Fall's overall lack of commercial glorification, while sundry notebook-bearing plagiarists ride around in style. And, among sundry songs that came along afterwards, that give you pause for just a little 'hmmmm....,' play Garbage's 'Stupid Girl' alongside 'Behind The Counter.' Hmmmm.

Elsewhere, 'Happy Holiday,' has a bass line borrowed from Tamla and the threat of a killer pop dance song living in the chorus, while Henry Cow's 'War' packs the ghost of 80s past, swiping its ascending bass line from scary 80s band Martha & the Muffins' 'Echo Beach,' and its chant from a Cossack hoedown. Smith later recalled losing his own copy of the Cambridge University avant garde-ists' 1975 album *In Praise Of Learning* sometime before deciding to attempt the song, so he recited the lyrics from memory.

(LIVE/STUDIO) date/venue unknown
9328. Behind The Counter (live)
ORIGINAL RELEASE: see Receiver label comps (appendix II)

THE FALL

MIDDLE CLASS
REVOLT

1994

What might otherwise have passed as just another year in the life of the Fall – a string of British, American and (a few) European dates ignited by the release of a new album, and bookended by a pair of Peel sessions (the band's 17th and 18th) – was granted a more remarkable air by Mark E Smith's debut on *Top Of The Pops*, clutching a lyric sheet like the last straw on earth, and looking perfectly underwhelmed by the entire experience. The only thing that spoiled it was, the Fall were not alongside him.

Smith's guest appearance on fellow Mancunians Inspiral Carpets' 'I Want You' single shoved Smith into 14 million living rooms at a time when his own music was itself pushing towards ever more fruitful ground. Talking to the American magazine *Pandemonium*, however, he admitted that he didn't understand why. Or so he hoped.

The Fall had now been around long enough for their first fans to be breeding new fans of their own, and Smith recalled, 'when I was 18 I used to laugh at people who were into the Grateful Dead, and they're now parents, having little Grateful Dead fans. It's always been part of the business, the band that's been around so long that, love 'em or hate 'em, you've got to admire them. Like Status Quo. I hope that's not the reason with us. But it's a frightening [thought]. The younger generation are turning into their parents. These kids are into psychedelic and the Beatles and all that, just like their mums and dads.'

Warming to the theme, he continued, 'the problem today is that the kids – if that's what we must call them – are so busy rediscovering what their parents listened to that they're missing everything else.' His skin, he shuddered, still crawled to recall a comment made early in the 1990s by one of Jesus Jones – right there, right then, the Billy Big Bananas of the British Baggy bag. 'It was something along the lines of "*Sgt Pepper's* is my favourite album because my mum used to play it to me every day." That says it all. Can you admit to *admitting* to liking the same records as your *mum*? The whole point of rock music is listening to music your parents *didn't* like. My dad was into George Formby and I listened to the Velvets. But if he'd listened to the Velvets, I'd have been into George Formby. And, if I caught my kids listening to my record collection, I'd kill them.'

Not that *Middle Class Revolt* would have sat well with anyone searching for more of the same comforting candy as the Inspiral Carpets or, indeed, the Beatles had delivered. Mocking the continued grind of Grunge, unaware that the movement's tragic denouement would come within weeks of the album's May 1994 release, Smith reached back to recall the popping of his gig-going cherry by hauling out the Groundhogs' 'Junk Man' – a heavily-laden distorted blues that made the Seattle scene's belly-aching sound anaemic by comparison.

So, just another year in the life? Not quite. The return of Karl Burns to reawaken memories of the old two drummer line-up was a pleasant surprise, while the Fall were midway through a reasonably relaxed summer schedule when, as Smith told *Vox* a year later, 'Brix called me up out of the blue. We hadn't spoken to each other for three years. I didn't even know where she was. Then she said she'd been rehearsing with Hole and was really pissed off with it.'

Courtney What's-her-name had barely been allowed time to recover from the death of husband Kurt Cobain, when Hole bassist Kristen Pfaff was found dead in June. Brix – herself out of the public eye since the second Adult Net folded in 1991 – was recruited just days later, but the prospect of surrendering her own creativity to another notorious dictator apparently didn't appeal as much as she'd originally thought. When Smith informed her that he was in a similar state of dissatisfaction, searching for 'either a really young kid or an old producer... to put some bite back into The Fall, to kick them all up the arse,' Brix leaped at the chance to reignite their former partnership.

Inspiral carpets WANT YOU featuring mark e smith

'When I told Brix [what was happening], she immediately said she'd do it and got on a plane. [And] she revitalised the new LP. I was flattered that she wanted to leave Hole to come back to the Fall. They could have paid her 1,000 a week...' as opposed to the 50 she'd get from the Fall. But she was adamant.'

By the time the band launched their next American tour, Brix was firmly back on board, responding to the inevitable curious questions by admitting, simply, she'd remembered how great the Fall were.

(MUSICIANS)

LINE-UP #23 (Jan-Aug) MARK E SMITH (vocals), CRAIG SCANLON (guitar), STEVE HANLEY (bass), DAVE BUSH (keyboards), SIMON WOLSTENCROFT (drums)

LINE-UP #24 (remainder) MARK E SMITH (vocals), CRAIG SCANLON (guitar), BRIX SMITH (guitar), STEVE HANLEY (bass), DAVE BUSH (keyboards), SIMON WOLSTENCROFT (drums), KARL BURNS (percussion)
(BBC SESSION) February 5, 1994
   9401. M5
   ORIGINAL RELEASE: on *The Peel Sessions* (1998)
   COMMENTS: see appendix I/BBC sessions

(SINGLE) I Want You by INSPIRAL CARPETS
   9402. I Want You
   ORIGINAL RELEASE: Mute DUNG24 (7-inch/CD/remix CD) Feb 1994
   COMMENTS: The Inspiral Carpets were an odd vehicle for Smith to hitch up with. His hostility towards the Madchester scene was legendary, after all, a bile that was half disapproving veteran tutting 'kids these days...', and half a genuine horror at the thought of what was passing itself off as 'music these days...' And he admitted, 'when they first came along, I thought the Inspiral Carpets were a right load of crap. But they called up and asked me to sing a song with them, so I went along and it was good fun. They were great.'
   A considerably tougher number than the Inspirals were renowned for, a blast of frenetic guitar and drums through which the title/chorus streaked like plunging space junk (and Stephen Holt's vocals echoed the Jam's 'Funeral Pyre'), 'I Want You' was a true collaboration – the verses and even snatches of the hook are the province of Smith's engaging rampage and who else, one wonders, could get a mention of the Dutch East India Company into the Top 30?
   Meaningfully or otherwise, 'I Want You' proved to be the Inspiral Carpets' final major hit.

(SINGLE) 15 Ways
   9403. 15 Ways
   9404. Hey! Student
   9405. The $500 Bottle Of Wine
   ORIGINAL RELEASE: Permanent 10/12/CD SPERM14, April 1994
   UK CHART PEAK: #65
   COMMENTS: Neither the Fall's finest single, nor the best possible induction into the forthcoming *Middle Class Revolt*, '15 Ways' is basically a melodic revision of Paul Simon's '50 Ways To Leave Your Lover,' less the engaging shopping list coda.
   Notwithstanding the rampaging rhythm co-opted from the 16 year old 'Hey Fascist,' 'Hey! Student' is similarly lacklustre, little more than a rhyming rendition of a rant Smith had exercised on several occasions in past interviews, which leaves

only the mutant bluesy '$500 Bottle Of Wine' to save the show – a job it really isn't up to.

(SINGLE) The League Of Bald-Headed Men
  9312. The League Of Bald-Headed Men
  9302. Why Are People Grudgeful?
  9304. The Re-Mixer
  9315. League Moon Monkey Mix
  ORIGINAL RELEASE: Matador 62 (USA) 1994
Easing towards the new album by restating a highlight of the last, this is the American EP that has baffled so many on-line Fall Discographies into either ignoring it, or just pulling a few random pledges out of thin air. The only track of true interest, of course, is the closing 'League Moon Monkey Mix,' Simon Rogers' remix of 'The League of Bald Headed Men' that sheds the misty mountain hoppiness of the original, but little else. Long unavailable elsewhere, it has since been appended to the Artful CD reissue of *The Infotainment Scam*.

(ALBUM) various artists: *Bend It! 94*
  9406. spoken word from Smith's appearance on TV's *Goal*.
  ORIGINAL RELEASE: Exotica Records PELE8CD, 1994

(ALBUM) *Middle Class Revolt aka The Vapourisation of Reality*
  9403. 15 Ways
  9407. The Reckoning
  9328. Behind The Counter
  9326. M5#1
  9408. Surmount All Obstacles
  9409. Middle Class Revolt!
  9324. War
  9410. You're Not Up To Much
  9411. Symbol Of Mordgan
  9412. Hey! Student
  9413. Junk Man
  9414. The $500 Bottle Of Wine
  9415. City Dweller
  9416. Shut Up!
  JAPANESE CD BONUS TRACKS
  9409a. Middle Class Revolt (Prozac Mix – by Drum Club)
  9409b. Middle Class Revolt (Orange In The Mouth Mix – by Drum Club)
  ORIGINAL RELEASE Permanent PERMLP16, May 1994
  REISSUE (1): Artful ARTFULCD23, 1999
  UK CHART PEAK: #48
  COMMENTS: When Smith remarked later in the year that he was looking for a new producer to give the Fall a kick in the pants, the myrmecological *Middle Class Revolt* was probably the first to stand up and applaud. By no means a bad album, in the way that, say, an REM or Phish album is bad, it was nevertheless an unconvincing (and, more seriously, unconvinced) offering, built around songs that were only halfway to completion and arrangements that seemed to know it.
  Smith's lyrics are louder and clearer than ever before, as if to disguise the fact

that the band seems simply to be busking or, worse still, merely cruising, with the paucity of ideas (or an exaggerated need to annoy) best illustrated by 'Symbol Of Mordgan,' a telephone conversation about football (and Manchester City) between Craig Scanlon and DJ John Peel, set to a low-fi twanging that sounds like an unrehearsed Garage band trying to play the Shadows.

It was no coincidence at all, then, that the best numbers were three covers – Smith's impassioned (if unintentional) reinvention of Henry Cow's 'War,' remixed from the previous year's 'Behind The Counter' single; another Monks number, the 60s Garage trash classic 'Shut Up!'; and – recalling the first live show Smith ever attended, a distorted bluesy plod through the Groundhogs' growling, gruelling 'Junk Man.'

(SINGLE) *Middle Class Revolt remixes*
   9409a. Middle Class Revolt (Prozac Mix)
   9409b. Middle Class Revolt (Orange In The Mouth Mix)
   ORIGINAL RELEASE: White label bootleg 12-inch
   COMMENTS: With imported copies of the Japanese CD at a premium, some enterprising soul took the two stray remixes and pressed up this club friendly platter. It is now even harder to find than the CD used to be.

(STUDIO) out-take
   9417. Glam Racket (Brix vocal)
   ORIGINAL RELEASE: see Receiver label comps (appendix II). No, really! It's worth it.

1995

Smith was right. Brix's return completely reinvigorated the Fall. She herself wondered just what she could bring to the band when she heard *The Infotainment Scam* and proclaimed it 'awesome.' But 1995's *Cerebral Caustic* was at least its equal and the live shows that now stretched ahead of the band were, accordingly, to see the band turn in some of their finest live performances in years.

You had to be sharp to catch them, though. The Fall played less than 20 shows all year – one reason, perhaps, why the two live albums that those shows produced (*Fall In The City* and *The 27 Points*) are so highly thought of.

Such apparent inactivity disguised much, however. In September, Smith crowned almost two decades of possibility by making his first ever solo spoken word appearance at an arts event in the Hague, Netherlands, performing what amounted to a series of monologues loosely and occasionally built around familiar Fall lyrics. It was an area towards which friends and associates had been pushing him for as long as some of them had known him. Lydia Lunch, in particular, spent years trying to 'entice him into doing [it] because I know that the lyrics, which one can only vaguely decipher on any of [the] records, are just beautiful.'

Only now, however, did Smith feel comfortable with the medium, and the years since have seen him perform thus on several occasions, including one date, in L.A. in 2001, where he did indeed share the bill with Lunch.

In December, meanwhile, the Fall made their 19th appearance on the John Peel show. That same month, however, also brought the news that both Craig Scanlon and Dave Bush had departed the Fall, Scanlon after more than a decade and a half on board, Bush to join Elastica.

The split came as a major shock, all the more so since Smith, in an *NME* interview, himself recently stressed the importance of the core line-up. 'Musicians aren't completely interchangeable. Craig, Simon and Steve have been with me a long time.'

But he also conceded, 'I still don't understand musicians. I find them completely unfathomable. I can't work out where they're coming from. They think new guitars and who's played with who is important, but I'm the sort who just yells at them: "Play D, E and A, fast and hard." So, obviously, I've chucked a few people out of the band. Half the time it was them jumping but the rest, yeah, it was me pushing. I get tired of them, you see, even though I never socialise with them and, when things become a routine it's easier just to let go. Most musicians just want to do the same old songs, but I won't have that.'

In their place, numerically if not instrumentally, came the unknown and untried Julia Nagle and Lucy Rimmer, a close friend of Smith's sister Caroline, to make their debut at the Peel session. The face – not to mention the sound – of the Fall was shifting once again.

(MUSICIANS)

LINE-UP #24 (Jan-Nov) MARK E SMITH (vocals), CRAIG SCANLON (guitar), BRIX SMITH (guitar), STEVE HANLEY (bass), DAVE BUSH (keyboards), SIMON WOLSTENCROFT (drums), KARL BURNS (percussion)

LINE-UP #25 (Dec) MARK E SMITH (vocals), JULIA NAGLE (guitar, keyboards), BRIX SMITH (guitar), STEVE HANLEY (bass), SIMON WOLSTENCROFT (drums), KARL BURNS (percussion), LUCY RIMMER (backing vocals)

(LIVE) Mar 20/21/22 (?) 1995 Roadhouse, Manchester
   9501. The Joke
   9502. Aphid
   9503. Dead Beat Descendant
   9504. Feeling Numb
   9505. War
   9506. Glam Racket
   9507. Pearl City
   9508. L.A.
   9509. Don't Call Me Darling
   9510. Bill is Dead
   9511. Behind the Counter
   9512. Edinburgh Man
   9513. Middle Class Revolt
   9514. Gut of the Quantifier
   9515. Life Just Bounces

ORIGINAL RELEASE: as *The Fall In The City*, Artful Records ARTFULCD3 – 1997

COMMENTS: Recorded during the same season of shows as the 1995 live collection *The Twenty-Seven Points*, and thus reiterating several of the same titles, *The Fall In The City* is nevertheless an extraordinarily different beast to that leviathan. For starters, it captures just one show in its entirety, as opposed to the piecemeal scissors and paste approach that glued *The Twenty-Seven Points* together; as such, of course, it stands and falls on the band's performance on the night. Which, as it happens, was a good 'un, with the closing salvo of three or four songs up there with the best of any available Fall live recordings. The return of Brix is, of course, a key selling point, celebrated over the resurrection of such old faves as 'Gut of the Quantifier' and 'LA,' although *The Fall In The City* was also significant as the band's first album for new label Artful.

(ALBUM) *Cerebral Caustic*
   9544. The Joke

9545. Don't Call Me Darling
9546. Rainmaster
9547. Feeling Numb
9548. Pearl City
9549. Life Just Bounces
9550. I'm Not Satisfied
9551. The Aphid
9552. Bonkers In Phoenix
9553. One Day
9554. North West Fashion
9555. Pine Leaves
ORIGINAL RELEASE Permanent PERMLP30, July 1995
REISSUE (1): Artful ARTFULCD24, 1999
UK CHART PEAK: #67
COMMENTS: One of the Fall's most studio-centric albums, *Cerebral Caustic* would receive uneven airings on the live circuit, while its virtual absence from either of the Fall's own 1990s retrospectives (one track apiece on *A World Bewitched* and *A Past Gone Mad*) has furthered its obscurity. As a consequence, the album itself has passed into history as one of the Fall's most obscure, yet it is also one of their purest, a demandingly upbeat collection that is most heavily tainted by Smith's continued fascination with the possibilities (if not the textures) of techno, but swinging between some strange extremes regardless.

'One Day' is a wicked highlight, Smith's treated vocals and the breakneck guitars not even trying to pace themselves for the three minute sprint, while a Scanlon-heavy attempt on Frank Zappa's *Freak Out*-era 'I'm Not Satisfied' does contrarily satisfy anyone who wondered what would happen if 'I'm Frank' were taken to its logical conclusion.

At the other end of the scale, 'Bonkers In Phoenix' is, indeed, slightly bonkers, an effects strewn semi-duet between the two Smiths, with Brix broaching the cute melody line in wistful Laughing Gnome tones, while Mark is restricted to a clutch of shattered sentences, and bursts of noisy interference shattering the otherwise gentle musical ambience. His interjected observations on the Fall's 1992 Glastonbury appearance are priceless, though ('vegetarian burgers to the left... meat burgers to the right'), while the apparently aimless mention of one M Riley at the end of the piece suggests that the former Creeper's recent rebirth as BBC radio's Lard had not gone unnoticed. 'I always said he should be in children's television,' Smith shrugged later.

The album's other key duet is 'Don't Call Me Darling,' a song whose juxtaposition of verse and shrieked chorus prompted further speculation in its own right. In fact, it's a glorious pop romp and its secrets, if there are any, should be left unsaid.

(LIVE) European tour, spring 1995 and others unknown
9516. Mollusc In Tyrol
9517. Return
9518. Ladybird (Green Grass)
9519. Idiot – Walk Out
9520. Ten Points
9521. Idiot Joy Showland

9522. Big New Prinz
9523. Intro – Roadhouse
9524. The Joke
9525. M.H.'s Jokes – British People In Hot Weather
9526. Free Range
9527. High Tension Line
9528. The League Of Bald-headed Men
9529. Glam Racket-Star
9530. Lost In Music
9531. Mr. Pharmacist
9532. Cloud Of Black
9533. Paranoia Man in Cheap Sh*t Room
9534. Life Just Bounces
9535. Outro
9536. Passable
9537. Glasgow Advice
9538. Middle Class Revolt – Simon, Dave & John
9539. Bill Is Dead
9540. Strychnine
9541. War
9542. Noel's Chemical Effluence
9543. Three Points – Up Too Much

ORIGINAL RELEASE: as *The Twenty Seven Points*, Permanent PERMLP36 7 August 1995

COMMENTS: Titled for the series of seemingly self-contradictory laws introduced by the Nazis during the 1930s, *The Twenty-seven Points* (but 28 tracks) round up an apparently random selection of (predominantly) live recordings highlighting the Fall's in concert activities of the previous year or so, with a handful dating back to the early 1990s. Live in Prague, Tel Aviv, London, Glasgow, New York... this isn't a rock'n'roll band, it's a travel agency.

Pulling most of its references from the last three studio albums, *The Twenty-Seven Points* is, ultimately, less an in-concert document than (with typical E Smithery) a summary of where the Fall were at the time of its release, a final consolidation before they went stomping off to another plane of resistance, to convince another generation of impressionable pop kids that the Fall is a secret which few other folk share.

As the American magazine *Alternative Press* put it, in its own review of *The Twenty-Seven Points*, "the Fall will never be superstars... [instead], they inculcate the cult of the outsider, and distance themselves so far from the norm that they could be rolling in hits and you'd still think they're obscure. In fact, they are rolling in hits, but they're secret ones, which is why *The Twenty-Seven Points* is one of the few double live albums which doesn't even boast an audience singalong. "Hey, Bratislava, I want you all to join in this one, it's called 'The League Of Bald-Headed Men'." Yeah, right.'

There again, anybody hoping for an orderly follow-up to *Cerebral Caustic* is in for something of a shock. Although the album can be regarded as more or less essential, especially in the face of what would soon become a numbing flood of shoddily packaged out-take and archive compilations, the generous track listing does itself mask some peculiar foibles – as the warning sticker says, PARENTAL

ADVISORY: EXPLICIT, INCOMPETENT MUSIC. The first of two versions of 'Idiot Joy Showland,' for example, lasts just 40 seconds before Smith calls a halt to the proceedings. Neither is the sanctity of individual performance respected, as evidenced by a most disconcerting medley of two versions of 'Glam Racket,' one featuring Brix, the other not.

What is not sacrificed is an eye for the sheer power of the Fall in full flight. With so many different sources in play, the sound quality is variable, but it is unlikely that anyone would want to sacrifice any of the performances included here for the sake of a clearer-sounding rendition – dynamic versions of 'Ladybird (Green Grass)' and 'The Joke' are a case in point. There's also a healthy helping of Smith spoken word on board, including a discussion of books about Frank Zappa – the only other man who, with perhaps deliberate irony, could regularly get away with such purposefully disjointed and disorientating collections as this. The difference is, most of Zappa's came out after he died.

(SINGLE) Heads Of Dead Surfers by LONG FIN KILLIE
9556. Heads Of Dead Surfers
ORIGINAL RELEASE: Too Pure PURE44, 1995 (7-inch/12" CD single)
COMMENTS: Scotland's ultra-art pop quartet Long Fin Killie were still the new kids on the block when Mark E Smith threw a few hyper-excited sentences into the sax and riff clattered middle eight of 'Heads Of Deep Surfers,' the band's second single, but only one of 13 fuzzed, warped weirdies on their *Houdini* album. Temperamentally, one could say that the public should never be forgiven for overlooking Long Fin Killie. In truth, one would have been extraordinarily shocked if they hadn't.

(LIVE/STUDIO)
9544a. The Joke
9557 Rainmaster (live)
ORIGINAL RELEASE: see Receiver label comps (appendix II)

1996

Another year, another record company. After two albums with Permanent, the Fall moved on once again, this time to Jet – historically renowned as one of Electric Light Orchestra's old homes, but now a part of the Trojan conglomerate of imprints, wherein mid-price reissues and compilations were far more familiar fodder than new releases. Indeed, that was how Smith himself first came in contact with the company, when the Receiver label approached him over licensing some of the band's back catalogue. A deeper, if ultimately problematic relationship developed from there.

The split with Permanent was precipitated by the same dispute that scarred the Fall's dealings with other labels – Smith's insistence on working at his own speed (that is, very fast), rather than sitting back for a couple of years after each album, as the rest of the music industry seemed content to do. The days, even a decade before, when a new album and a couple of singles a year were the foundation stone of any band's career were long gone. Now, even the hottest shot newcomers could spend an eternity scratching together a follow-up, and no-one batted an eyelid.

Permanent also baulked at releasing the group's next single, 'The Chiseller'; Jet, on the other hand, were more than happy with it, viewing it as the flagship within an archive-trawling exercise whose sheer breadth took the breath away. With the Fall's next album, *The Light User Syndrome*, not scheduled for release until early summer, the first half of 1996 was devoted to realigning the band's back catalogue in the form of three compilations, *Sinister Waltz*, *Fiend With A Violin* and *Oswald*

Defence Lawyer.

With Rough Trade's simultaneous reactivation of the age-old Acklam Hall bootleg, suitably and self-reverentially retitled *The Legendary Chaos Tape*, one might have been excused for imagining that Smith's entire attention was focussed towards the past. March, however, brought another of his guest appearances, 'Plug Myself In,' a collaboration with Manchester dance act DOSE for Pete (ex-Stock, Aitken &) Waterman's Manchester-based dance label Coliseum. Smith told the local *City Life* fanzine, 'Someone who was doing a film for The Fall began working with Pete Waterman and he sent me a tape of what he was involved in. I liked it so I went down and did my bit.'

The union, of course, between the man who brought us Kylie and he who gave us 'Australians In Europe' caused raised eyebrows across the spectrum, but Smith was impervious. 'He was alright, quite an unassuming fellow. He didn't really interfere and I was impressed with the set up. I'm so used to going into the studio and seeing stoned freaks behind the tape deck. These kids at his studio worked around the clock. I actually like some of his trashier stuff. "I'd Rather Jack" [a 1989 hit for the Reynolds Girls] was a great record.'

The Light User Syndrome duly arrived in June, a lower-key release than the Fall were accustomed to, at least in terms of media coverage, although Smith himself wasn't unduly concerned – 'I can't complain, we've had a fair bit of attention.' Besides, well-received performances at the Roskilde and Phoenix festivals certainly confirmed the Fall's still-formidable presence on the live circuit, while there was also a short swing of shows through the UK in October, deliberately hitting towns that few bands (Smith himself, as he readily admitted) even knew existed – Cannock, Cheltenham, South Shields, Kings Lynn and Worthing, among them.

It was there, in these lands that rock forgot, that Brix Smith bowed out again, a departure that took her bandmates completely by surprise. Her final show was in Cheltenham on October 4th, a week before the tour was set to conclude.

The departure, once more, was her own idea; 'I feel like I've done the Fall, enjoyed it, given the most I could to it and got the most out of it. But now it's time to move on.' She would be returning to her own career; the Fall, though fuming over the suddenness of her departure, would simply get on with theirs.'

(MUSICIANS)

LINE-UP #25 (Jan-Oct) MARK E SMITH (vocals), JULIA NAGLE (guitar, keyboards), BRIX SMITH (guitar), STEVE HANLEY (bass), SIMON WOLSTENCROFT (drums), KARL BURNS (percussion), LUCY RIMMER (backing vocals), MIKE BENNETT (backing vocals)

LINE-UP #26 (remainder) MARK E SMITH (vocals), JULIA NAGLE (guitar, keyboards), STEVE HANLEY (bass), SIMON WOLSTENCROFT (drums), KARL BURNS (percussion)

(SINGLE) The Chiselers
9601. The Chiselers
9602. Chilinist
9603. Interlude (CD, cass only)
9604. Chilinism (CD, cass only)

ORIGINAL RELEASE: Jet JET/CD/MC 500, Feb 1996
UK CHART PEAK: #60
COMMENTS: The last Fall recording to feature Craig Scanlon and Dave Bush, cut shortly before their November departures, 'The Chisellers' was also the final flashpoint in the Fall's relationship with Permanent. Scheduled by Smith to be the band's next single, the label, he accused, 'didn't like it. They reckoned it sounded like an LP track.' And, with an overall length of 16 minutes, featuring nine separate movements, 12 different speeds and eight different vocal arrangements (introducing new auxiliaries Lucy Rimmer and producer Mike Bennett to the family), they may have been correct.

However unappetizing such a description might sound, however, 'The Chisellers' remains one of the Fall's greatest achievements of the 1990s. Its opening section – that which was sliced out for the basic 7-inch single – returns once again to the Glammy feel of 'Big New Prinz' *et al*, driven by gutsy glitter guitars and locomotive drums, a motif that regularly returns through the succeeding soundscapes of 'Chilinist,' 'Interlude' and 'Chilinism' (the latter pair, familiar from live performance as the formative 'Tunnel,' were also destined for inclusion on the new album).

As for what the suite is about, Smith noted (on the single's own liner notes) that 'this song is relevant to the recent experiences of Halifax Football Club,' who in early 1996 were battling for their very survival, both on and off the field. Whether such under-doggerel could also be applied to the Fall's own state of being is, of course, up to the individual to decide.

Permanent were not alone in doubting the value of 'The Chisellers.' Producer Grant Showbiz, who worked with the band on the basic track, told *Tape Op*, 'What you see is people going over their peak. I was thinking "Well, you're not making any sense anymore." It came to a head for me when we made "Chilinist." I was up there working on it and Craig Scanlon, who was one of the great guitarists of the Fall, had gotten a clarinet and we tried really hard to get it to work, to get a good sound. Then Mark heard it and said, "What the fuck is there a clarinet on this song for?" He told us to wipe it off the track. We played the mix again and Mark was like "This is shit. Where is the clarinet? That was the best thing on the track"'

(ALBUM) *The Light User Syndrome*
  9605. D.I.Y. Meat
  9606. Das Vulture Ans Ein Nutter-Wain
  9607. He Pep!
  9608. Hostile
  9609. Stay Away (Old White Train)
  9610. Spinetrak
  9603. Interlude
  9604. Chilinism
  9611. Powder Keg
  9612. Oleano
  9613. Cheetham Hill
  9614. The Coliseum
  9615. Last Chance To Turn Around
  9616. The Ballad Of J. Drummer
  9617. Oxymoron

9618. Secession Man
BONUS TRACKS
9601. The Chiselers
9602. Chilinist
ORIGINAL RELEASE Jet Records JETCD 1012, February 1996
REISSUE (1): Receiver RRCD264 (CD) 1999 with bonus tracks
REISSUE (2): Castle CMRCD470 (CD) 2002 with bonus tracks
UK CHART PEAK: #54
COMMENTS: *'Waleed lives in Baghdad. He wants to hear the Fall. Penelope
is a teacher. She lives in Honey Grove, Texas, and heard the Fall on the BBC world
service. Sebastian works in Hamburg. He's a doctor and roams the internet in
search of Fall information. Not all the time, mind. Jeff does the same. He lives in
Ipswich and has compiled an authoritative Fall Discography. William is my son. He
said, "Fall LPs don't really need sleeve notes, Dad". He's right, of course' – from
John Peel's liner notes.*

The Light User Syndrome found the Fall swimming against the prevailing
musical tide in a manner that they themselves must have forgotten they'd ever
needed to. After five or six years spent at least flirting with the parameters of
mainstream approval, the emergence of the Britpop movement pushed the band
firmly back into the shadows – a sidelining that was all the more ironic for the
obvious reverence in which the movement's most significant acolytes held the Fall.

Elastica (musically) and Pulp (laconic-lyrically) made little musical secret of
their debt to the group, while the Justine Frischmann-era Suede actually looked to
the Fall for guidance during their own early years. The group helped them out with
several support slots during 1991-92, and Suede repaid the favour by writing
'Implement Yeah' about their mentors. (The song would finally be recorded by a
later incarnation of Suede in 1999.) No doubt it would have been the easiest thing
in the world for the Fall to concoct an album that fed straight into the same
preoccupations that so cooled Britannia... so, *of course*, they created one that flew
in the face of everything.

The Light User Syndrome is a frighteningly LOUD album, fast and loud and
delighting in walking the tightrope over total chaos. Later years would see Julia
Nagle's keyboard-playing provoke considerable comment from the Fall faithful, not
all (or even most) of it complimentary. Listening back to *The Light User Syndrome*
with that in mind is informative – 'Das Vulture Ans Ein Nutter Violin,' a song
widely proclaimed as Smith's tribute to Kraut Rock is riddled with discordant
organ, while Nagle's ability to create noise from notes is one of the album's edgiest
qualities.

Defiant, too, is the employment of Brix's backing vocals as a light-and-dark
contrast to the clatter into which she is imposed. 'Spinetrak,' which employs a brutal
60s beat band rhythm *a la* 'Barmy,' is reasonably conventional, while the brooding
'Hostile' carries a chorale that wouldn't have been out of place on 'Waking Up In
The Sun,' but still sounds akin to a Beanotown Red Indian rock band.

A couple of purposefully dissolute revivals add to the sheenless beauty of the
proceedings – a semi-Stax-packed take on Gene Pitney's 'Last Exit To Brooklyn' is
rendered so unrecognisable that a change of title (to 'Last Chance To Turn Around')
is the least of its problems, while Karl Burns' rendition of country veteran Johnny
Paycheck's '(Stay Away) Old White Train' sounds like a pub drunk karaoke boogie.

Burns is not the album's only unexpected vocal frontman. Producer Mike

Bennett, too, takes the lead on Smith's paean to suburban Manchester's 'Cheetham Hill,' setting the stage for the duets (and more) that would characterise the band's forthcoming tour. Some nights, the pair would perform side by side; on others, Smith would not even appear on stage for some songs, singing from the dressing room while Bennett alone held the centre of the stage. It was a disconcerting sight that would be compounded by an increasingly slovenly-looking Smith's apparently racing onstage unhappiness – and would culminate in the Fall's so-messy disintegration two years later.

In the wider world, however, the most attention was devoted to 'Powder Keg,' a brutal invocation of violence built around the refrain 'retreat from Enniskillen,' but marked out by the verse 'I had a dream... it going to hurt me, Manchester city centre.' Less than a week after the album was released, a massive IRA bomb ripped that very location apart and few interviews that year would pass without Smith being asked to comment on the coincidence. Finally, he'd had enough. 'I'm a fucking psychic. Fuck off.'

(SINGLE) Plug Myself In by DOSE FEAT MARK E SMITH
    9619. Plug Myself In
    ORIGINAL RELEASE: Coliseum Records/PWL TOGA001CD, 1996
The presence of Smith dignifies, but never really salvages, what is basically a slice of workaday techno – impressive, no doubt, from a technical point of view, and certainly compulsive when extended over a hot dance floor. But, sitting at home with it bouncing out of a boom box, there are better ways of spending four minutes, let alone the eight further mixes spread across the original two CD EPs.

(LIVE) June 26 1996, Astoria, London
    9620. Chilinist
    9621. Don't Call Me Darling
    9622. 15 Ways (To Leave Your Man)
    9623. D.I.Y. Meat
    9624. Pearl City
    9625. Feeling Numb
    9626. L.A.
    9627. Big New Prinz
    9628. Mr. Pharmacist
    9629. Everything Hurtz
    9630. The Mixer
    9631. Das Vulture Ans Ein Nutter-Wain
    9632. M5 6-7PM
    9633. Return
    9634. The Reckoning
    9635. Hey! Student
    ORIGINAL RELEASE: as *15 Ways To Leave Your Man*, Receiver RRCD239, August 1997
    COMMENTS: Recorded just days after the release of *The Light User Syndrome* – which, surprisingly, supplies just three songs to the proceedings – *15 Ways* is one of the apparent multitude of unnecessary live and studio recordings issued by the Receiver family of labels during the 1990s, good sound quality failing to mask a less than thrilling performance. The Fall are not quite going through the motions, but

they certainly fail to rise to the occasion.

(LIVE/STUDIO) unknown
    9601a. Interlude – Chilinism (actually 'The Chiselers')
    9601b. The Chiselers
    9615a. Last Chance To Turn Around
    9636. U.S. 80's – 90's (live)
    9637. White Lines
    9638. Italiano
    9639. Birthday
    ORIGINAL RELEASE: 9636 on free various artists EP with German *What's That Noise?* fanzine, issue 16; remainder see Receiver label comps (appendix II)

1997

The compilations were flying thick and fast now, as the Trojan labels' remorseless grip on the back catalogue was joined by Cog Sinister's own exhumation of the Fall's live archive. Aligned now with underground specialists Voiceprint, Cog Sinister at times seemed set to rival even the band's underground tape trading audience in terms of output, with the actual quality of the recordings often a long way down the totem.

In terms of the band's own career, 1997 brought a relatively low-key new album, *Levitate*, created while the Fall lay again without a record deal, as they departed Jet in late 1996. Recorded in Edwyn Collins's studio, after Smith guested on the former Orange Juice-r's gleeful 'Seventies Night,' the band was initially working with techno outfit DOSE, intending – as they had in the past – to come up with an album so good that no label in its right mind would be able to turn it down. Instead, Smith told *The Wire* later, the duo 'went dead rocky. I felt like a real corrupter. They obviously read a book on how to be a rock producer, or how to behave. I said, "If I wanted a bad rock producer, I'd have got one. I want you to do what you did when I worked with you [on 'Plug Myself In']".' The partnership was scrapped after just one week, with only one track – eventual DOSE single 'Inch' – completed.

There was also a studio encounter with former keyboard player Dave Bush, and his own latest band, Elastica. Three years had passed since 'Connection' *et al* established the group among the very vanguard of the Britpop movement, three years during which nothing whatsoever had happened. Nor did it seem likely to.

Attempts by Smith to cut a duet with vocalist Justine Frischmann, on a new Smith song called 'We Want You' ('it's about Gary Numan,' he explained, unhelpfully) were abandoned when Smith discovered his publicist, classically trained singer Koulla Constantinou, made a much better job of it.

'You've been sitting in this studio for a year with your fingers up your arses,' Smith told the watching Elastica-ns. 'And this girl's better than the four of you put together.' A total of four songs would ultimately be recorded, but it would be another two years before either Elastica or the fruits of their collusion with Smith again saw the light of day.

The year's most significant events, then, were reserved for the last months, as the Fall headed out for their latest tour in support of what finally emerged as the PWL-produced *Levitate*.

The line-up was less than stable all year. Gigs through the early part of the year saw various stand-in guitarists replacing the departed Brix, before Tommy Crooks joined in May, alongside the returning (again) Karl Burns – only for fellow drummer Simon Wolstencroft to depart in August (he would continue working behind the scenes with Smith).

Crooks was already known to the Fall faithful as the (uncredited) artist responsible for the inside cover art of *The 27 Points*. When Craig Scanlon left the group, he immediately contacted the Fall's office to ask if he could try out for the vacant spot. Months passed without a word before he finally received a letter asking if he could make a gig in Manchester in May 1997, just two weeks hence. It was accompanied by a list of the songs the band would be playing, and Crooks spent the next fortnight learning them – only to Discover, onstage at Jilly's Rockworld, that not one of them was in the set.

For a moment, the Fall appeared to have settled down. But, kicking off in Ireland, the *Levitate* tour was just three nights old when the Fall arrived in Belfast on November 7th – and promptly disintegrated. The following Monday's *Belfast Telegraph* reported, 'Smith was apparently in poor spirits when he arrived in town after a concert in Dublin." According to Mark Erskine, manager at the Empire, he left the tour bus, and headed straight onto the stage, where he started kicking things around. 'Then he sacked the band and they went away. Smith also upset the staff of the venue by flinging a bottle of tomato sauce backstage, hitting the door of the main office. The manager, Mike Gatt, promptly issued Smith with a mop and ordered him to clean it up.'

Vaguely, Smith contemplated salvaging the musician-less gig. Backstage, he was visited by Terri Hooley, founder of Belfast's Good Vibrations record label and a former concert promoter – he staged the Fall's show at Belfast's Harp Lounge back in September 1978. 'After renewing their friendship,' the *Telegraph* continued, 'the singer and the record boss entertained the idea of performing without music. Mark E Smith would sing Beach Boys songs, while Hooley and his friend, Angus Daye, would provide backing vocals. This plan was eventually shelved.'

Smith responded, through his Circus management company, with a withering denial. 'The show goes on. The Fall do not cancel tours! Contrary to erroneous reports, the Fall tour is definitely going ahead. The Belfast show November 7 was cancelled by the promoter rather than the band, and the group are looking to perform a replacement show in the near future.' Not, he added, that it mattered. 'If it's me and your granny on bongos, then it's a Fall gig.'

In fact, the band would reconvene the following week, to relaunch the tour in

Manchester on November 13th, but the writing – of course – was already on the wall. By the following April, Hanley, Burns and Crooks would all be out, this time for keeps.

(MUSICIANS)

LINE-UP #26 (Jan-May) MARK E SMITH (vocals), JULIA NAGLE (guitar, keyboards), STEVE HANLEY (bass), SIMON WOLSTENCROFT (drums)

LINE-UP #27 (May) MARK E SMITH (vocals), JULIA NAGLE (guitar, keyboards), ANDY HACKETT (guitar), STEVE HANLEY (bass), SIMON WOLSTENCROFT (drums), KARL BURNS (percussion)

LINE-UP #28 (May-Aug) MARK E SMITH (vocals), JULIA NAGLE (guitar, keyboards), TOMMY CROOKS (guitar), STEVE HANLEY (bass), SIMON WOLSTENCROFT (drums), KARL BURNS (percussion)

LINE-UP #29 (remainder) MARK E SMITH (vocals), JULIA NAGLE (guitar, keyboards), TOMMY CROOKS (guitar), STEVE HANLEY (bass), KARL BURNS (drums)

(LIVE) unknown venue/date
9701. Everybody But Myself
9702. Spencer Must Die
9703. Ol' Gang
ORIGINAL RELEASE: 9701 *Levitate* bonus CD (1997), remainder 'Masquerade' single (1998)

(LIVE) Jan 28 1997, Bristol Bierkeller
9704. Das Vulture Ans Ein Nutter-Wain
9705. Spinetrak
9706. Behind the Counter
9707. Hip Priest
UNR. Ol Gang
UNR. He Pep
UNR. Pearl City
UNR. 10 Houses of Eve
UNR. I'm Going to Spain
UNR. Oleano
UNR. Cheetham Hill
UNR. M5
UNR. Powder Keg
UNR. Masquerade
UNR. The Chiselers
UNR. The Mixer
ORIGINAL RELEASE: *Live Various Years* (1998)

(ALBUM) *Levitate*
9708. Ten Houses Of Eve

9709. Masquerade
9710. Hurricane Edward
9711. I'm A Mummy
9712. The Quartet Of Doc Shanley
9713. Jap Kid
9714. 4 1/2 Inch
9715. Spencer Must Die
9716. Jungle Rock
9717. Ol' Gang
9718. Tragic Days
9719. I Come And Stand At Your Door
9720. Levitate
9721. Everybody But Myself
BONUS CD
9722. Powderkex
9723. Christmastide
9724. Recipe For Fascism
8322. Pilsner Trail
9701. Everybody But Myself
ORIGINAL RELEASE Artful CDX9, November 1997
COMMENTS: Having so suddenly fired DOSE as producers, Smith turned for a replacement to the duo's own mentor, Pete Waterman's hi-tech PWL. The result was a devastating, almost-but-not-quite techno set that Smith promptly proclaimed 'one of the few LPs I can listen to all the way through.' Naturally.

Levitate is a thrilling album, but an awkwardly unsatisfying one. Its reliance on the latest studio technology and trickery has certainly allowed it to date somewhat – strip away Smith's vocals, and there really isn't too much going on. Some gripping highlights scream out, though – American 50s voice-over specialist and novelty songsmith Bob McFadden's 'I'm A Mummy,' is recast as such urgent Garage Punk that some reviewers mistakenly reported that the original was just as wild (Smith Discovered this comic slice of Egyptology on the second *Incredibly Strange Music* compilation), while '4 _ Inch' and 'Spencer Must Die' rely on agit-prop drums and slashing effects to conjure up a mood not too far removed from the dislocated dance of the Fall's early 1980s work. 'The Ten Houses of Eve,' meanwhile, burbles yowlingly and, perhaps, comfortingly along a fairly basic breakbeat jungle rhythm before splintering into a smoky nightclub, all tinkling piano and wistful vocal.

Slipping out of some odd vision of David Bowie's Berlin trilogy, Julia Nagle's piano instrumental 'Jap Kid' (which then reappears behind 'I Come And Stand At Your Door') is delicate, too, but the highlight has to be the frantically synth-whipped recreation of 'Jungle Rock,' a neat slab of obscure 50s rockabilly that was suddenly reactivated in spring 1976, first by the then-unknown Shaking Stevens, then when Hank Mizell's reissued original went racing to #3. Retaining the spirit of the original, while purposefully torpedoing the delivery, 'Jungle Rock' should probably have been pulled as the Fall's next single. Which might well be why it wasn't.

'Jungle Rock' was a song that Smith had considered recording for some years. He told *The Independent* in 1990, 'When I started the band in 1977 there weren't a lot of really raw records around like this, plus it was the only thing we could play.

It's got those really corny jungle drums – dumma-dumma-dumma-dum – done on a floor tom that I'm always a sucker for, and the vocals are a sort of clipped, hillbilly whine. If in doubt, sing out of the corner of your mouth in a high voice – that's what I do – it's pretty unpopular. The bass line's pretty corny too, it's just running up and down the scale. It's always been one of my strengths, not knowing how to play – you can sound quite good on an instrument until you get familiar with it.

'I've had 'Jungle Rock' for years and still get something out of it every time – things like that are very rare. I don't know what the words are about… something about the animals all having a party in the jungle…. '

Of the five tracks on the bonus CD, 'Powderkex' is a vital DOSE working of 'Powderkeg,' while 'Christmastide' revisits 'Xmas with Simon.' There is also, at long last, an official release for 'Pilsner Trail,' taken from a bootlegged live performance from 1983.

(ALBUM) *I'm Not Following You* by Edwyn Collins
    9725. Seventies Night
    ORIGINAL RELEASE: Epic 68716
    COMMENTS: Beauty meets the beast. On a slowly percolating rhythm loosely appropriated from St Etienne's collaboration with Frenchman Etienne Daho, Smith's roughshod vocals grind effectively alongside a scrapbook of period chants and effects on a darkly dancey paean to the Disco-glitter days that both men seem to find so fascinating.

Collins told the American CMJ magazine, '[Mark and I] were just talking about this ongoing '70s revival on the High street level – kids wearing polyester novelty print shirts and all this. Everywhere I go in the world, they still have '70s nights, not in a high fashion level, but on a High street level. And we were talking about this, and what it was like growing up in the '70s, and that's what we describe in the vocals. 1977 was the year Punk broke, but it was also a transitional period between Disco and Punk. For me this song evokes that period, because you have the kind of Studio 54 slinky, sophisticated for its time, backing track we're trying to copy. Juxtaposed with that, you have the horrible, guttural nasty Mark E Smith sound. For me it makes for a really good tension of these two. They're opposites.' Rather like the song's creators.

(SESSION) with ELASTICA
    9726. How He Wrote Elastica Man
    9727. KB
    UNR. We Want You
    UNR. title unconfirmed
    ORIGINAL RELEASE: on *Elastica*, Deceptive BLUFF071CD, 23 August 1999 (CD)
    COMMENTS: Utilising just two of the four songs Smith recorded with the band, the six track EP with which Elastica marked their comeback after five years searching for a follow-up formula did little to restate the minimalist brilliance of their first album, but at least indicated that they weren't prepared to rest on what remained of their laurels. 'KB' is mid-90s Fall by proxy, a slurring, skirling guitar and bass pattern interrupted by Orbital electronics and pushing even Justine Frischmann's vocals to the back of the room; the amusingly punning 'How He Wrote "Elastica Man"' is more in keeping with reputation, but loses its past echoes

beneath distorted vocals, Grunge guitar and an awful lot of yelling. It is, of course, no relation to the Fall song of almost the same title.

(SINGLE) Inch by INCH FEAT MARK E SMITH
    9728. Inch
    ORIGINAL RELEASE: Regal REG27CD, 1999
    COMMENTS: Originally destined for inclusion on *Levitate* (wherein it would fit like an only slightly-outsized glove) 'Inch' was the first – and only – track completed by producers DOSE, before Smith fired them. DOSE's Simon Spencer elaborated, 'The music was written for inclusion on *Levitate*, and we went to London with the band as producers. [But] we didn't really get on with Mark as well as we hoped and once we'd got the vocals for "Inch" we ran off back to Manchester with the tapes. Then we cut about 20 CDs of the finished mix, sent it to Peel, *NME*, other radio stations etc. which was a bit naughty really....' Smith, however, agreed to allow DOSE to reclaim the track for a single of their own and, after what Spencer described as 'months of being fucked around by one label, it came out on another.' A total of four mixes appear on the single.

1998

'You give musicians space, and trust them, then you come back and everything's in complete bloody chaos,' Smith told *NME* in February 1998. 'That's what happened in Belfast. Someone kicked a guitar stand over at rehearsal, and it was like... open rebellion! And I was very poorly at the time, I had the flu badly. Which they all got a week later, which says something. But I couldn't hear what anyone was saying, and the moment you relax they're all going, "We want this, we want that." People smell a bit of weakness. You're dealing with people, in the main, who think they're in Oasis. Think you're a millionaire. Think you've got a harem upstairs. Think you're on drugs all the time. And they start to think: "What am I doing in the bleeding Fall playing drums to 1,000 people in fucking Wales?"'

On March 30th, the Fall opened their first American tour in four years with a performance at New York City's Coney Island High. It was a scrappy gig, and one that set the tone for the remainder of the outing. The on-line Rocktropolis Allstar Daily News all-but began its review with the assurance, 'there were no firings at the sold-out... show, though there might have been a fight at some point prior to the gig – Smith sported a black eye as he walked onstage....' In fact, Nagle had just whacked him around the head with a telephone.

The action was even closer to the audience three nights later in nearby Passaic Park, as Crooks and an apparently drunken Smith seemed constantly on the verge of a brawl, before Smith himself left the stage and the band completed the show with the guitarist taking over lead vocals. The next night was fine, but the night after that, in Philadelphia, saw Smith alternate between stalking off stage and leaving the band to get on with it, and walking back to unplug their equipment.

Finally, one incursion too many into Hanley's territory saw the two come close to blows, before Burns, Crooks and Hanley himself decided that they'd suffered enough. All three walked off, leaving Nagle and Smith alone to complete a seriously truncated set with a bizarre and clearly unexpected sample and vocal duet through 'Cheetham Hill.'

The following night in DC, faced with unfamiliar equipment after her own keyboards were stolen in New York (together with a guitar and a bag of cymbals), it was Nagle who left the spotlight, just a few numbers in. But it was back in New York where everything fell apart. Onstage, the Fall got through just six songs and at least two fights before, once again, Smith and Nagle were left to close the set alone; offstage, at the Quality Hotel Eastside, Smith was involved in an argument with Nagle herself, a row that ended only when New York police turned up and arrested him. That night's scheduled show was cancelled, and Smith spent the night instead in a cell.

Arraigned two days later on charges of misdemeanour assault and harassment charges, Smith posted bail of $1,000, then vanished – immediately prompting wild rumours that he had gone missing; might have jumped bail; and, as the Chinese whispers spread, was even on the run. In fact, he was simply keeping his head down before the court case on April 14th. There he was ordered to undergo alcohol treatment, told to submit monthly reports to the court, and observe "a limited order of protection" regarding Nagle – one that separated them on personal terms, but permitted them to share a stage.

Smith was also ordered to return to the court later in the year – at which point, according to the band's then current schedule, they would be preparing for another US tour, as part of a monster retro Punk package co-starring Pere Ubu, the Stranglers and the Buzzcocks. The tour, in the event, never happened, and the charges – which even the presiding judge acknowledged were absurdly exaggerated – were ultimately dropped.

Nevertheless, Smith told *Melody Maker*, 'I had to go over to America and sit in a hotel room for three days and they were all like, "Good, you turned up." Of course I turned up! I'm not daft y'know. [But] nothing happened. It's like a pub fight breaking out and the police arrive and arrest the fella who's sat in the corner quietly. But I'm not gonna run away from it or anything, cos I haven't done anything. The judge said 'Why do we just keeping dragging this man from England? They've accepted that I work and live in Britain and it's a different thing over there.'

Still, it was clear that this incarnation of the band had run its course. Crooks, Hanley and Burns were planning their own new group, Ark, before they even returned to England, and when the Fall next appeared in public, for three shows in London and Reading at the end of April, it was as a Spartan trio of Nagle, Smith and hastily recruited Polythene drummer Kate Methan alone. (Michael Clark also added some vocalising, bass and chair-juggling to the first London gig.)

The shows were correspondingly brittle and the media loved it all, painting a picture of the Fall in absolute disarray. Smith, however, shrugged their concerns away as easily as he seemed to wipe off the scars of the band's demise. 'Tommy was really just a hired guitar. It's the same as if the triangle player out of Phil Collins' band had left. Karl is out too. If Steve leaves for good, we'll just get another bassist. I just picked the wrong men to take to New York. I don't really know why they left, they don't communicate with me. It's all arse about tit. Everything you read, the opposite is true. It's like one of those films where a fellow's minding his own business and he gets attacked.'

Smith would elaborate further on the subject with the two part 'I'm Bobby,' from *The Post Nearly Man*, the spoken-word album released in August that was the nearest the year would come to a new Fall album. Meantime, he continued working to meld the new line-up into a cohesive whole.

Slowly, the core of Smith and Nagle was augmented by a gathering crowd. Bassist Karen Leatham arrived from Wonky Alice and Mark Burgess' Sons of God. Martin Bramah came close to returning to the band once more, before unknowns Nev Wilding and Adam Bromley seemingly appeared out of nowhere, while drummer Thomas Patrick Murphy was the younger brother of one of Smith's friends, brought in after Smith heard a tape of 'Zappa-esque stuff' he'd recorded. 'I'm lucky to get him,' Smith enthused later. 'He's brilliant. He does exactly what you want. He'd played jazz, Country & Western; he can play anything – I mean, really play it. It used to take days, weeks and months sometimes, before the drummer got it right.'

Smith continued, 'I outgrew the last group. The new one is more amenable to my ideas. They're a lot younger and they're not Fall fans. I don't recruit Fall fans because they have a pre-set idea that you've got to be miserable.'

In this seemingly tentative form, the Fall played a handful more shows around the UK as the year leeched away. None of them were especially successful, none of them exactly wowed the Fall-watchers who, like the press, seemed more interested in attending a funeral than witnessing any form of rebirth. That, however, was what they got – by the final gig of the year, what started out looking like a desperate mismatch had evolved into an spellbindingly dynamic unit.

A Peel session in November further proved the strengths of the new line-up, with Peel himself moved to tell the BBC's website, 'The Fall, in my head at least, is the band by which all others must be judged.' This was their 22nd session for his program, 'and I hope I'm around to hear many more."

(MUSICIANS)

LINE-UP #29 (Jan-Apr) MARK E SMITH (vocals), JULIA NAGLE (guitar, keyboards), TOMMY CROOKS (guitar), STEVE HANLEY (bass), KARL BURNS (drums)

LINE-UP #30 (Apr) MARK E SMITH (vocals), JULIA NAGLE (guitar, keyboards), KATE METHAN (drums)

LINE-UP #31 (Aug) MARK E SMITH (vocals), JULIA NAGLE (guitar, keyboards), KAREN LEATHAM (bass) THOMAS MURPHY (drums)

LINE-UP #32 (Oct-Nov) MARK E SMITH (vocals), JULIA NAGLE (guitar, keyboards), NEV WILDING (guitar), KAREN LEATHAM (bass), THOMAS MURPHY (drums), SPETH HUGHES (special effects)

LINE-UP #33 (Dec) MARK E SMITH (vocals), JULIA NAGLE (guitar, keyboards), NEV WILDING (guitar), ADAM BROMLEY *aka* HALAL (bass), KAREN LEATHAM (bass), THOMAS MURPHY *aka* TOM HEAD (drums)

(SINGLE) Masquerade
    9709a. Masquerade (remix)
    9801. Ivanhoe's Two Pence (CD 1 only)
    9702. Spencer Must Die (live) (CD 1 only)
    9708a. 10 Houses of Eve (remix) (CD 1 only)
    9802. Calendar (CD 2 only)
    9803. Scareball (CD 2 only)
    9703. Ol' Gang (live) (CD 2 only)
    9709b. Masquerade (Mr. Natural mix)
    9709c. Masquerade (PWL mix)
    ORIGINAL RELEASE: Artful CD/CX/10 ARTFUL 1 Feb 1998 (CD #1)
    UK CHART PEAK: #69
    COMMENTS: While the Fall apparently foundered, 'Masquerade' was belatedly hauled from *Levitate*, to plug what looked like being a barren year. Or maybe its spluttered condemnation of banking, profit and financial corruption had a

subtext whose topicality Smith alone truly recognised.

'Calendar' features guest Damon Gough *aka* Badly Drawn Boy – he first came in contact with the Fall, apparently, after Smith mistook his car for a late night mini-cab and demanded he be driven home. Gough agreed, but only after Smith agreed to record a BDB song called 'Tumbleweed.'

(ALBUM) *The Post Nearly Man* by MARK E SMITH
    9804. The Horror in Clay
    9805. Shad Segment
    9806. The Caterer
    9807. I'm Bobby part 1
    9808. The CD in Your Hand
    9809. Enigrammatic Dream
    9810. Visit of an American Poet 1
    9811. Segment
    9812. Visitation of an American Poet
    9813. Visit of an American Poet 2
    9814. I'm Bobby part 2
    9815. Typewriter
    9816. Dissolute Singer
    9817. A Lot in a Name
    ORIGINAL RELEASE Artful CD14 September 1998
    COMMENTS: Notebooks out, analysts! Credited to 'Mark E Smith' rather than The Fall, *The Post Nearly Man* is the long threatened spoken word CD built around the short stories, lyrics and poetry Smith accumulated 'while I've been stuck doing my day job.' The bare minimum of keyboards, rhythm and sound effects (contributed by Nagle and Leatham) broke the rhythmic spell of Smith's voice, and it's diverting attempting to identify the little snatches of recognisable music that crops up as background accompaniment. 'Sleep Debt Snatches' surfaces within 'Typewriter,' 'Ol Gang' during the Lovecraft-ian 'The Horror In Clay,' 'Free Range' in 'The Caterer,' and so on. There are also a few pieces inserted simply to confound expectations – the windy whistling 'Shad Segment' lasts all of 17 seconds, 'Enigrammatic Dream' is an experiment with the varispeed function on a tape recorder, and 'Segment' is completely silent.

The heart of the album, however, is Smith, as he half-conducts/half misleads the listener through a joyously bewildering mass of cryptic ideas, incredible episodes and anecdotal opinions. An enjoyable, humorous and informative listen, it was best summed up by Smith himself, with an offhand 'shouty, violent, and nothing like a Radio 4 play.'

(ALBUM) various artists: *Brazil Classics: Beleza Tropical Volume 2*
    9818. Rios, Pointes and Overdrives by CHICO SCIENCE and NACAO ZUMBI
    ORIGINAL RELEASE: Warner Bros 46275, Nov 1998
    REISSUE (1): Luaka Bop 49025
    COMMENTS: Nothing to get *too* excited about, although the combination of sententious former Talking Heads mainman David Byrne, and a pair of Brazilian rappers doing their thing on a compilation destined for the World Music section of your friendly neighbourhood megamart, probably isn't the first place you'd look for an instantly recognisable Mark E Smith sample.

1999

After the eruptions of the previous year, the Fall deserved a year of quiet reflection and that, for the most part, was what they received. A year dominated by the continuation of Cog Sinister's back catalogue reissue program also brought a pair of great singles, 'Touch Sensitive' and a slash through the Tommy Blake rockabilly classic 'F-'oldin' Money,' the long-awaited (and much-delayed) appearance of a Peel sessions compilation (*The Sunday Times*' Record of the Week), and a new album, *The Marshall Suite*. And Smith made his silver screen acting debut, appearing in a couple of shorts by director Mark Aerial Waller, *Glow Boys* and *Midwatch*.

However, it also became apparent, this time around, that the Fall was less a band, more a floating aggregation of musicians who dropped in and out as Smith saw fit – borrowing from the latest buzzword in the footballing lexicon, he described it as 'squad rotation.' Nagle, Nev Wilding, Leatham, Adam Bromley (Halal) and Murphy (Head) would each perform alongside Smith as the year went on, but seldom all at one time.

This new regime made its debut with three shows at Ashton's Witchwood at the end of February, the first shots fired in what became one of the band's most active live spells in some years – and highlighted by some of Smith's most exhilarating (not to mention enthusiastic) performances in just as long.

'This new band is great," Smith told *The Wire*. 'It's a pleasure to be on stage now, which is the first time it's been like that for a bit. A lot of the things that were frustrating me have disappeared. A lot of things that were put down to me rambling and all that was in fact the group, that last group. They were efficient, lazy, old fashioned, I thought, everything the Fall shouldn't be.'

(MUSICIANS)
LINE-UP #33 (all) MARK E SMITH (vocals) – from: JULIA NAGLE (guitar, keyboards), NEV WILDING (guitar), ADAM BROMLEY *aka* HALAL (bass), KAREN LEATHAM (bass), THOMAS MURPHY *aka* TOM HEAD (drums)

(SINGLE) Touch Sensitive
  9901. Touch Sensitive
  9901a. Touch Sensitive (Dance Mix)

160

9902. Antidote
ORIGINAL RELEASE: Artful 12/CD ARTFUL2, Feb 1999
COMMENTS: Previewing the Fall's forthcoming next album (provisionally and revealingly entitled *The New*), 'Touch Sensitive' is a loosely played Garage reinterpretation of the Velvets' 'Waiting For The Man,' shot through with Gary Glitter drums and Johnny Rotten yowls, growling at the mixed moralities of modern society – political correctness on the one hand, isolationist fear on the other: 'in the cars or on the street, if you smile you are a creep.'

'We were looking for something a bit more savage,' Smith explained. 'I've been using rhythm machines, but using them properly and distorting things. I still want that basic rockabilly thing that I think we've been losing in the past year or two.' A churning cello and a compulsive chant serve up a backdrop that drives 'Touch Sensitive' home, even in its regular album incarnation. The dance mix, however, is sonic dynamite.

(ALBUM) *The Marshall Suite*
9901. Touch Sensitive
9903. F-'oldin' Money
9904. Shake-Off
9905. Bound
9906. This Perfect Day
9907. (Jung Nev's) Antidotes
9908. Inevitable
9909. Anecdotes + Antidotes In B#
9910. Early Life Of The Crying Marshal
9911. The Crying Marshal
9912. Birthday Song
9913. Mad.Men-Eng.Dog
9914. On My Own
LP BONUS TRACK
9915. Finale: Tom Raggazzi
ORIGINAL RELEASE Artful ARTFULCD17 (CD, LP) April 1999 (CD)
COMMENTS: Rejoicing in the unspoiled enthusiasm of this latest Fall line-up, wherein Nagle alone had 'been around,' Smith reinvented the group for the umpteenth time. The result was one of the band's most reassuring records in recent years. Surprisingly, perhaps, the trailing singles ('Touch Sensitive' and 'F-'oldin' Money') were as representative as anything on what was, at its heart, a joyously noisy Garage-art album, although the strengths that they confer serve primarily to spotlight the moments where *The Marshall Suite* moves seriously off kilter.

'Shake Off' is fabulous, a corposant wall of darkly symphonic synth rearing behind a Smith lyric that contemplates the perils of hip parenting (and, terrifyingly, a Simple Minds reunion), but it is only the curtain raiser to the split two-parter '(Jung Nev's) Antidote' and 'Anecdotes + Antidotes In B#' which utilises many of the same elements, but renders them ever darker. The oasis between the pair, meanwhile, could not be more jarring – 'Inevitable' is almost painfully clunky, although its thumpy bass and toytown keyboard possess an almost immaculate charm when encountered amid the insensate stygia that surrounds them.

It's disappointing, however, to discover that the finest face of this version of the Fall was turned towards a radio session, broadcast by XFM on April 15. Rousing versions of the best of the album ('Shake Off,' 'F-'oldin' Money,' 'Touch Sensitive,' 'Antidotes' and 'Inevitable' (oh, and a plodding 'This Perfect Day') were accompanied by a storming 'Ten Houses of Eve' and, keeping the tapers very happy indeed, the New York Dolls' Glam-Punk classic 'Jet Boy.'

(SINGLE) F-'oldin' Money
9903. F-'oldin' Money
9916. Perfect Day (new version) (CD 1 only)
9917. The REAL Life of the Crying Marshal (new version) (CD 2 only)
9915a. Tom Raggazzi (new mix) (CD 2 only)
9912a. Birthday Song (new mix) (CD 1 only)
ORIGINAL RELEASE: Artful CD/CDX ARTFUL3, June 1999 (CD)
COMMENTS: A country boogie gem, expertly recreated in the image of the Milkshakes, Tommy Blake's 'F-'oldin' Money' was rattling around the one-time Sun label star's repertoire for some four years before he finally recorded it in 1959, as his first single for the Recco label. Its musical qualities (and lyrical truths) notwithstanding, 'F-'oldin' Money' probably also appealed to Smith for its maker's own story – never rising out of the rockabilly third division, Blake spent his last years lost in drug and alcohol, before being accidentally shot by his wife on Christmas Eve, 1985.

Of the remixed album tracks that complete the twin CDs, nothing leaps out as desperately different, but one should pause to consider 'This Perfect Day' (in any incarnation), as Smith allows his attention to wander over one of the Fall's own Punk-era peers, Australia's The Saints. In truth, the band's roughshod R&B nihilism fitted as uneasily in the Punky basket as the Fall themselves, a point pushed home by this hard retread of their second album's title track.

In fact, it was a marriage that spent almost 20 years awaiting consummation. Way back in 1981, Smith told *NME* about his love for the dissolute Australian R&B Punk band the Saints – a primal influence on discerning young Australians before they relocated to the UK in early 1977. 'I saw them right back at the beginning of '77, and they were, like, the best,' Smith enthused. 'But did you ever see them on *Top Of The Pops*? They were doing "This Perfect Day," I think, and they looked, y'know, just slightly wrong. They all had these pullovers on, and they were really, like, dirty, and really over the top, and the singer stood at this strange angle, I think he had a pint in his hand, y'know ... fuckin' great! That was the great thing about them, there was no way the English could televise them. Yeah, I still play all their singles.'

(LIVE) Monarch, Camden April 19 1999 with THE CLINT BOON EXPERIENCE
9919. I Wanna Be Your Dog
ORIGINAL RELEASE: b-side, Artful Records 7ARTFUL31, June 1999 (7-inch, CD single)
COMMENTS: Recorded live, the b-side of Artful labelmate (and former Inspiral Carpets keyboard player) Boon's 'You Can't Keep A Good Man Down' 45 opens with the guesting Smith complaining, in a tone caught midway between a belligerent drunk and a drunker Jim Morrison, that the band won't let him go home. But he throws himself violently into the old Stooges chestnut, with a few lyric changes in the second verse to personalise the performance far beyond the Experience's straightforward rendering of the original's murky riff.

2000

Another year of stability haunted, as before, only by the ghosts of sundry past Fall incarnations, rattling chains that were far removed from the band's own latest adventures. It didn't matter where you looked, either – even tuning into Posh Spice's TV chat show left you facing the Fall's 12-year-old version of the Kinks' 'Victoria,' while emigrating to San Francisco only placed you in range of the world's first Fall tribute band, Triple Gang (featuring former members of Faith No More, Clarke Nova, Fudge Tunnel and Horsey), as they performed *This Nation's Saving Grace* in its entirety. Including the CD bonus tracks. And, proving that lightning can strike twice, another tribute band promptly turned up in Hull, Mark E Banks and Santa's Buggerboyz.

The Fall themselves gigged only sporadically through the year. The main bursts of activity were during May and November, with the new album, *The Unutterable*, trailing the latter. Having shed drummer Murphy in October, the latter shows introduced Spencer Birtwistle – a former bandmate of Nagle's in a long ago combo, who then found acclaim as a member of mid-90s electronica heroes Intastella.

(MUSICIANS)

LINE-UP #34 (Jan-Oct) MARK E SMITH (vocals) – from: JULIA NAGLE (guitar, keyboards), NEV WILDING (guitar), ADAM BROMLEY *aka* HALAL (bass), THOMAS MURPHY *aka* TOM HEAD (drums)

LINE-UP #35 (Nov-Dec) MARK E SMITH (vocals), JULIA NAGLE (guitar, keyboards), NEV WILDING (guitar), ADAM BROMLEY *aka* HALAL (bass), SPENCER BIRTWISTLE (drums)

(SINGLE) Fistful Of Credit – Mild Man Jan/Mark E Smith
  0001. Fistful Of Credit
  ORIGINAL RELEASE: Atlantis SWALF 1 (7-inch) October 2000
  COMMENTS: A fascinating, vaguely Tricky-esque collaboration between Smith and Manchester artist Spencer Marsden. Limited edition (500 copies) pink vinyl 45.

(ALBUM) *The Unutterable*
　0002. Cyber Insekt
　0003. Two Librans
　0004. W.B.
　0005. Sons of Temperance
　0006. Dr. Buck's Letter
　0007. Hot Runes
　0008. Way Round
　0009. Octo Realm – Ketamine Sun
　0010. Serum
　0011. Unutterable
　0012. Pumpkin Soup and Mashed Potatoes
　0013 Hands up Billy
　0014. Midwatch 1953
　0015. Devolute
　0016. Das Katerer

ORIGINAL RELEASE Eagle EAGCD164 6 November, 2000 (CD)

COMMENTS: Subsequently dismissed by Smith himself as 'a bit arty,' but elsewhere described as one of the Fall's more 'personable' albums, *The Unutterable* is certainly one of the most purposefully light-hearted – where, as Smith himself demands in 'Devolute,' would we be 'without music and humour'? So, he chuckles his way through 'Dr Buck's Letter' – a tribute to bucolic author Charles Bukowski; then unleashes his bandmates on 'Octo Realm,' a brief interlude that has every member in turn introduce themselves in a variety of odd voices, before they slam into the stand-out 'Ketamine Sun.' A certain second cousin to Lou Reed's 'Kill Your Sons,' the song discusses the recent promotion of a veterinary anaesthetic to the realms of teenaged kicks, packing a hazed intensity that ranks it alongside either 'Totally Wired' or 'Rowche Rumble' (you choose) as the Fall's most significant drug song. (Unless you want to count 'Serum,' later in the cycle.)

Indeed, *The Unutterable* has precious few moments that, considering the full spectrum of Fall releases, can be considered groundbreaking. Reuniting the band with producer Grant Showbiz, its sonic templates range from brutal electronics to purposefully thin Garage guitars, with the old rockabilly rhythms still a favourite form of propulsion. Where it does stand alone is in the increasing attention to songwriting detail that now characterises Smith's work – even his most intemperate rants have a structure that might have been anathema to an earlier Fall.

Other points: the conjoined riffery that saw 'Serum' revisit *Levitate*'s 'Crying Marshall,' the rockabilly jangle 'Hot Runes' (a distinct cousin to 'Guest Informant'), 'Pumpkin Soup and Mashed Potatoes,' which marks the band's first stab at jazz, and 'Midwatch 1953,' which isn't simply the shortest (seven words, repeated twice) lyric in the Fall's vocabulary, it is also one of the most obscure. What did happen in 1953?

2001

The line-up changes that commenced in November 2000, with the departure of Tom Head, continued as the Fall prepared to play their first show of 2001, in Dublin. Out went Nev Wilding and Adam Helal, in came the similarly unknown Ben Pritchard and Jim Watts. By summer, Julia Nagle, too, would have gone, while her replacement, guitarist B Fanning, would hang on only until October (manager Ed Blaney also appeared on stage as a guitarist during this period).

Spencer Birtwistle would follow them out in November – *his* successor, Dave Millner, was given precisely 45 minutes of rehearsal immediately before his first show, in Manchester on November 29. All of which meant, of course, that the Fall left 2001 in completely different form to that in which they entered it.

Around these disruptions, the band's live schedule was understandably spotty, with the greatest concentration of gigs falling first during the spring, and then in the autumnal run-up to the new album, *Are You Missing Winner* (ironically released around the same time as the Fall's first single in two years; the three-song *The Present* EP was canned).

Short British and European tours were followed by a brief, but utterly triumphant American outing – their first since the ill-fated shows of four years previous. The itinerary concentrated on the Fall's established coastal strongholds, largely based around appearances at the famed Knitting Factory chain of clubs. A new live album, 2002's *2G+2*, was recorded during this latter sequence

(MUSICIANS)

LINE-UP #36 (Jan-July) MARK E SMITH (vocals) JULIA NAGLE (guitar, keyboards), BEN PRITCHARD (guitar), JIM WATTS (bass), SPENCER BIRTWISTLE (drums)

LINE-UP #37 (July-Oct) MARK E SMITH (vocals) B FANNING (guitar), ED BLANEY (guitar, vocals), BEN PRITCHARD (guitar), JIM WATTS (bass), SPENCER BIRTWISTLE (drums)

LINE-UP #38 (Nov-Dec) MARK E SMITH (vocals) BEN PRITCHARD (guitar), ED BLANEY (guitar, vocals), JIM WATTS (bass), DAVE MILLNER (drums)

(SINGLE) Rude (All The Time)
 0101. Rude (All The Time)
 0102. I Wake Up in the City
 ORIGINAL RELEASE: Flitwick MK45 1FG (7-inch ltd ed of 500 copies)
 COMMENTS: A special release prepared as a subscription giveaway to members of the Flitwick label's singles club – a successor to similar offerings made by Sub Pop and Rough Trade. The Spores, Keith John Adams, Gag (proud purveyors of 'the most annoying song ever written,' 'Roast'), Flitwick (Bedfordshire) bands one and all, rank among the other beneficiaries of the label's largesse. The Fall's release, meanwhile, was promoted with the simple hope, 'we think there's a bright future for them in the business. Happy to give them a leg up.' (http://www.flitwick-records.co.uk/)

(LIVE) Los Angeles Knitting Factory, November 15
 0103. Ibis-Afro Man
 0104. I Am Damo Suzuki

(LIVE) Seattle, November 20 2001
 0105. The Joke

(LIVE) New York Knitting Factory, November 23
 0106. Bourgeois Town
 0107. Mr. Pharmacist

(LIVE) New York Knitting Factory, November 25
 0108. My Ex-Classmates' Kids
 0109. Enigrammatic Dream
 0110. Kick the Can
 0111. F-'Oldin' Money
 ORIGINAL RELEASE: on *2G+2* (2002)
 COMMENTS: The Fall performed a more or less stable set list throughout their American visit, of which the tracks selected for the next live album were at least a representative sampling. Also available for selection from the same shows were versions of the following: Touch Sensitive / 2 Librans / Cyber Insekt / And Therein / F-'oldin' Money / Way Round / Crop-Dust / Jim's New Fall / Dr. Buck's Letter /

Antidotes / Sons of Temperance / I Wake up in the City / Ey Bastardo.
(ALBUM) *Are You Missing Winner*
    0112. Jim's "The Fall"
    0113. Bourgeois Town
    0114. Crop-Dust
    0115. My Ex-Classmates' Kids
    0116. Kick the Can
    0117. Gotta See Jane
    0118. Ibis-Afro Man
    0119. The Acute
    0120. Hollow Mind
    0121. Reprise: Jane – Prof Mick – Ey Bastardo
    ORIGINAL RELEASE Cog Sinister COGVP131CD, November 2001 / COGVP131LP (2LP picture disc ltd ed) January 2002
    COMMENTS: Odd, given the Fall's long-running flirtation with Iggy Pop and/or the Stooges, that, over the course of 25 years the only overt tribute to them in the band's entire catalogue was Smith's performance on the Clint Boon Experience's 'I Wanna be Your Dog.' Odder still, however, that when the Fall did finally give in, they chose one of the least Iggy-like songs of them all, *New Values'* closer 'African Man.' 'That's funny,' Iggy himself agreed. 'Every album of mine, there's always one track where people say – "okay, he's finally lost it." That was the one for *New Values.*'

Retitled 'Ibis-Afro Man,' to account for Smith's lyrical revisions and additions, the inclusion of snatches of 'Race With The Devil' and 'Birthday' further the song's resolute disjointedness, while the possibility that Smith is duetting with a monkey should not be discounted either. The nigh-on ten-minute end result is one of those occasional numbers that works a lot better live than on record (although the version on *2G+2* isn't especially brilliant, either).

Are You Missing Winner is a difficult album – difficult in that you want to enjoy it, but it steadfastly holds your ears at arm's length, as the sense of delighted exploration that underpins the soul of the Fall seems to have been sent out of the room for half an hour. Too much of the album is unformed, too many songs are uneven, and too often the noise is simply unbearable.

The opening 'Jim's "The Fall",' a gnarly statement of intent for the latest line-up of the group, is as cumbersome as early reviews of the line-up always said it was, while a tumultuous version of Leadbelly's 'Bourgeois Town' does an okay job of reiterating the song, but adds nothing even vaguely interesting to the proceedings.

Elsewhere, a rockabilly-ish return to the R Dean Taylor songbook, this time for 'Gotta See Jane,' lacks much of the foreboding polish that cloaked 'There's A Ghost In My House,' with Smith's vocal sounding more like a rehearsal-time run through than a finished performance. But the reappearance of the song's basic rhythm during the closing 'medley' does make you want to take another listen to its first airing. Well, it's either that or sit through the rest of the medley.

Further highlights are restricted to just a couple of moments, pinned between the plodders. 'Hollow Mind' is one of those joyous Sing-a-long-a-Smith rambles that nails itself to a memorable melody and a bad-temperedly unplugged backing, although you can't help thinking you've maybe heard it somewhere before. The acerbic 'My Ex-Classmates' Kids,' meanwhile, has a relentlessly snot-nosed Punkish feel that reminds one of the early Rough Trade albums (or 'Spirit In The

Sky' played by the Velvet Underground). Unfortunately, such virtues are largely superficial, a flaw that is echoed by the country-ish 'The Acute' – it's fun the first few listens, but quickly loses its appeal.

Nevertheless, no matter what else the Fall accomplish over the next ten years, two tracks at least are shoo-ins for their next decade-spanning 'best of.' 'Crop Dust' has a visceral, rolling, momentum that follows 'Jim's "The Fall"' into the gabba-gabba-hatefulness mapped out by America's industrial citizenry, but adds a gentle Stuka guitar motif to break the monotony of the machines, while 'Kick The Can' has a lazy-but-so-anthemic feel, carried on hand-rolled riff and lackadaisical slur, before settling into a twangy passage that doesn't do much, but has a great time not doing so.

After all that, searching for positive points on this album remains easy. In a career whose very longevity is built on the trampled remains of previous laurels, the odd wrong move is inevitable – Smith's done it before, he'll do it again. Meanwhile, his refusal, even after all these years, to sink into the quixotic quagmire that long ago swallowed his Punk-era contemporaries can only be applauded – not for the Fall a comfortable berth on Post-punk Gold FM, or the umpteenth recycling of things he used to be good at, for an audience that simply wants to grow old nostalgically.

(SINGLE) *The Present*
    0115. My Ex-Classmates' Kids
    0122. New Formation Sermon
    0123. Distilled Mug Art
    ORIGINAL RELEASE: Artful – unissued
COMMENTS: After several months anticipation, *The Present* was canned in early autumn. 'My Ex-Classmates Kids,' of course, was available on *Are You Missing Winner*; the remaining cuts, 'New Formation Sermon,' and the loosely reggaefied 'Distilled Mug Art' would be held over for the 2002 live album *2G+2*.

2002

25 years. It seems a lot longer.

In common with most everybody else that erupted out of the Manchester Punk scene, the Fall were handed the optimum stage upon which to celebrate their longevity with the movie *24 Hour Party*, based around *So It Goes* TV host (and Factory Records head) Tony Wilson's own reminiscences. Apparently, Smith turned down the opportunity for any kind of major role in the film, but did make a cameo appearance, among the punters seen lining up for the opening night of Wilson's Factory Club.

Instead of looking back, then, the year kicked off with one of the Fall's largest tours in recent years, close to a month in Europe, followed by a string of UK dates leading up to two nights at All Tomorrow's Parties in April. In fact, an even heavier itinerary was on the cards until a mix-up over visas necessitated the cancellation of a quick return to the United States. The outing was cancelled and quickly rescheduled for later in the year – only for this, too, to be canned, a disappointment that was widely seen as precipitating the departure of manager Ed Blaney, after two years overseeing the band.

Although a new single, *The Fall vs 2003*, arrived just in time to wave 2002 goodbye, there was no new studio album this year, only the live *2G + 2*, recorded on the US tour in 2001, while fans of Smith's spoken word activities were granted *Pander! Panda! Panzer!* Live, however, steps towards the next epoch of the Fall were taken when Smith's new wife Elena moved in on keyboards – following

Blaney's ouster, she would also take over the band's management.

All of which amounted to a curiously low-key way of celebrating a quarter of a century of the Fall – which in turn means it was a typically Fall-like way of doing so. Smith, however, carried no regrets. The year ended with readers of the *Manchester Evening News* website (www.manchesteronline.co.uk) overwhelmingly electing him the Greatest Mancunian, streaking ahead of everyone from Ian Brown and Morrissey to Elizabeth Gaskill and Harrison Ainsworth.

Working on songs for the band's next album, scheduled for spring 2003, Smith paused only to tell *The Independent*, 'I don't really think I've changed since I was 18. If anything, I'm worse. There are a lot of twats around, and I don't like them. I reckon the 18-year-old me would think I was all right.'

(MUSICIANS)

LINE-UP #38 (Jan-summer) MARK E SMITH (vocals) BEN PRITCHARD (guitar), ED BLANEY (guitar, vocals), JIM WATTS (bass), ELENA SMITH (occasional keyboards), DAVE MILLNER (drums)

LINE-UP #39 (remainder) MARK E SMITH (vocals) BEN PRITCHARD (guitar), JIM WATTS (bass), ELENA SMITH (occasional keyboards), DAVE MILLNER (drums)

(ALBUM) *2G+2*
    0105. The Joke
    0108. My Ex-Classmates' Kids
    0109. Enigrammatic Dream
    0110. Kick the Can
    0111. F-'Oldin' Money
    0106. Bourgeois Town
    0103. Ibis-Afro Man
    0107. Mr. Pharmacist
    0104. I Am Damo Suzuki
    0122. New Formation Sermon
    0102. I Wake Up in the City
    0123. Distilled Mug Art
    ORIGINAL RELEASE: Action Records TAKE18CD 10 June, 2002 (CD)
    COMMENTS: Recorded during the Fall's short (eight shows, four cities) American visit in November 2001, *2G+2* sadly lines up alongside all the other live albums best recommended to collectors, and left to linger on the shelf by everyone else.

There is little wrong with the sound quality, the energy levels are generally high, and 'I Am Damo Suzuki' offers up a movingly atmospheric finale. But none of the performances really excel over their studio counterparts and even arch completists will be more excited about the inclusion (randomly inserted in between live tracks) of three of the Fall's better-known latter-day rarities – 'New Formation Sermon' and 'Distilled Mug Art' were salvaged from the withdrawn *The Present* EP, 'I Wake Up in the City' hails from the limited edition Flitwick label 7-inch.

(ALBUM) *Pander! Panda! Panzer!*

0201. Mount Street Sermon
0202. PPP – The End
0203. Enigrammatic Dream
0204. Life Just Bounces
0205. Copenhagen 'Set-Up'
0206. Dissolute Singer
0207. Lucifer Over Lancashire
0208. Lakeland Opus 1
0209. Sport Duet
0210. Idiot Joy Showland
0211. 5 Previously Unreleased Sentences
ORIGINAL RELEASE: Action Records TAKE19CD, September 2002
COMMENTS: Mark E Smith spoken word album. The CD is mastered as one continuous track. Several pieces feature extrapolations on previously released Fall songs.

(ALBUM) various artists: *FABRICLIVE.07 John Peel*
8606a. Mr Pharmacist (remix)
ORIGINAL RELEASE: Fabric FABRIC14, December 2002

COMMENTS: Actually less a remix, more a case of slamming some echo onto the song's conclusion. Unlike other volumes in the Fabric series, #7 allows its contents to stand all but unaltered, barring the occasional insertion of some Liverpool FC commentary. An excellent disc for anybody stranded far from Peel's nearest radio broadcasts, swooping through a wealth of genres and timespans, from bluegrass to noise and back again, *Fabriclive.07* reminds us just how he has survived for so long as the top of his game. Him and certain other people.

(SINGLE) *The Fall vs 2003*
0212. Susan vs Youthclub
0213. Janet vs Johnny
0212a. Susan vs Youthclub (remix) (CD only)
ORIGINAL RELEASE: Action TAKE 20/CD (7-inch, CD) December 2002
UK CHART PEAK: #64
A mighty electroblurge dominated by one of Smith's most stentorian (almost Dalek-esque) vocals in a while, 'Susan Vs Youthclub' half-tells the story of a woman slammed back to her mid-teens following an unspecified accident. It's a showcase more for a near industrial barrage of sound than anything else – the remix is especially impenetrable – but it posits some brutal futures for the Fall.

Equally captivating, but considerably easier to listen to, 'Janet vs Johnny' is an absolute comedown in the midst of such raging, Smith all but crooning his way through a gentle, but so foreboding electronic nursey rhythm. Oddly, if you slice the riff in half, it could lead off into folkie Davey Graham's 'Anji,' although why anyone would want to do that is another matter entirely.

APPENDIX I
The Fall on Air: BBC Radio Sessions 1977-2002

'The Fall have given me more pleasure, over a longer period of time, than any other band. And when people ask me why, I always say gnomically "They're always different, always the same". I'm not sure that that means anything but it sounds reasonably good. They're just the Fall – a band by which in our house all the others are judged' – John Peel, 1998.

'In the flow and jetsam of modern society, only John Peel stands out as the modicum of 'respectability-alternative'. Without John, all children would be weeping – their kindred looking towards heavens for signals, none apparent' – Mark E Smith, 1999.

Through the early-mid 1970s, John Peel was one of the few BBC DJs who were not afraid to go out on a limb. He broadcast late, 10pm on weekday evenings, and thought nothing of devoting great swathes of his show to a new album by one of the bands he held holy, or a session by someone that his listeners had probably never heard of. When the first stirrings of Punk rock began making themselves felt, it was inevitable that Peel would investigate. Indeed, the first 'Punk' record aired on the John Peel Show was the Ramones' debut album, in May, 1976. Peel himself had only just got hold of the record, 'and [that night], I put in five or six tracks from it. I immediately got a lot of letters from people saying "you must never do that again," and of course, that always excites me.'

By late August, Peel was playing Nick Lowe's Stiff Records debut 'Sound Of The City' on a nightly basis; on September 29, he opened the show with the Saints' "I'm Stranded" (and then played Stevie Wonder's new album in its entirety). On October 12, the Vibrators became the first of the new wave bands to record a session; and on November 30, the Damned brought pure Punk rock screaming into studios which just weeks, even days before, such doughty warriors as folkie Alan Hull, the Climax Chicago Blues Band and Stackridge had made their own.

Through 1977, even as Punk made greater and greater inroads into the UK chart consciousness, Peel remained its greatest champion, forever one step ahead of even the hippest of his fellow DJs, and several more in front of the journalists and jerks that were forever raising another half-chord wonder to the heights of Next Big Thingdom.

The onus of selecting bands for the sessions fell squarely on Peel and producer John Walters. Both were regular gig-goers, with Walters taking his brief so seriously that he referred to Punk shows as 'lack-of-talent spotting' exercises, the 'lack of (conventional, serious musicianly) talent,' of course, being what he and Peel found so delightful about the entire movement.

It was Walters who first heard the Fall, heading down to Croydon Greyhound to catch Siouxsie and the Banshees, but remembering journalist Danny Baker's recommendation that he see the support band as well. Days later, on May 15th, he contacted Smith. 'You don't know me but I know you,' he wrote. 'The band seems to have the kind of defiant non-musical approach which ought to be encouraged.' And the encouragement he could offer was, the opportunity to record a session for Peel. The Fall were booked into Maida Vale studios on May 30.

With Steve Davis, a friend of manager Kay Carroll, guesting on incongruous congas, the Fall's maiden Peel session comprised two songs plucked from their latest live set, 'Rebellious Jukebox' and 'Mother Sister,' and two more dating back to the Tony Friel era, 'Industrial Estate' and 'Futures and Pasts.' It was a dramatic debut and one, of course, that ignited a love affair between DJ and band that is as strong today as ever. 'Things like the Sex Pistols don't seem to have stood the test of time,' Peel once remarked. 'But if you listen to… the [early] Fall, they sound as good as they ever did. That's unusual in any area of popular music.'

On another occasion, he enthused, 'they're the great miracle of my musical life. I just adore them. If they made a bad record, I wouldn't know. All they have to do is turn up and that's enough.'

With the exception of comedian Ivor Cutler, no single performer can claim a stronger hold on the heart of DJ John Peel's near-nightly radio sessions than the Fall. Between 1978 and 1998, the band recorded more than 30 studio and concert sessions at the BBC, 22 of them for Peel alone (the 23rd was taped in February 2003), while the DJ has also hosted four separate live broadcasts, including two from the Phoenix Festival and one more from his own 50th birthday party.

In the face of so much activity, the Fall have been strangely under-represented within the various BBC sessions discs released in the years since that particular archive was first cracked open in the late 1980s. Although a rendering of their second session was included among the earliest of all *Peel Sessions* EPs, plans for a full-length album compiling Peel's own favourite moments from all of the sessions dragged on for over a decade – the album was first mooted in 1987, at the inception of the Strange Fruit label, but remained a mere promise until 1998. And, of course, it merely scratched the very tip of the diamond.

The releases that have made it out, however, have included some significant moments, including the first ever 7-inch single released by the Strange Fruit label that was, for many years, the primary source of BBC archive releases.

The following represents a full catalogue of all of the Fall's BBC sessions and broadcasts.

INDEX OF FALL BBC SESSIONS 1977-2002

PROGRAMME: John Peel #1
RECORDED: 30 May 1978
FIRST BROADCAST: 15 June 1978
UNR. Futures And Pasts
UNR. Mother – Sister!
7802. Rebellious Jukebox
UNR. Industrial Estate
Produced by Tony Wilson, engineered by Mike Robinson. Mark E Smith – vocals; Martin Bramah – guitar, bass, backing vocals; Yvonne Pawlett – keyboards; Karl Burns – drums; Steve Davis – congas.

PROGRAMME: John Peel #2
RECORDED: 27 November 1978
FIRST BROADCAST: 6 December 1978
7817. Put Away
7818. Mess Of My
7819. No Xmas For John Quays
7820. Like To Blow
Produced by Bob Sargeant, engineered by Dave Dade & Brian Tuck. Mark E Smith – vocals; Martin Bramah – guitar, bass, backing vocals; Yvonne Pawlett – keyboards; Marc Riley – bass; Karl Burns – drums.

PROGRAMME: John Peel #3
RECORDED: 16 September 1980
FIRST BROADCAST: 24 September 1980
8010. The Container Drivers
UNR. Jawbone And The Air-Rifle
8011. New Puritan
8012. New Face In Hell
Produced by John Sparrow. Mark E Smith – vocals; Marc Riley – guitar; Craig Scanlon – guitar; Steve Hanley – bass; Paul Hanley – drums.
COMMENTS: Source of two of the tracks lifted for the 'Kicker Conspiracy' bonus single, 'The Container Drivers' and a radical reinvention of 'New Puritan.'

PROGRAMME: John Peel #4
RECORDED: 24 March 1981
FIRST BROADCAST: 31 March 1981
8101. C'n'C-Hassle Schmuck
8102. Middle Mass
UNR. Lie Dream Of A Casino Soul
UNR. Hip Priest
Produced by Dale Griffin, engineered by Martyn Parker. Mark E Smith – vocals; Marc Riley – guitar; Craig Scanlon – guitar; Steve Hanley – bass; Paul Hanley – drums; Dave Tucker – clarinet.
COMMENTS: An excellent 'C'n'C-Hassle Schmuck' includes Smith's apparently ad-libbed thoughts on Arthur Askey.

PROGRAMME: John Peel #5
RECORDED: 26 August 1981
FIRST BROADCAST: 15 September 1981
UNR. Deer Park
UNR. Look, Know
8117. Winter (Hostel Maxi)
UNR. Who Makes The Nazis?
Produced by Dale Griffin, engineered by Nick Gomm. Mark E Smith – vocals; Marc Riley – guitar; Craig Scanlon – guitar; Steve Hanley – bass; Paul Hanley – drums.

PROGRAMME: John Peel #6
RECORDED: 21 March 1983
FIRST BROADCAST: 23 March 1983
8302. Eat Y'self Fitter
UNR. Smile
UNR. Garden
UNR. Hexen Definitive – Strife Knot
Produced by John Porter, engineered by Dave Dade. Mark E Smith – vocals; Craig Scanlon – guitar; Steve Hanley – bass; Paul Hanley – drums; Karl Burns – drums.

PROGRAMME: John Peel #7
RECORDED: 12 December 1983
FIRST BROADCAST: 3 January 1984
UNR. Pat Trip Dispenser
8401. Words Of Expectation
8402. 2 X 4
UNR. c.r.e.e.p.
Produced by Tony Wilson, engineered by Martin Colley. Mark E Smith – vocals; Brix Smith – guitar, vocals; Craig Scanlon – guitar; Steve Hanley – bass; Paul Hanley – drums; Karl Burns – drums.
COMMENTS: 'Words Of Expectation' includes one of Smith's all-time great slices of self-analysis… 'if we carry on like this, we're gonna end up like King Crimson.'

PROGRAMME: David Jensen
RECORDED: 19 February 1984
FIRST BROADCAST: 1 March 1984
UNR. Lay Of The Land
UNR. God Box
UNR. Oh! Brother
UNR. C.R.E.E.P.
Produced by Dale Griffin, engineered by Mike Engles. Mark E Smith – vocals; Brix Smith – guitar, vocals; Craig Scanlon – guitar; Steve Hanley – bass; Paul Hanley – drums; Karl Burns – drums.

PROGRAMME Janice Long
RECORDED: 9 September 1984
FIRST BROADCAST: 17 September 1984
8419. Stephen Song
8420. No Bulbs

UNR. Draygo's Guilt
UNR. Slang King
Produced by Dale Griffin, engineered by Mike
Engles. Mark E Smith – vocals; Brix Smith –
guitar, vocals; Craig Scanlon – guitar; Steve
Hanley – bass; Paul Hanley – drums; Karl
Burns – drums.

PROGRAMME: *Saturday Live*
BROADCAST live to air 29 September 1984
UNR. Copped It
UNR. Elves
UNR. Fortress
UNR. Marquis Cha-Cha
Produced by Mark Radcliffe, engineered by
Ted de Bono. Mark E Smith – vocals; Brix
Smith – guitar, vocals; Craig Scanlon – guitar;
Steve Hanley – bass; Paul Hanley – drums;
Karl Burns – drums.

PROGRAMME: John Peel #8
RECORDED: 14 May 1985
FIRST BROADCAST: 3 June 1985
UNR. Couldn't Get Ahead
8502. Spoilt Victorian Child
8503. Gut Of The Quantifier
8504. Cruiser's Creek
Produced by Mark Radcliffe, engineered by
Mike Walters. Mark E Smith – vocals; Brix
Smith – guitar, vocals; Craig Scanlon – guitar;
Steve Hanley – bass; Simon Rogers – guitar,
keyboards; Karl Burns – drums.

PROGRAMME: John Peel #9
RECORDED: 29 September 1985
FIRST BROADCAST: 7 October 1985
UNR. L.A.
UNR. The Man Whose Head Expanded
8520. What You Need
UNR. Faust Banana
Produced by Dale Griffin, engineered by Mike
Engles. Mark E Smith – vocals; Brix Smith –
guitar, vocals; Craig Scanlon – guitar; Steve
Hanley – bass; Simon Rogers – guitar,
keyboards; Karl Burns – drums.
COMMENTS: The unexpected return to the
two year old 'The Man Whose Head
Expanded' offers a dramatic rearrangement of
the familiar song, in keeping with the
dynamics of the then-current live version.

PROGRAMME: John Peel #10
RECORDED: 29 June 1986
FIRST BROADCAST: 9 July 1986
UNR. Hot Aftershave Bop
UNR. R.O.D.
UNR. Gross Chapel – British Grenadiers
UNR. U.S. 80's-90's
Produced by Dale Griffin, engineered by Mike
Engles. Mark E Smith – vocals; Brix Smith –

guitar, vocals; Craig Scanlon – guitar; Steve
Hanley – bass; Simon Rogers – guitar,
keyboards; Karl Burns – drums.

PROGRAMME: John Peel #11
RECORDED: 28 April 1987
FIRST BROADCAST: 19 May 1987
8706. Athlete Cured
UNR. Australians In Europe
UNR. Twister
UNR. Guest Informant
Production details unknown. Mark E Smith –
vocals; Brix Smith – guitar, vocals; Craig
Scanlon – guitar; Steve Hanley – bass; Simon
Rogers – guitar, keyboards; Simon
Wolstencroft – drums.

PROGRAMME: Janice Long
RECORDED: 13 May 1987
FIRST BROADCAST: 19 May 1987
UNR. Frenz
UNR. Get A Hotel
UNR. There's A Ghost In My House
UNR. Haf Found Bormann
Produced by Pete Watts, engineered by
Martyn Parker and Fred Kay. Mark E Smith –
vocals; Brix Smith – guitar, vocals; Craig
Scanlon – guitar; Steve Hanley – bass; Simon
Rogers – guitar, keyboards; Simon
Wolstencroft – drums.

PROGRAMME: *In Concert*
RECORDED: 25/5/87, Nottingham Rock City
FIRST BROADCAST: 25/5/87 (live)
8707. Australians In Europe
8708. Shoulder Pads
8709. There's A Ghost In My House
8710. Hey! Luciani
8711. Terry Waite Sez
8712. Fiery Jack
8713. Lucifer Over Lancashire
Produced by Phil Ross. Mark E Smith –
vocals; Brix Smith – guitar, vocals; Craig
Scanlon – guitar; Steve Hanley – bass; Simon
Rogers – guitar, keyboards; Simon
Wolstencroft – drums.

PROGRAMME: John Peel #12
RECORDED: 25 October 1988
FIRST BROADCAST: 31 October 1988
8863. Dead Beat Descendant
UNR. Cab It Up
UNR. Squid Lord
UNR. Kurious Oranj
Produced by Mike Robinson. Mark E Smith –
vocals; Brix Smith – guitar, vocals; Craig
Scanlon – guitar; Steve Hanley – bass; Marcia
Schofield – keyboards, vocals; Simon
Wolstencroft – drums.

PROGRAMME: John Peel's 50th Birthday
Party (live at Subterrania)
RECORDED: 29/8/89
FIRST BROADCAST: 30/8/89
UNR. Mere Pseud Mag Ed
UNR. I'm Frank
UNR. Arms Control Poseur
UNR. Fiery Jack
8903. Race with the Devil
UNR. Carry Bag Man
UNR. Mr. Pharmacist
Mark E Smith – vocals; Martin Bramah –
guitar; Craig Scanlon – guitar; Steve Hanley –
bass; Marcia Schofield – keyboards, vocals;
Simon Wolstencroft – drums; Kenny Brady –
fiddle.

PROGRAMME: John Peel #13
RECORDED: 17 December 1989
FIRST BROADCAST: 1 January 1990
UNR. Chicago Now
9001. Black Monk Theme Part I
UNR. Hilary
UNR. Whizz Bang (never broadcast)
Produced by Dale Griffin, engineered by Mike
Engles. Mark E Smith – vocals; Martin
Bramah – guitar; Craig Scanlon – guitar;
Steve Hanley – bass; Marcia Schofield –
keyboards, vocals; Simon Wolstencroft –
drums; Kenny Brady – fiddle.
COMMENTS: The unbroadcast, unreleased
'Whizz Bang' offered an early version of
'Butterfly 4 Brains.'

PROGRAMME: John Peel #14
RECORDED: 5 March 1991
FIRST BROADCAST: 23 March 1991
UNR. The War Against Intelligence
9101. Idiot Joy Showland
UNR. A Lot Of Wind
UNR. The Mixer
Produced by Mike Robinson. Mark E Smith –
vocals; Craig Scanlon – guitar; Steve Hanley –
bass; Simon Wolstencroft – drums; Kenny
Brady – fiddle.

PROGRAMME: John Peel #15
RECORDED: 19 January 1992
FIRST BROADCAST: 15 February 1992
9201. Return
9202. Kimble
9203. Free Range
UNR. Immortality
Produced by Dale Griffin, engineered by Mike
Engles & James Birtwistle. Mark E Smith –
vocals; Craig Scanlon – guitar; Steve Hanley –
bass; Dave Bush – keyboards; Simon
Wolstencroft – drums.

PROGRAMME: Sound City
RECORDED: 21/4/92 (Waterfront, Norwich)
FIRST BROADCAST: 21/4/92 (live)
UNR. And Therein
UNR. Blood Outta Stone
UNR. Time Enough At Last
UNR. Free Range
UNR. Idiot Joy Showland
UNR. Gentlemen's Agreement
UNR. Edinburgh Man
Mark E Smith – vocals; Craig Scanlon –
guitar; Steve Hanley – bass; Dave Bush –
keyboards; Simon Wolstencroft – drums.

PROGRAMME: John Peel #16
RECORDED: 28 February 1993
FIRST BROADCAST: 13 March 1993
UNR. Ladybird (Green Grass)
9301. Strychnine
UNR. Service
UNR. Paranoia Man In Cheap Sh*t Room
Produced by Mike Robinson, engineered by
James Birtwistle. Mark E Smith – vocals;
Craig Scanlon – guitar; Steve Hanley – bass;
Dave Bush – keyboards; Simon Wolstencroft –
drums.

PROGRAMME: Sound City
RECORDED: 7 April 1993 (Hallam
University, Sheffield)
FIRST BROADCAST: 7 April 1993 (live)
UNR. Why are People Grudgeful?
UNR. Ladybird (Green Grass)
UNR. Glam-Racket
UNR. Free Range
UNR. I'm Going to Spain
UNR. League of Bald-Headed Men
UNR. Lost in Music

PROGRAMME: Mark Goodier
RECORDED: 1 May 1993
FIRST BROADCAST: 17 May 1983
UNR. Glam Racket
UNR. War
UNR. 15 Ways
9316. A Past Gone Mad
Produced by Paul Long, engineered by Julian
Markham. Mark E Smith – vocals; Craig
Scanlon – guitar; Steve Hanley – bass; Dave
Bush – keyboards; Simon Wolstencroft –
drums.

PROGRAMME: John Peel (repeat of Mark
Goodier Session)
RECORDED: 11 September 1993
FIRST BROADCAST: 17 May 1993
Tracks and details as above.
COMMENTS: The repeat broadcast replaced
a proposed new session scheduled to be
recorded on September 3rd, but cancelled

because the Fall were in the US.

PROGRAMME: John Peel #17
RECORDED: 8 December 1993
FIRST BROADCAST: 5 February 1994
9401. M5
UNR. Behind The Counter
UNR. Reckoning
UNR. Hey! Student
Produced by Tony Worthington. Mark E Smith
– vocals; Craig Scanlon – guitar; Steve Hanley
– bass; Dave Bush – keyboards; Simon
Wolstencroft – drums.

PROGRAMME: John Peel
RECORDED: December 8 1993, Manchester
Roadhouse
FIRST BROADCAST: 29 April 1994
UNR. M5
UNR. Behind the Counter
UNR. Ladybird (Green Grass)
UNR. League of Bald Headed Gentlemen
UNR. War
UNR. A Past Gone Mad
UNR. I'm Frank
UNR. Glam Racket
UNR. Wrong Place
UNR. The Mixer
UNR. Lost in Music
UNR. Cab Driver
UNR. Paranoia Man in Cheap Sh*t room
UNR. Free Range
Mark E Smith – vocals; Craig Scanlon –
guitar; Steve Hanley – bass; Dave Bush –
keyboards; Simon Wolstencroft – drums.

PROGRAMME: John Peel #18
RECORDED: –
FIRST BROADCAST: 17 December 1994
UNR. Glam Racket – Star
UNR. Jingle Bell Rock
UNR. Hark The Herald Angels Sing
UNR. Numb At The Lodge
Mark E Smith – vocals; Brix Smith – guitar;
Craig Scanlon – guitar; Steve Hanley – bass;
Dave Bush – keyboards; Simon Wolstencroft –
drums; Karl Burns – drums.

PROGRAMME: John Peel
RECORDED: 14/7/95 (Phoenix Festival)
FIRST BROADCAST: 14/7/95 (live)
UNR. Pearl City
UNR. Behind the Counter
UNR. Free Range
UNR. Don't Call Me Darling
UNR. Feeling Numb
UNR. Idiot Joy
UNR. Edinburgh Man
UNR. Glam Racket
Mark E Smith – vocals; Brix Smith – guitar;

Craig Scanlon – guitar; Steve Hanley – bass;
Dave Bush – keyboards; Simon Wolstencroft
– drums; Karl Burns – drums.

PROGRAMME: John Peel #19
RECORDED: 17 December 1995
FIRST BROADCAST: 22 December 1995
UNR. He Pep!
UNR. Oleano
UNR. Chilinist
UNR. The City Never Sleeps
Mark E Smith – vocals; Brix Smith – guitar;
Steve Hanley – bass; Julia Nagle –
keyboards; Simon Wolstencroft – drums; Karl
Burns – drums; Lucy Rimmer – vocals.

PROGRAMME: John Peel
RECORDED: 21/7/96 (Phoenix Festival)
FIRST BROADCAST: 21/7/96 (live)
UNR. He Pep!
UNR. U.S. 80's 90's
UNR. The Chisellers
UNR. 15 Ways
UNR. Pearl City
UNR. Powder Keg
UNR. Behind the Counter
Mark E Smith – vocals; Brix Smith – guitar;
Steve Hanley – bass; Julia Nagle –
keyboards; Simon Wolstencroft – drums; Karl
Burns – drums.

PROGRAMME: John Peel #20
RECORDED: –
FIRST BROADCAST: 18 August 1996
UNR. D.I.Y. Meat
UNR. Spinetrak
UNR. Spencer Must Die
UNR. Beatle Bones 'N' Smokin' Stones
Mark E Smith – vocals; Brix Smith – guitar;
Steve Hanley – bass; Julia Nagle –
keyboards; Simon Wolstencroft – drums; Karl
Burns – drums.
COMMENTS: An early vision of 'Spencer
Must Die' is a virtual Nagle showcase, a
synth spectacular that certainly conjures a
very different mood to the *Levitate* take.
'Beatle Bones...' is a *Strictly Personal* era
Captain Beefheart number.

PROGRAMME: John Peel #21
RECORDED: 3 February 1998
FIRST BROADCAST: 3 March 1998
UNR. Calendar
UNR. Touch Sensitive
UNR. Masquerade
UNR. Jungle Rock
Produced by Mike Robinson. Mark E Smith –
vocals; Steve Hanley – bass; Julia Nagle –
keyboards, guitar; Karl Burns – drums; John
Rolleson – backing vocals.

PROGRAMME: John Peel #22
RECORDED: 18 October 1998
FIRST BROADCAST: 4 November 1998
UNR. Bound Soul One
UNR. Antidotes
UNR. Shake-Off
UNR. This Perfect Day
Mark E Smith – vocals; Julia Nagle –
keyboards, guitar; Neville Wilding – guitar;
Karen Leatham – bass, keyboards; Tom Head
– drums; Speth Hughes – special effects.

PROGRAMME: Robert Elms (BBC GLR)
Broadcast live: 15 April 1999
UNR. Antidotes
UNR. F-'Oldin' Money/
Mark E Smith – vocals; Neville Wilding –
guitar; Karen Leatham – bass; Adam Helal –
bass; Tom Head – drums.

AND AN HONOURABLE (OR OTHERWISE) MENTION FOR...

PROGRAMME: John Peel
RECORDED: 11 October 1988
FIRST BROADCAST: 19 October 1988
Psycho Mafia
My New House
Rowche Rumble
Victoria
Performed by SONIC YOUTH with EPIC
SOUNDTRACKS. 'Sonic Youth seemed to
make a career out of being like us. They did a
Peel session of Fall stuff that was atrocious.
Being told you're responsible for Sonic
Youth... you lose sleep over that' – Mark E
Smith.

APPENDIX II
Compilations and Anthologies

Fall compilations are not like buses. You never have to wait for another one. The following details all compilations released in the UK between 1977-2002, plus major foreign releases. Please note, to better illustrate the full remit of each release, tracks are listed in chronological order, as opposed to their appearance on the actual disc.

(ALBUM) *77-Early Years-79*
7706. Bingo Master's Breakout
7707. Psycho Mafia
7708. Repetition
7815. It's The New Thing
7816. Various Times
7913. Rowche Rumble
7914. In My Area
7918. Dice Man
8001. Fiery Jack
8002. 2nd Dark Age
8003. Psykick Dancehall 2
(*) BONUS TRACKS
7704. Stepping Out
7705. Last Orders
ORIGINAL RELEASE: Step Forward SFLP6 (LP) September 1981
REISSUE – as *Early Fall 77-79*, Cog Sinister COGVP123CD (CD) with bonus tracks (*)
UK INDIE CHART PEAK: #6
COMMENTS: The first of what would one day become an epidemic of Fall compilations and, for many years, one of the most useful of them all. A straightforward gathering of the formative band's earliest single and EP releases, all of which were now out-of-print, *77-Early Years-79* would remain unsurpassed

for much of the next two decades, until the arrival of the Cog Sinister reissue.
(ALBUM) *Hip Priests & Kamerads*
8118. Lie Dream of a Casino Soul
8119. Fantastic Life
8201. The Classical
8203. Hip Priest
8204. Fortress – Deer Park
8205. Mere Pseud Mag. Ed.
8220. Look, Know
8221. I'm Into C.B.
8253. Hard Life In Country
8254. Room to Live
CD/CASSETTE ONLY BONUS TRACKS
8258. Who Makes The Nazis?
8259. Just Step S'ways
8260. Jawbone And The Air-Rifle
8261. And This Day
ORIGINAL RELEASE Situation Two SITU/SITL13 (LP, CD, cassette) March 1985
UK INDIE CHART PEAK: #4
COMMENTS: A neat corralling of (some of) the best of the Fall's Kamera label output, *Hip Priests and Kamerads* was (like *Early Fall* before it) a handy round-up of long deleted singles for anybody not looking to fork over collectors' prices – at the same time as the previously

unavailable live CD/cassette bonus tracks offered a nice incentive for those collectors as well. Unfortunately the lack of sound quality control can grow wearing after a time – the CD itself suffers from having been mastered from vinyl, an iniquity that would become all too common among future Fall reissues.

(ALBUM) *Nord-West Gas*
8418. C.R.E.E.P.
8421. Lay of the Land
8429. Disney's Dream Debased
8430. No Bulbs
8505. Couldn't Get Ahead
8506. Rollin' Dany
8509. Barmy
8511. Bombast
8514. L.A.
8516. My New House
8517. Paintwork
8518. I am Damo Suzuki
ORIGINAL RELEASE: Funf Und Vierzig (FRG) LP08 (LP) 1986
COMMENTS: Well-compiled German collection highlighting material from *The Wonderful and Frightening World Of...* and *This Nation's Saving Grace*.

(SINGLE) *The Peel Session*
7817. Put Away
7818. Mess Of My
7819. No Xmas For John Quays
7820. Like To Blow
ORIGINAL RELEASE: Strange Fruit SFPS 028 (12-inch) May 1987
UK INDIE CHART PEAK: #3
COMMENTS: The Fall's second John Peel session, from November 1978, not only captures the live chaois of the group, it refines it to a thing of genuinely listenable beauty. The versions of 'Put Away' and 'Like To Blow' are especially incandescent. See appendix I/BBC sessions

(ALBUM) *Domesday Pay-Off (Triads Plus)*
8606. Mr. Pharmacist
8610. R.O.D.
8612. Shoulder Pads #1
8613. Gross Chapel – British Grenadiers
8614. U.S. 80's-90's
8615. Terry Waite Sez
8617. Riddler!
8618. Shoulder Pads #2
8621. Hey! Luciani
8702. There's A Ghost In My House
8703. Haf Found Bormann
ORIGINAL RELEASE RCA/Big Time 6039 (USA) (CD) 1987
COMMENTS: The Americans bend *Bend Sinister* around a track listing that included

the singles 'Hey! Luciani,' 'There's A Ghost In My House' and 'Haf Found Bormann,' but somehow omitted 'Dktr. Faustus' and the doomy bass of 'Auto-Tech Pilot.' Nevertheless, there's a cohesion to the album that belies the hostility of sundry Fall-bores and, though it offers nothing that a good-looking collection won't already have, chasing it through from beginning to end presents a vision that defies you to call the Fall impenetrable.

(ALBUM) *in – Palace of Swords Reversed*
8008. How I Wrote `Elastic Man'
8013. Totally Wired
8014. Putta Block
8015. Pay Your Rates
8104. An Older Lover, Etc
8105. Prole Art Threat
8106. Fit and Working Again
8252. Marquis Cha-Cha (LP version)
8316. The Man Whose Head Expanded
8318. Kicker Conspiracy
8319. Wings
8412. Neighbourhood of Infinity
CD BONUS TRACKS
8009. City Hobgoblins
8108. Leave The Capitol
(*) BONUS CD
8212. Look, Know
8213. Tempo House
8214. I'm into C.B.
8215. Mere Pseudo Mag. Ed..
ORIGINAL RELEASE: Cog Sinister COG1 (LP) December 1987
REISSUE (1) – Cog Sinister COGVP 107 (CD) February 1998 with bonus disc (*)
UK INDIE CHART PEAK: #1
It is possible to become way too possessive of the Fall's Rough Trade era, all the more so since the Kamera and Beggar's Banquet years in particular offered far greater variety, intensity and, if you wish, subversion. However, the clatter-and-bang *sturm und drang* that was the group's calling card through this period should never be under-rated – and rarely is.
The first Cog Sinister release was also one of the finest, even after the anthologies really started to flow a decade later. A straightforward selection of early 1980s highlights is bolstered by one previously unissued live track, plus a handful of interspersed live snippets and introductions ('another dynamic entrance,' deadpans Smith in the preamble to 'Putta Block'), and a thoughtful sequencing that allows *in – Palace Of Swords Reversed* to stand as an album altogether in its own right, in the same way that old Stones and Kinks comps can often be considered 'real' LPs. In the search for a good early 80s Fall retrospective, one might be

tempted to pass this over in favour of *Totally Wired*. One would be very stupid to do so.

(ALBUM) *458489 A Sides*
8413. Oh! Brother
8416. c.r.e.e.p.
8433. No Bulbs 3
8505. Couldn't Get Ahead
8506. Rollin' Dany
8514. L.A.
8521. Cruiser's Creek
8602. Living Too Late
8606. Mr. Pharmacist
8621. Hey! Luciani
8702. There's A Ghost In My House
8714. Hit The North part 1
8801. Victoria
8852a. Jerusalem
8862. Big New Prinz
8864. Wrong Place Right Time 2
8881. Dead Beat Descendant

ORIGINAL RELEASE: Beggars Banquet BEGA111, September 1990
UK CHART PEAK: #47
COMMENTS: A straightforward summary of the Fall's Beggars-era a-sides and, in its exposure of one of the late 1980s' most reliable minor hitmakers, a revelatory document.

(ALBUM) *458489 B Sides*
8414. God Box
8417. Pat-trip Dispenser
8430. No Bulbs
8431. Draygo's Guilt
8432. Clear Off!
8434. Slang King 2
8507. Petty (Thief) Lout
8508. Vixen
8603. Hot Aftershave Bop
8604. Living Too Long

8607. Lucifer Over Lancashire
8608. Auto Tech Pilot
8622. Shoulder Pads #1B
8623. Entitled
8703. Haf Found Bormann
8704. Sleep Debt Snatches
8705. Mark'll Sink Us
8715. Hit the North part 2
8720. Northerns in Europ
8802. Tuff Life Boogie
8803. Guest Informant
8804. Twister
8865. Acid Priest 2088
8901. Cab it Up!
CD BONUS TRACKS
8415. O! Brother
8418. C.R.E.E.P.
8719. Australians in Europe
8721. Mark'll Sink Us (live)
8814. Bremen Nacht Run Out
8867. Kurious Oranj
8868. Hit the North
ORIGINAL RELEASE: Beggars Banquet BEGA116, December 1990
COMMENTS: Double LP partner to the a-sides collection. Note – the entire Fall Beggars Banquet catalogue appeared as an 8CD Japanese box set in 1996.

(SINGLE) Kimble
8101. C'n'C-Hassle Schmuck (John Peel 31/3/81) (7/12-inch only)
8401. Words Of Expectation (John Peel 3/1/84) (12-inch, CD only)
8502. Spoilt Victorian Child (John Peel 3/6/85) (12-inch, CD only)
8503. Gut of the Quantifier (John Peel 3/6/85) (CD only)
9202. Kimble (John Peel 15/2/92)
ORIGINAL RELEASE: Strange Fruit SFPS 7/0/CD 87, March 1993
COMMENTS: Pre-dating the better-known assault on 'Why Are People Grudgeful?' by less than a month, the Fall's take on Lee Perry's 'Kimble' was the first single to be released by Strange Fruit, some five years after they launched the best-selling series of *Peel Session* 12-inch EPs. 'Kimble' itself dated back to Perry's years alongside producer Joe Gibbs, originally appearing as a b-side to the Pioneers' 'Jackpot' 45, and featuring Perry in the character of the *Fugitive* TV hero of the same name. See appendix I/BBC sessions

(ALBUM) *The Collection*
7926. Intro – Fiery Jack
7928. Muzorewi's Daughter
7930. Choc-Stock
8004. Cary Grant's Wedding

8008. How I Wrote Elastic Man
8009. City Hobgoblins
8013. Totally Wired
8019. The Container Drivers
8020. Impression of J. Temperance
8022. W.M.C.-Blob 59
8103. Middle Mass
8107. Slates, Slags etc.
8108. Leave the Capitol
8109. The N.W.R.A.
8110. Hip Priest
8304. Smile
8835. A Day in the Life
8320. Medical Acceptance Gate
ORIGINAL RELEASE: Castle CCSCD365
March 1993 (CD)
COMMENTS: A reasonably adventurous
gathering of Rough Trade era cuts gains minor
kudos from the inclusion of the charity 'A Day
In The Life' recording, and the otherwise
unavailable *Perverted By Language*-era out-
take 'Medical Acceptance Gate.'

(ALBUM) *Backdrop*
7701. Dresden Dolls (*Dresden Dolls* EP)
8245. Backdrop (*Fall in a Hole*)
8252a. Marquis Cha-Cha (Kamera 7-inch)
8301. Plaster on the Hands (live)
8501. Wings (*Bugs on the Wire* LP)
8605. L.A. (*Fruitcakes and Furry Collars* LP)
8607a. Lucifer over Lancashire (*Vinyl Conflict* EP)
8609. The Man Whose Head Expanded (*Bang Zoom* tapezine)
8620. Hey! Luciani (*Sounds Showcase* EP)
8701. U.S. 80's-90's (*Head over Ears* LP)
8722. Mark'll Sink Us (*Frenz Experiment* 7-inch)
8814. Bremen Nacht Run Out (*Frenz Experiment* 7-inch)
8831. Guest Informant (*Sniffin' Rock* EP)
8903. Race with the Devil (John Peel birthday party)
9301. Strychnine (see appendix I/BBC Sessions, 1993)
— spoken word on How I Wrote *Elastic Man* / City Hobgoblins
ORIGINAL RELEASE: Pseudo Indie PILO 5CD (bootleg CD) 1994
REISSUE (1) – Cog Sinister 127 2001
COMMENTS: It's chaotic appearance
notwithstanding, *Backdrop* ranks among the
most crucial of all Fall collections, a labour-of-
love round-up of the vast majority of odds,
ends and one-offs that the band distributed
around sundry compilations during the
1980s, topped up with unreleased material
that had long since attained 'legendary' status
– 'Race With The Devil' from John Peel's
birthday party, for example, and the formative

fuzz of the 1977 demo 'Dresden Dolls.'
Marking the album's obvious genesis as a
bootleg, the sound quality is of less concern
than the scarcity of the material and, granting
the set an official reissue seven years later,
Cog Sinister made no attempt to clean things
up. They didn't need to – with less than a
handful of noticeable omissions, *Backdrop* is
the ultimate Fall rarities collection.

(ALBUM) The Receiver Label compilations
Between 1996-1997, the Trojan group of
companies released and/or licensed eight Fall
compilations drawing from a stockpile of
some 40 rehearsal, live and out-take
recordings, dating in the main between 1983-
1992 (bulked out with cuts drawn from the
Light User Syndrome studio and *15 Ways*
live albums), but with not a jot of information
as to who, what, when or even why. Across
the course of these compilations, this material
has been widely duplicated – the following
notes the contents of all eight, with each
individual compilation numbered thus:
Sinister Waltz (1)
Fiend With A Violin (2)
Oswald Defence Lawyer (3)
Oxymoron (4)
The Less You Look, The More You See (5)
Cheetham Hill (6)
Archive Series (7)
Northern Attitude – Alternative Selection (8)
7932. E.S.P. Disco (4, 8)
8316a. The Man Whose Head Expanded (techno remix) (2, 5, 7, 8)
8319a. Wings (1, 5)
8323a. Eat Y'self Fitter (6)
8328b. I Feel Voxish (2, 5, 7, 8)
8422a. Fiend With A Violin (*aka* 2 x 4) (2, 8)
8422b. Fiend With A Violin (vox) (2, 7)
8435. 2 x 4 (3, 5)
8505a. Couldn't Get Ahead (alternate) (1, 5)
8507a. Petty (Thief) Lout (2, 5)
8512a. What You Need (2, 5)
8513a. Spoilt Victorian Child (2)
8515a. Gut of the Quantifier (1, 5, 7)
8522. Bombast (live) (2, 5)
8523. Bombast (live) (3, 5, 8)
8524. L.A. (2, 5, 8)
8611a. Dktr. Faustus (1, 7)
8614a. U.S. 80's-90's (6)
8714e. Hit The North (6)
8803a. Guest Informant (3, 5, 7, 8)
8805a. Frenz (3)
8807a. Get a Hotel (3, 5, 7)
8812a. Oswald Defence Lawyer (3, 5, 7, 8)
8813a. Bremen Nacht (3, 8)
8872a. Big New Prinz (3, 5)
8878. Victoria (live) (3, 5, 8)
8879. Bad News Girl (live) (3, 5, 7)

8880. Carry Bag Man (live) 3, 5, 7)
9002c. Telephone Thing (1, 5, 8)
9006a. Bill Is Dead (4)
9007a. Black Monk Theme Part I (1, 5)
9010a. Chicago, Now! (1)
9031a. White Lightnin' (6)
9032a. Blood Outta Stone (1, 5, 7)
9042. Life Just Bounces (live) (4)
9103a. Idiot Joy Showland (6)
9104a. Edinburgh Man (1, 5, 7, 8)
9109a. You Haven't Found It Yet (live) (2, 5)
9111a. A Lot Of Wind (1, 5)
9204a. Free Range (6)
9210a. Time Enough At Last (6)
9215a. Gentlemen's Agreement (2, 5)
9216a. Married, 2 Kids (2, 5)
9218. Arid Al's Dream (1, 5, 7)
9234a. Ed's Babe (6)
9235a. Pumpkin Head Xscapes (1, 7)
9236a. The Knight the Devil and Death
(alternate) (1, 5)
9238. Birmingham School Of Business
School (live) (4)
9239. Just Waiting (live) (3, 5, 7)
9417. Glam Racket (Brix vocal)
9328. Behind The Counter (live) (4)
9544a. The Joke (6)
9557. Rainmaster (live) (4)
9601a. Interlude – Chilinism (actually 'The
Chisellers') (4)
9601b. The Chiselers (6)
9606. Das Vulture Ans Ein Nutter-Wain (8)
9607. He Pep! (4)
9608. Hostile (4, 5)
9610. Spinetrak (6)
9611. Powder Keg (4)
9611. Powder Keg (8)
9612. Oleano (6)
9613. Cheetham Hill (6)
9614. The Coliseum (6)
9615a. Last Chance To Turn Around (6)
9617. Oxymoron (9)
9617a. Oxymoron (4, 5)
9618. Secession Man (6)
9624. Pearl City (live) (4)
9628. Mr. Pharmacist (8)
9632. M5 6-7PM (8)
9637. White Lines (4)
9638. Italiano (4, 8)
9639. Birthday (1, 5)
Sinister Waltz (Receiver Records RRCD 209,
January 1996)
COMMENTS: The nightmare begins. Or so
some people would have you believe. The fact
is, if this material was ever recompiled with
attention to dates and details, it would rival
any Fall alternative anthology you could
conceive – even Backdrop lolls its tongue in
astonishment. Only the labels' clumsily
merciless permutations of the material truly

scarred the series – indeed, by 1998, Smith
himself was recommending that Fall fans
contact the Trading Standards office to
register their disapproval. 'It's been a matter
of growing concern to The Fall, and fans of
the band, that "compilations" of Fall material
have been released on a "flood the market"
type basis. Some of these recordings have
prompted complaints from fans on various
issues, such as – ill conceived track listings,
regurgitating tracks that are already available
(some of them on other Receiver
compilations), and all manner of matters of
dissatisfaction.'
Of the eight albums in the series, Sinister
Waltz is probably the best (Oxymoron runs it
close, though), especially as it includes what
might well have been one of the band's most
recent recordings. What better time, after all,
could there have been for the Fall to record
an old Jeff Lynne song (a playful, Brix-led
version of the Idle Race's 'Birthday'), than in
celebration of signing to the Electric Light
Orchestra's old label? 'Al Arid's Dream,'
hitherto available only via the Volume
fanzine, also makes a welcome appearance,
while 'Edinburgh Man' and 'A Lot Of Wind'
sound so close to their Shift-work prototypes
that one is hard-pressed to figure out what is
alternate about them. If anything.
'Telephone Thing' offers a magnificent semi-
dub mix that is considerably darker than any
of the released versions, a shade slower and
with the bass a pummelling force at the very
forefront of the proceedings. Elsewhere,
'Couldn't Get Ahead' unveils the raw, maybe-
live, maybe-rehearsal feel that would become
the series' hallmark, a mood carried on over a
raging 'Blood Outta Stone.' An instrumental
re-take of 'The Knight, The Devil and Death,'
meanwhile, visits a b-side that always
demanded more prominence that it received.
An electrifying live-ish version of 'Wings' and
a strong studio take of 'Gut Of The Quantifier'
wrap up Sinister Waltz's highlights, leaving
an album that, for all the faults that
reputation assigns it, is as enjoyable as any
collection of odds, sods and out-takes could
be.
Fiend With a Violin (Receiver Records RRCD
211 19 February 1996); reissued Sanctuary
DVD-audio DVA588099, 2002
COMMENTS: Fiend With A Violin is
dominated by material from the early Beggars
Banquet era and, again, is let down more by
shoddy research (retitling '2 x 4' as the title
track, to resemble a previously unheard Fall
song, is its most iniquitous sin) than the
actual music – although, one can barely
imagine who thought it was a good idea to

reissue *Fiend* in DVD-Audio in 2002. Unless you really need theatre-quality surround-sound to appreciate the sort-of-techno remix of 'The Man Whose Head Expanded'? 'What You Need' does little that the familiar take doesn't, although the guitar is implausibly filthier, while 'Petty Thief Lout' is more brooding than you could ever imagine – and that despite a jovial organ overdub that wholly subverts the guitars. There are also great, booming live versions of 'L.A.' and 'Bombast,' the latter prefaced by a short, but effective slap of the verbals. But what is one to make of 'You Haven't Found It Yet,' which takes what sounds like a perfectly good studio out-take, then dubs on an audience? Or maybe it is live? Of such intrigue are these albums' reputation made.

Oswald Defence Lawyer (Receiver Records RRCD 213, 1996)
COMMENTS: With its contents apparently dating wholly from the *Frenz Experiment/ Kurious Oranj* era, *Oswald Defence Lawyer* is, superficially, the least interesting of the three original compilations, although again, one cannot help but think that, had someone only taken the trouble to date/define its contents – beyond the obvious fact that much of it was recorded either live or in rehearsal/soundcheck – it could have been worth so much more. The title track sounds more like Phil Spector's 'Be My Baby' than ever before, while 'Big New Prinz' is nothing less than a swampy Gary Glitter, a walk on gilded sparkles.
To the surprise of possibly no-one whatsoever, these releases called down a hail of rage from the Fall faithful. However, further compilations drawn from the same stockpile of material continued to emerge, beginning with the utterly unambitious 3CD box set *The Other Side Of The Fall* (Receiver RRXCD 506), comprising all three original albums.

Oxymoron
ORIGINAL RELEASE: Receiver RRCD246 (CD) 1997
COMMENTS: The usual mix of live and studio recordings, *Oxymoron* concentrates on the *Light User Syndrome* era, but with excursions back into the earlier 1990s. The Brix vocal version of 'Glam Racket,' presumably taped at a soundcheck, is a genuine highlight, marred only by the boomy sound quality.
Less enticing are okay-but-better-elsewhere live versions of 'Behind the Counter,' 'The Birmingham School of Business School' and an incoherent 'Rainmaster.' 'Bill Is Dead' is even more Disconcerting, although the loose and looned feel, sprawling through feedback

and distortion, actually works well. It is difficult to tell, however, whether it's a live recording or, possibly, a rehearsal tape, a problem that also afflicts several other numbers, and is exacerbated by some unusual studio manipulation – the merging of 'The Chiselers' (mistitled 'Interlude – Chilinism') into a seriously edited live 'Life Just Bounces' is just plain unnecessary, while the aforementioned 'Bill Is Dead' segues strangely into the most unexpected track on the entire album, the 1979-vintage 'E.S.P. Disco' revision of 'Psykick Dancehall.'

Finally, two new songs, 'White Lines' and 'Italiano,' emerge as rough instrumental backing tracks, which several sources, including *Mojo*'s Pat Gilbert have suggested may not actually be by the Fall in the first place.

The Less You Look, The More You Find
ORIGINAL RELEASE: Snapper SMDCD 132, 1997

COMMENTS: Possibly the best way into the Receiver labyrinth, with 32 tracks spread across two CDs and rounding up what is generally regarded as the best of the batch.... And, had 'Glam Racket' been included, it would have been.

Cheetham Hill
ORIGINAL RELEASE: Receiver RRCD247, 1997
COMMENTS: *Cheetham Hill* apparently wrapped up Receiver's share of the archive, its contents (many from the *Light User*-era) remaining uncollected anywhere else.

Archive Series – The Fall
ORIGINAL RELEASE – Rialto Records RMCD214, 1997

COMMENTS: Certainly the least adventurous in the series, with the chief criteria for inclusion apparently being that a song ought to have appeared on at least two other collections first. In other words, precisely the kind of pointless rip-off that gives market-saturating overkill a bad name.

Northern Attitude
ORIGINAL RELEASE: Music Club MCCD350, 1998
COMMENTS: The track selection stretches from the usual suspects, through to the Fall's two conventional Trojan family releases, *The Light User Syndrome* and the *15 Ways* live album.

(ALBUM) *The Peel Sessions*
7802. Rebellious Jukebox
7818. Mess of My
8012. New Face in Hell
8102. Middle Mass
8116. Winter (Hostel Maxi)
8303. Smile
8402. 2 x 4
8504. Cruiser's Creek
8520. What You Need
8706. Athlete Cured
8863. Dead Beat Descendent
9001. Black Monk Theme Part I
9101. Idiot Joy Showland
9203. Free Range
9301. Strychnine
9316. A Past Gone Mad
9401. M5
ORIGINAL RELEASE: Strange Fruit SFRSCD048 – 1998 (CD)
COMMENTS: First proposed in 1987, and scheduled for release more or less annually for the next 11 years, there was never going to be an easy way around the long-anticipated Fall BBC sessions album, even within the already vast remit of the series. True, a single disc recounting of their 1987 *In Concert* broadcast had already appeared, various compilations and singles culled further odds and ends, and hope springs eternal that the two sessions recorded for Janice Long might eventually appear within Strange Fruit's Night Tracks subsidiary's series. As of 1998, however, the Fall had recorded 22 separate sessions for Peel, totalling some 90 tracks – enough to stuff a box set and then some. The final solution was the ultimate compromise – 17 songs, drawn from 17 different sessions, were brought together to illustrate the entire history of the Fall, from the rambunctious blur of 'Rebellious Jukebox,' cut at their first ever session in 1978, through to 'M5' from a 1994 airing. And, beyond the

sense that everything Mark E Smith does in the name of the Fall fits somehow into an overall masterplan, continuity was the first thing to go out of the window. Even tracing the group step-by-step subjects the listener to some vast swings in mood and momentum and, well-intentioned though *The Peel Sessions* certainly is, it is ultimately as frustrating as it is fabulous, a road map with all the roads rubbed out. Truly, that box set still sounds like a grand idea.
NOTE: An earlier version of the album, with a track listing compiled by Stephen Fall of *The Biggest Library Yet* fanzine, was briefly scheduled for release around 1992. It featured 'Words of Expectation,' 'C 'n' C Hassle Schmuk,' 'New Puritan,' 'The Man Whose Head Expanded,' 'Whizz Bang,' 'Rebellious Jukebox,' 'Mess of My,' 'Deer Park.' 'Winter (Hostel Maxi),' 'Australians in Europe,' 'Twister,' 'Guest Informant,' 'Athlete Cured,' 'Garden,' 'What You Need,' 'New Face in Hell,' 'Kurious Oranj,' 'Black Monk Theme,' 'A Lot of Wind.' (see also appendix I/BBC sessions)

TITLE – *Smile...It's The Best Of*
7927. Rowche Rumble (live)
7931. Spectre vs Rector 2
8005. That Man
8006. New Puritan
8007. No Xmas For John Quays
8015. Pay Your Rates
8017. New Face In Hell
8020. Impression of J. Temperance
8104. An Older Lover Etc.
8105. Prole Art Threat
8111. Totally Wired
8112. Lie Dream Of A Casino Soul
8327. Smile
8329. Tempo House
9605. D.I.Y. Meat
9607. He Pep!
9617. Oxymoron
ORIGINAL RELEASE: Castle CCSCD823 March 1998 (CD)
COMMENTS: A budget priced studio and live collection, delving into the Rough Trade catalogue, but also – confusingly – throwing in some *Light User Syndrome* cuts as well. An odd vision of 'the best of' the Fall, but certainly packing highlights a-plenty... so long as you don't own anything else.

(ALBUM) – *Live Various Years*
9317. Dead Beat Descendant
9318. Big New Prinz
9319. Why Are People Grudgeful?
9320. Free Range
9321. Shift-work

9322. Strychnine
9704. Das Vulture Ans Ein Nutter-Wain
9705. Spinetrak
9706. Behind the Counter
9707. Hip Priest
8832. Carry Bag Man
8833. Yes, Oh Yes
8834. U.S. 80's-90's
ORIGINAL RELEASE: Cog Sinister
COGVP111CD, August 1998
COMMENTS: An eclectic ragbag of sounds
and sources, hauling together two CDs worth
of performances that truly might have been
better served had entire shows been
preserved, as opposed to a random gathering
of what may or may not be the highlights.
Certainly there is little about any of these
performances that screams 'essential' at the
casual buyer, although the Munich material
packs quite a punch and the Sonics'
'Strychnine' (a song otherwise best
experienced via its appearance in a 1993
John Peel session) is certainly a latter-day Fall
classic.

(ALBUM) *A Past Gone Mad*
9006. Bill Is Dead
9038. High Tension Line
9112. Rose
9204. Free Range
9209. Birmingham School of Business School
9306. Lost in Music
9308. I'm Going to Spain
9309. It's a Curse
9313. A Past Gone Mad
9323. Behind the Counter
9412. Hey! Student
9552. Bonkers in Phoenix
9708. 10 Houses of Eve
9808. The CD in Your Hand
9901. Touch Sensitive
9903. F-'Oldin' Money

9904. Shake Off
9907. (Jung Nev's) Antidotes
ORIGINAL RELEASE: Artful ARTFULCD17,
April 1999
COMMENTS: The first of two extraordinarily
enjoyable collections rounding up the Fall's
1990s output, singling out *The Infotainment
Scam* and *The Marshall Suite* (with four
tracks apiece) as the decade's most important
releases, and *Light User's Syndrome* (with
none) apparently as its least. That, of course,
is arguable, as is the underplaying of
Extricate, rated no more deserving (one song)
than *Cerebral Caustic* and *Levitate*. However,
with the Fall's late-1990s output certainly
patchier than any other sequence of albums
in the band's history, *A Past Gone Mad* does
offer an enticing introduction to the whole.

(ALBUM) *Psykick Dancehall*

7704. Stepping Out
7705. Last Orders
7706. Bingo Master's Breakout
7707. Psycho Mafia
7708. Repetition
7815. It's the New Thing
7816. Various Times
7901. Frightened
7905. No Xmas for John Quays
7907. Industrial Estate
7912. Music Scene
7913. Rowche Rumble
7914. In My Area
7915. Psykick Dancehall
7917. Printhead
7918. Dice Man
7921. Muzorewi's Daughter
7922. Flat of Angles
7925. Put Away
8001. Fiery Jack
8002. 2nd Dark Age
8008. How I Wrote Elastic Man
8025. Middle Mass – Crap Rap
8028. That Man

8030. Male Slags
8036. Spectre vs Rector
8013. Totally Wired
8015. Pay Your Rates
8016. English Scheme
8017. New Face in Hell
8019. The Container Drivers
8105. Prole Art Threat
8106. Fit and Working Again
8108. Leave the Capitol
8118. Lie Dream of a Casino Soul
8119. Fantastic Life
8201. The Classical
8202. Jawbone and the Air Rifle
8203. Hip Priest
8204. Fortress – Deer Park
8206. Winter (Hostel Maxi) (Hostel Maxi)
8208. Just Step S'ways
8211. And This Day
8220. Look, Know
8328. I Feel Voxish
8252. Marquis Cha-Cha
8253. Hard Life in Country
8316. The Man Whose Head Expanded
8318. Kicker Conspiracy
ORIGINAL RELEASE: Eagle EEECD010
August 2000 (3CD)
COMMENTS: After six years of tat, crap and
recycled nonsense, just the thought of another
budget-priced compilation was sufficient to
induce a sleepiness verging on nausea... and
three discs worth of the stuff as well? Pass
me the Guns'n'Roses CD now.
Psykick Dancehall, then, stunned everybody.
A 3CD box set, it could match any fan's pre-
Beggars best of in every department bar the
packaging – a utilitarian booklet that tells the
story, but surrenders few details. As far as the
music goes, though, from *Short Circuit*
through *Perverted By Language*, from 'Bingo
Master' to 'Kicker Conspiracy,' from Baines to
Brix, *Psykick Dancehall* doesn't put a foot
wrong (well, maybe one – it would have been
nice to see something from the Total Eclipse
bootleg EP on board), at the same time as
reminding us why the oft-demanded prospect
of a career-spanning Fall box is unlikely ever
to materialise. If the first six years devour
three discs, how many would 25 years
consume?

(ALBUM) *A World Bewitched (The Best Of
1990-2000)*
9004. Sing! Harpy
9007. Black Monk Theme Part I
9030. Repetition (Tackhead featuring MES)
9032. Blood Outta Stone
9041. Theme From ERROR-ORROR!
9103. Idiot Joy Showland
9110. The Mixer

9208. The Legend of Xanadu
9211. Immortality
9218. Arid Al's Dream
9234. Ed's Babe
9302. Kimble
9303. Glam Racket
9302. Why Are People Grudgeful?
9314. Light – Fireworks
9327. Happy Holiday
9322. Strychnine
9326. M5#1
9402. I Want You (The Inspiral Carpets
featuring MES)
9409. Middle Class Revolt
9515. Life Just Bounces
9542. Noel's Chemical Effluence
9553. One Day
9556. The Heads Of Dead Surfers (Long Fin
Killie featuring MES)
9611. Powder Keg
9619. Plug Myself In (DOSE featuring MES)
9711. I'm a Mummy
9714. 4 1/2 Inch
9725. Seventies Night (Edwyn Collins with
MES)
9727. KB (Elastica featuring MES)
9802. Calendar (The Fall featuring Badly
Drawn Boy)
9806. The Caterer
9908. Inevitable
9918. The Real Life of the Crying Marshall
9919. Now I Wanna Be Your Dog (The Clint
Boon Experience with MES)
0001. Fistful of Credit (Mild Man Jan with
MES)
ORIGINAL RELEASE: Artful ARTFULCD35,
February 2001 (2CD)
COMMENTS: The companion volume to *A
Past Gone Mad*, still paying short shrift to
certain albums, but compensating with a
second disc that rounds up many of Smith's
90s-era collaborations with other artists,
several of which have become extremely hard
to come by in their original state. Once again,
the overall portrait is of a decade packed with
more highlights than listening to the actual
albums would suggest – but isn't that the
point of such exercises?

(ALBUM) *Totally Wired*
7927. Rowche Rumble
8004. Cary Grant's Wedding
8005. That Man
8006. New Puritan
8008. How I Wrote Elastic Man
8009. City Hobgoblins
8013. Totally Wired
8015. Pay Your Rates
8016. English Scheme
8017. New Face in Hell

8019. The Container Drivers
8023. Gramme Friday
8103. Middle Mass
8104. An Older Lover Etc.
8105. Prole Art Threat
8106. Fit and Working Again
8108. Leave the Capitol
8109. The N.W.R.A.
8110. Hip Priest
8112. Lie Dream of a Casino Soul
8116. Winter (Hostel Maxi)
8316. The Man Whose Head Expanded
8317. Ludd Gang
8318. Kicker Conspiracy
8319. Wings
8328. I Feel Voxish
8323. Eat Y' Self Fitter
8326. Hotel Blôedel
8327. Smile
8329. Tempo House
8330. Hexen Definitive/Strife Knot
ORIGINAL RELEASE: Castle 461, 2002
COMMENTS: 2CD collection concentrating exclusively on the Rough Trade years, essentially negating the usefulness of (almost) all previous label anthologies, and adding one previously unreleased cut, in the shape of an alternate 'I Feel Voxish,' similar to – but about 10 seconds longer than – that featured among the receiver label collections.

(SINGLE) *Singles Box*
8008. How I Wrote *Elastic Man*
8009. City Hobgoblins
8013. Totally Wired
8014. Putta Block
8316. The Man Whose Head Expanded
8317. Ludd Gang
8318. Kicker Conspiracy
8319. Wings
8019. The Container Drivers
8006. New Puritan
ORIGINAL RELEASE: Castle 526, 2002
COMMENTS: The Fall's four original Rough Trade 45s spread across five CD singles to take into consideration the bonus disc delivered with 'Kicker Conspiracy' – a gesture, sadly, that is completely undermined by the inclusion of the wrong versions of 'The Container Drivers' and 'New Puritan.' The original single featured John Peel session cuts; the box set simply pulls the regular released versions.

(ALBUM) *High Tension Line*
9037. Life Just Bounces
9038. High Tension Line
9103. Idiot Joy Showland
9110. The Mixer
9204. Free Range

9209. Birmingham School Of Business School
9211. Immortality
9302. Why Are People Grudgeful?
9303. Glam Racket
9310. Paranoia Man In Cheap Sh*t Room
9312. The League Of Bald-Headed Men
9313. A Past Gone Mad
9323. Behind The Counter
9324. War
9404. Hey! Student
9409. Middle Class Revolt
9532. Cloud Of Black
9542. Noel's Chemical Effluence
9545. Don't Call Me Darling
9552. Bonkers In Phoenix
9702. Spencer Must Die
9710. Hurricane Edward
9719. I Come And Stand At Your Door
9720. Levitate
ORIGINAL RELEASE: Recall/Snapper SMDCD443, September 2002
COMMENTS: Budget-priced 2CD anthology of 1990s material, redundant in the face of *A Past Gone Mad* and *A World Bewitched*, but a reasonably sound selection regardless.

(ALBUM) *Listening In – Lost Singles Tracks 1990-92*
9002a. Telephone Thing (Extended)
9002b. Telephone Dub
9016. Butterflies 4 Brains
9017. Zandra
9032. Blood Outta Stone
9033/4/5. Zagreb (Movements I & II & III)
9036. The Funeral Mix
9037. Life Just Bounces
9039. Xmas With Simon
9040. Don't Take The Pizza
9102a. So What About It? (Remix 1)
9102b. So What About It? (Remix 2)
9102c. So What About It? (Remix 3)
9234. Ed's Babe
9235. Pumpkin Head Xscapes
9236. The Knight The Devil And Death
9237. Free Ranger
ORIGINAL RELEASE: Cog Sinister COGVP132CD, November 2002
COMMENTS: The Fall released six singles during their time with Fontana (1990-93), a total of over two dozen tracks, from which *Listening In* gathers up those that did not find full release on one or other of the band's albums and/or compilations. There are a few stragglers, chiefly confined to barely altered 7-inch mixes of the a-sides, but *Listening In* nevertheless presents a fascinating, and fascinatingly askance look at the development of the band through what hindsight now portrays as their last truly stable era.

(ALBUM) *Early Singles*
7706. Bingo-Master's Break-Out!
7707. Psycho Mafia
7708. Repetition
7815. It's The New Thing
7816. Various Times
7913. Rowche Rumble
7914. In My Area
8001. Fiery Jack
8002. 2nd Dark Age
8003. Psykick Dancehall No.2
8118. Lie Dream Of A Casino Soul
8119. Fantastic Life
8220. Look, Know
8221. I'm Into C.B.

8252a. Marquis Cha-Cha
8254. Room To Live
ORIGINAL RELEASE: Cog Sinister
COGVP136CD, December 2002
COMMENTS: Ending the Fall's 25th year
with a reminder of their first four, *The Early
Singles* is, as one would expect, a
compilation of all the group's Step Forward a
and b-sides (1978-80), plus the three
Kamera 45s from 1982. The inclusion of the
all-but unissued 'Marquis Cha-Cha' confirms
the set's claim to completeness, although the
24 bit remastering only just disguises the fact
that the original master tapes remain AWOL –
the source here was vinyl.

APPENDIX III
Miscellaneous Cog Sinister Releases

Mark E Smith's own Cog Sinister label originally launched in November 1986, with a much-needed compilation of the Fall's Rough Trade era, *in: Palace Of Swords Reversed*. Over the next few years, the label's fortunes were very much tied to the Fall's own, with releases linked to whichever other company the band was signed to.

Attempts by Smith to operate Cog Sinister as an outlet for other favoured artists' work were swiftly abandoned – one reason, he complained, was the flood of demo tapes he received from bands who themselves sounded like the Fall. Of the label's non-Fall releases, Czech musician Phil Schoenfelt was a former associate of Marcia Schofield.

Since 1997, Cog Sinister has operated separately from the band, through the auspices of reissue specialists Voiceprint, and has maintained a solid catalogue of both unreleased archive recordings and rereleased albums.

One unfortunate caveat – the 'official' status of these releases is no guarantee of quality. Several releases, as noted below, were drawn from less-than-pristine master sources including, on one notorious occasion (the *Fall In A Hole* live album), an already poorly sourced German bootleg.

ALBUMS

COG 1 *in: Palace of Swords Reversed* (LP)
COGCD 1 *in: Palace of Swords Reversed* (CD)

COG 2 various artists: *The Disparate Cogscienti* (LP)
Features: God, John the Postman, OB Men, The Hamsters, etc

COGVP 101CD *The Legendary Chaos Tapes*
COGVP 102CD *In A Hole* (vinyl remaster)
COGVP 103CD *Live At The Witch Trials* (vinyl master)
COGVP 104CD *Perverted By Language*
COGVP 105CD *Room To Live* (vinyl master)
COGVP 106CD *Grotesque* (vinyl master)
COGVP 107CD *in: Palace of Swords Reversed* (vinyl master)
COGVP 108CD *Live To Air In Melbourne '82*
COGVP 109CD *Live In Zagreb*
COGVP 110CD *Nottingham 92*
COGVP 111CD *Live Various Years 93-97*
COGVP 112CD
COGVP 113CD *Dragnet*

COGVP 114CD *Live 1977*
COGVP 115CD *Live In Cambridge 1988*
COGVP 116CD
COGVP 117CD
COGVP 118CD *Live In Liverpool '78*
COGVP 119CD *Hex Enduction Hour*
COGVP 120CD
COGVP 121CD
COGVP 122CD *Extricate*
COGVP 123CD *Early Years 77-79* (+ bonus tracks)
COGVP 124CD
COGVP 125CD *Live in Reykjavik (Austurbae Jarbio)*
COGVP 126CD
COGVP 127CD *Backdrop*
COGVP 128CD
COGVP 129CD
COGVP 130CD
COGVP 131CD *Are You Are Missing Winner?* (CD)
COGVP 131LP *Are You Are Missing Winner?* (LP)
COGVP 132CD *Listening In (Singles 1990-2001)*
COGVP 133CD *Code: Selfish*

COGVP 134CD *Shift Work*
COGVP 135CD
COGVP 136CD *Early Singles (1978 – 1982)*
COGVP 137CD *In A Hole*
COGVP 138CD *Live at the Witch Trials* (+ bonus tracks)
COGVP 139CD *Room To Live* (+ bonus tracks)
COGVP 140CD *Dragnet* (+ bonus tracks)
COGVP 141CD *Hex Enduction Hour* (+ bonus tracks)
COGVP 142CD
COGVP 143CD *Live In America* (released Feb 2003)

COG SINISTER SINGLES

SIN 1 ANDREW BERRY – Unsatisfied
SIN 2 PHIL SCHOENFELT – Charlotte's Room
SIN 3
SIN 4 Telephone Thing
SIN 5 Popcorn Double Feature
SIN 6 White Lightning
SIN 7 High Tension Line
SIN 8 Free Range
SIN 9 Ed's Babe

The Fall Tribute Album

Organised by Douglas Wolk of the American label Dark Beloved Cloud, a Fall tribute album was planned for release during 1996. For a variety of reasons, it never came out. Wolk himself recalls, 'the whole thing was recorded, and a handful of the bands ended up putting out their tracks elsewhere' – God Is My Co-Pilot's 'Totally Wired' wound up on their Atavistic *Best Of*, the Wedding Present track was released as a b-side. Walk continued, 'It would've been a great tribute album, since virtually every band tried to do something radically different from the original versions of the songs. Contrary to prevailing opinion, I think it *is* possible to make a great tribute album-as-album – *Red Hot & Blue* and *Whore* both come to mind.'

PROPOSED TRACK LISTING (artist/title)
Airlines – Leave The Capitol
Alan Smithee – Prole Art Threat
Bugskull – There's A Ghost In My House
Dustdevils – Big New Prinz
Eeyore Powertool – Copped It
Ferret – Stephen Song
Fifth Column – No Xmas For John Quays
Fire in the Kitchen – I Feel Voxish
Fly Ashtray – Joker Hysterical Face
Gamma Rays – Look, Know
Garden Gnomes – Bug Day
Giant Mums – Last Orders
God is my Co-Pilot – Totally Wired
Jowe Head – Two Steps Back
Jupiteria – Edinburgh Man
Lid – Telephone Thing
Lovefish – Fantastic Life
Nipple – Hilary
Nothing Painted Blue – The Steak Place
Number – Your Heart Out
Smack Dab – I am Damo Suzuki
Television Personalities – Bingo Master's Break-out
Uncle Wiggly – Papal Visit and/or Winter
Versus – The Classical
VPN – ROD
Wedding Present – Jumper Clown (Marc Riley & the Creepers)
Wingtip Sloat – Mark E Smith and Brix (Barbara Manning)

The Covers Collection

An at-a-glance guide to the original/easiest sources for original versions of the Fall's studio, session and best-known live covers.

A Day In The Life – the Beatles (LP *Sgt Pepper's Lonely Hearts Club Band* 1967)
African Man – Iggy Pop (LP *New Values* 1979)
Beatle Bones n Smokin' Stones – Captain Beefheart (LP *Strictly Personal* 1968)
Black Monk Theme *aka* I Hate You – The Monks (LP *Black Monk Time*, 1966)
Black Night – Deep Purple (single 1970)
F'Oldin' Money – Tommy Blake (single 1959)
Gotta See Jane – R Dean Taylor (single 1968)
I'm a Mummy – Bob McFadden (compilation *Incredibly Strange Music Vol 2*)
I'm Going To Spain – Steve Bent (compilation *The World's Worst Record*)
I'm Not Satisfied – Mothers of Invention (LP *Freak Out* 1967)
Jet Boy – New York Dolls (LP *New York Dolls* 1974)
Jungle Rock – Hank Mizell (single 1958)
Junkman – Groundhogs (LP *Split* 1971)
Just Waiting – Hank Williams (as Luke The Drifter) (single 1951)
Kimble – Lee Perry (single 1967)
Last Chance To Turn Around – Gene Pitney (single 1965)
Legend of Xanadu – Dave Dee, Dozy, Beaky, Mick & Tich (single 1968)
Lost In Music – Sister Sledge (single 1979)
Louie Louie – Richard Berry (single 1957)
Mr Pharmacist – the Other Half (single 1968)
Oh, How To Do Now – the Monks (LP *Black Monk Time*, 1966)
Popcorn Double Feature – the Searchers (single 1967)
Race With The Devil – Gene Vincent (single 1956)
Rollin' Dany – Gene Vincent (LP *Gene Vincent Rocks & The Blue Caps Roll* 1958)
Shut Up – the Monks (LP *Black Monk Time*, 1966)
Stay Away (Old White Train) – Johnny Paycheck
Strychnine – the Sonics (LP *Here Are The Sonics* 1965)
There's A Ghost In My House – R Dean Taylor (single 1974)
This Perfect Day – the Saints (LP *Eternally Yours* 1978)
Victoria – the Kinks (single 1970)
War – Henry Cow (LP *In Praise Of Learning* 1975)
White Lightning – the Big Bopper (LP *Chantilly Lace* 1958)
Why Are People Grudgeful? – the Pioneers (single 1968)

APPENDIX IV
Directory of Former Members

BAINES, UNA (keyboards 1976 – spring 1978)
'Sod Mo Tucker, Una Baines is the new heroine' – Julian Cope.

Founding member of the Fall, and the originator of the Snoopy piano sound that became so integral to their early presence. Silent following her departure from the Fall, she resurfaced in 1979 when she and boyfriend MARTIN BRAMAH formed the Blue Orchids. Following the couple's marriage, she worked briefly with a new band, the Fates, before the birth of their first child. The pair briefly reformed the Blue Orchids in 1985.

SELECTED DISCOGRAPHY
BLUE ORCHIDS
45 Disney Boys/After The Flood (Rough Trade) 1980
45 Work/The House That Faded Out (Rough Trade) 1981
LP *The Greatest Hit (Money Mountain)* (Rough Trade) 1982
EP *Agents Of Change* (Rough Trade) 1982
45 Sleepy Town/Thirst (Racket) 1985

THE FATES
LP *Furia* (Taboo) 1982

BENNETT, MIKE (backing vocals January-October 1996)
Producer of the Fall's *Light User Syndrome*

album, Bennett has also written and produced for Ian Brown ('Golden Gaze'), the Muppets (!), Bananarama and the Utah Saints, and handled a number of reggae remix projects. One half of the Trance Visionary project with former Wishbone Ash's Andy Powell, he also wrote and directed the acclaimed *All Cloned Up* stage show.

BIRTWISTLE, SPENCER (drums November 2000-October 2001)
A founding member, in 1985, of Manchester indie band Laugh, Birtwistle was also active in the studio, engineering Madchester also-rans World Of Twist's 1990 single 'The Storm' among other things. (Coincidentally, 'The Storm' appears immediately beforehand the almost-Fall's 'Theme From ERROR-ORROR' on the 1990 compilation album *Home*). Laugh became Intastella in 1991 following the arrival of vocalist Stella Gray. Since departing the Fall, he has continued to work alongside the now solo Stella. JULIA NAGLE, with whom he'd played in an early 1980s band, introduced Birtwistle to the Fall.

SELECTED DISCOGRAPHY
LAUGH
EP *Take your Time Yeah* (Debris) 1986
45 Paul McCartney/Come On (Remorse) 1987
45 Time To Lose It/Time To Abuse It (Remorse) 45
LP *Sensation* (Sub Aqua) 1988

EP *Sensation #1* (Sub Aqua) 1988

INTASTELLA
45 Dream Some Paradise/Some Dreams
(MCA) 1991
45 People/Bendy (MCA) 1991
LP *And The Family Of People* (MCA) 1991
45 Century/Strawberry Jam (MCA) 1991
EP *Drifter* (with Shaun Ryder) (Planet 3)
1993
EP *In The Night* (Planet 3) 1995
LP *What You Gonna Do* (Planet 3) 1995
EP *Grandmaster* (Planet 3) 1996

STELLA
EP *Now and Then I Get High* (Phenomenon)
2001

BLANEY, ED (guitar July 2001-summer 2002)
The Fall's manager and occasional musician
throughout his two-year tenure with the group.

BRAMAH, MARTIN (guitar 1976 – May 1979, May 1989-August 1990)
Founding member who was originally the
Fall's singer. Left in 1979 to form the Blue
Orchids with UNA BAINES, establishing
themselves as one of the better acts on the
post-Punk club circuit both in their own right
and across a stint spent working as Nico's
backing band. Bramah and Baines married in
1982 and placed the band on hiatus, before
reforming in 1985 for a one-off single, 'Sleepy
Town,' released on TONY FRIEL's co-operative
Racket label. Bramah next linked with KARL
BURNS (and his wife Carrie) in Thirst, named
for the final Blue Orchids b-side. He turned
down an offer to become lead vocalist with
the infant Inspiral Carpets, before returning to
the Fall in 1989 to replace Brix Smith.
Sacked alongside MARCIA SCHOFIELD during
the Australian tour in 1991, he re-formed The
Blue Orchids with former Smiths/Adult Net
guitarist Craig Gannon and a guest appearance
from Schofield. With a changing line-up,
Bramah maintained the group until 1995,
recording a second album, *Dark Matter* aka
The Sleeper. It was never issued and the band
split that same year. Bramah himself came
close to rejoining the Fall in 1998.

SELECTED DISCOGRAPHY
BLUE ORCHIDS
45 Disney Boys/After The Flood (Rough
Trade) 1980
45 Work/The House That Faded Out (Rough
Trade) 1981
LP *The Greatest Hit (Money Mountain)*
(Rough Trade) 1982
EP *Agents Of Change* (Rough Trade) 1982
45 Sleepy Town/Thirst (Racket) 1985

THIRST
EP *Riding The Times* (Rough Trade) 1987

BLUE ORCHIDS
45 Diamond Age/Moth (As Is) 1991
LP *A View From The City* retrospective
(Playtime) 1991
EP *Secret City* (Authentic – unreleased)
1992
LP *A Darker Bloom* retrospective (Cherry Red)
2002

BROMLEY, ADAM (see HALAL, ADAM)

BROWN, JOHNNIE (bass Jan – spring 1978)
Short-lived stand-in, who designed the sleeve
for the 'Bingo Master's Break-out" single.

BURNS, KARL (drums June 1977–February 1979, May 1981–May 1986, January 1993–April 1998)
The Fall's second drummer, replacing the
mysterious Dave, was a former member of
Nuclear Angel, alongside TONY FRIEL.
According to Mark E Smith, Burns' entire
career since then seems to have been divided
between playing with the Fall and planning to
give up music. However, he joined Friel in an
early incarnation of ex-Buzzcock Steve
Garvey's Teardrops in late 1979 and was
briefly on board John Lydon's Public Image
Ltd, where he replaced Richard Dudanski.
However he neither recorded nor gigged with
the group. The following year, Burns was
credited among the conspirators behind John
Cooper Clarke's *Snap Crackle And Bop*
album. 1985 saw him working alongside
MARTIN BRAMAH in the band Thirst.

BUSH, DAVE (keyboards August 1991-November 1995)
A former drummer who gravitated to
keyboards once he started recording his own
dance music at home, Bush was a member of
the Fall's road crew when he first suggested
Smith allow him to do some programming for
the band – a move which, once Smith agreed,
was regarded with some hostility by the
band's following. A member of the Fall for four
years, Bush quit in November 1995 and, the

following spring, was confirmed as Elastica's new keyboard player. It was Bush who introduced Smith to that band, paving the way for Smith's contributions to their comeback EP in 1999. Shortly before Elastica's October 2001 split, Bush released a solo album.

SELECTED DISCOGRAPHY
ELASTICA
EP *Elastica* (Deceptive) 1999
LP *The Menace* (Deceptive) 2000
45 The Bitch Don't Work/No Good (Wichita) 2001

DAVE BUSH AND FOOD
LP *The Big One* (The Orchard) 2001

CROOKS, TOMMY (guitar August 1997-April 1998)

Scottish artist who first entered the Fall's orbit as the (uncredited) painter whose work helped decorate the *27 Points* album. Having proiginally applied for the guitarist slot following CRAIG SCANLON's departure, he was eventually employed as the replacement for BRIX SMITH.

His time with the Fall ended, alongside KARL BURNS and STEVE HANLEY on the spring 1998 US tour.

This trio promptly formed Ark – however, Crooks departed following early rehearsals, since when he has returned to his artwork.

DAVE (drums, May 1977)

The Fall's first drummer, present for their first four shows in 1977, the historically surname-less Dave is otherwise best remembered for his staunchly Conservative beliefs, and the one stab at songwriting that he offered to the group, the pro-Thatcher prophecy of 'Landslide Victory.'

DAVIS, STEVE (congas, percussion – spring 1978, spring 1980)

Introduced to the Fall by then-manager Kay Carroll, Davis added congas to the band's first Peel session in 1978. He reappeared in 1980 while a member of the Gong/Can covers band Mushroom Tango, when Smith asked him to stand-in on the band's forthcoming Dutch tour. Today, Davis runs a samba school.

ERIC ? (bass – spring 1978)

A former member of John Cooper Clarke's Curious Yellows, the frequently revolving line-up that backed the Salford poet at many 1977-era shows, and also appear on his *Innocents* EP. (Eric remains mysteriously and, perhaps, dole-office-defyingly surnameless on that record's credits as well.) According to Clarke himself, the band was so-named because they always had hepatitis.

FANNING, B (guitar July-October 2001)

Strangely obscure stand-in!

FERRET (bass – spring 1978)

'An oily little beast,' recalled Marc Riley, and one that was dismissed after he stopped playing mid song to light a cigarette.

FRIEL, TONY (bass 1976 – December 1977)

Founder member, having previously played with the metal band Nuclear Angel alongside KARL BURNS. Departed the Fall in December 1977 to form the Passage with Manchester Musicians Collective mainstay Dick Witts. (The *NME Book of Modern Music* (1978) also records an early, shortlived union with the formative Magazine.) Friel also recorded as Contact with another MMC member, Duncan Prestbury, a project that remained in operation even after Friel departed the Passage, following the release of the band's debut album.

Again alongside Burns, Friel was briefly involved with ex-Buzzcock Steve Garvey's Teardrops during 1979-1980, but spent much of the next 20 years playing in semi-professional R&B bands, while operating the independent Racket label, where he briefly reunited with MARTIN BRAMAH and UNA BAINES in 1985. He is now a member of the Woodbank Streetband.

SELECTED DISCOGRAPHY
CONTACT
EP *Future/Past* (Object 1979)

THE PASSAGE
EP *New Love Songs* (Object 1978)
EP *About Time* (Object 1979)
LP *Pindrop* (Object 1980)
45 Devils and Angels/Watching You Dance (Night & Day 1981)

HACKETT, ANDY (guitar May-August 1997)

Another strangely obscure stand-in!

HALAL, ADAM (bass December 1998-December 2000)

He arrived from nowhere and, sadly, appears

to have returned there.

HANLEY, PAUL (drums June 1980 – June 1986)

Younger brother of STEVE HANLEY, Hanley was just 15 when he joined the Fall. Silent following his departure from the Fall, he resurfaced in 1998 alongside his brother in a new band, Ark.

HANLEY, STEVE (bass June 1979 – April 1998)

Brother of PAUL HANLEY. One of the longest serving of all Fall members, Hanley's first band of note was the Sirens, alongside MARC RILEY and CRAIG SCANLON and Fast Cars frontman Steven Murray. Hanley and Scanlon alone went on to Staff 9, before they were recruited to the Fall. Hanley departed following the spring 1998 US tour and initially intended launching his own band, Ark, alongside fellow departing members KARL BURNS and TOMMY CROOKS. A six song CD was reportedly ready for immediate release, but the line-up fizzled swiftly, and Hanley redesigned the group around brother Steve before Ark finally released their debut album.

SELECTED DISCOGRAPHY
ARK
LP *Brainsold* (Urban Pyramid) 2002

HEAD, TOM (drums August 1998-October 2000)

The younger brother of one of Smith's friends, Tom Head (aka Murphy) was recruited after Smith heard a tape he made.

LEATHAM, KAREN (bass August 1998-1999)

A founder member of the Oldham based Wonky Alice, Leatham was also a member of former Chameleons' vocalist Mark Burgess' highly-acclaimed Sons of God touring outfit (alongside Wonky's Yves Altana). Following her departure from the Fall, Leatham was involved in a Wonky Alice reunion.

SELECTED DISCOGRAPHY
WONKY ALICE
EP *Insects and Astronauts* (Pomona) 1991
EP *Sirius* (Pomona) 1991
LP *Atomic Raindance* (Pomona) 1993
EP *Atom* (Pomona) 1993

MARK BURGESS & THE SONS OF GOD
LP *Manchester 1993* (Pivot) 1994

LEIGH, MIKE (drums February 1979 –June 1980)

Awesome drummer, recruited from (and, eventually, despatched back to) the rock'n'roll revival circuit.

METHAN, KATE (drums April 1998)

American-born drummer with Polythene, recruited as stand-in drummer following the disastrous 1998 US tour.

MILLNER, DAVE (drums November 2001-present)

MURPHY, THOMAS (see HEAD, TOM)

NAGLE, JULIA (keyboards December 1995-July 2001)

A key member of the Fall throughout the turmoil of the late 1990s. Although never regarded by fans as one of the most natural musicians/performers Smith ever worked with, her distinctive keyboards and writing frequently ranked among the era's highpoints.

PAWLETT, YVONNE (keyboards spring 1978 – May 1979)

Still teenaged when she joined the Fall, Pawlett apparently relocated to Poland to work as a DJ following her departure from the band. Apparently.

PRITCHARD, BEN (guitar January 2001 – present)

RILEY, MARC (bass, guitar, keyboards summer 1978 – November 1982)

Ex-Sirens, where he played alongside CRAIG SCANLON and STEVE HANLEY, Riley was still in his teens when he joined the Fall. Sacked in 1982, he promptly formed the distinctly Fall-inflected Creepers, signing to In Tape, a label formed by manager (and Creepers keyboard player) Jim Khambatta. Yeah Yeah Noh, Terry & Gerry and SIMON WOLSTENCROFT's Weeds were also on the label.

Critical favourites for much of the mid-1980s, the original Creepers petered out around 1985, but a new line-up kept the flag flying until 1988, when Riley rechristened them The Lost Soul Crusaders. When that folded, Riley moved into radio, eventually re-emerging as Lard, and co-hosting a successful Radio One show with Mark Radcliffe.

SELECTED DISCOGRAPHY
MARC RILEY & THE CREEPERS
45 Favourite Sister/Carry Mi Card (In Tape) 1983
45 Jumper Clown/Violin (in Tape 1984
EP *Creeping At Maida Vale* (In Tape) 1984
LP *Cull* retrospective (In Tape) 184
45 Polystiffs/Railroad (In Tape) 1984
LP *Gross Outs* (In Tape) 1984
EP *Shadow Figure* (In Tape) 1984
LP *Fancy Meeting God* (In Tape) 1985
EP *4 As from Maida Vale* (In Tape) 1985
LP *Warts'n'All – Live In Amsterdam* (In Tape) 1985
45 Baby's On Fire/Another Song About Motorbikes (In Tape) 1986
LP *Miserable Sinners* (In Tape) 1986
EP *Brute* (Red Rhino) 1987
LP *Rock'n'Roll Liquorice Flavour* (Red Rhino) 1988

THE SHIREHORSES (with Mark Radcliffe)
LP *The Worst Album In The World... Ever* (Columbia) 1997
LP *Our Kid Eh?* (Columbia) 2001

RIMMER, LUCY (backing vocals December 1995-October 1996)
Distinctive addition to the *Light User Syndrome* era.

ROGERS, SIMON (keyboards, bass June 1985 – December 1986)
As well known as a producer and remixer as he is a musician, Rogers was originally recruited to Adult Net, before becoming largely responsible for the sea-changes wrought on the Fall's mid-1980s (and beyond) sound. A former member of the panpipes-led Incantation, he is now a regular on sundry Ministry of Sound dance/electro collections, often appearing alongside such electro maven as Sasha & Digweed, Dave Seaman and Paul Oakenfeld. He has also worked with Peter Murphy (*Love Hysteria* and *Deep),* Boy George *(Martyr Mantras)*, Terry Hall *(Home)* and more.

SCANLON, CRAIG (guitar June 1979 – November 1995)
Ex-Sirens, alongside MARC RILEY and STEVE HANLEY. Scanlon and Hanley then formed Staff 9, from whence they were recruited to the Fall in 1979. A member of the band for the next 16 years, before departing.

SCHOFIELD, MARCIA (keyboards May 1987-August 1990)
Brooklyn born Schofield left the New York post Punk underground in the early 1980s (the 1981 *White Column Noise Festival Tape* captures her in action alongside the Swans, Lydia Lunch, Sonic Youth and others), moving to London with Czech musician Phil Schoenfelt, to form Khmer Rouge. A musical successor to Gang of 4, the band cut an EP with producer John Leckie shortly before he launched his own relationship with the Fall. (Schoenfelt later issued a solo single on Mark E Smith's Cog Sinister label.)

She also recorded with Lynn Todd, Barry Adamson (during his 'Man With The Golden Arm' period), Barkmarket and US Ape. She came to the Smiths' attention after Khmer Rouge opened for the Fall in early 1985 – Schofield would go on to work with both the Fall and Brix's Adult Net. Alongside MARTIN BRAMAH, she was dismissed from the band during the 1990 Australian tour. Since that time, she has worked with Bramah's reformed Blue Orchids and, again, Adamson, among others.

SELECTED DISCOGRAPHY
KHMER ROUGE
EP *City Primeval* (Vision) 1985

KID CONGO POWERS & MARCIA SCHOFIELD
EP *Cat Tabu* (RTD 1987)

SMITH, BRIX (guitar, vocals September 1983 – May 1989, August 1994-October 1996)
The first Mrs Mark E Smith was born in Los Angeles, attended college in Vermont, and

finally moved to Chicago in search of a record deal with her band Banda Dratzing. There she met Smith in spring 1983, returning to the UK with him and marrying that same year. A member of the Fall until the couple broke up during 1989, Brix also maintained a parallel career with her own Adult Net, cutting four great singles (and an unreleased LP) during 1985-86. She revived the band shortly before departing the Fall, rerecording much of the abandoned album as *The Honey Tangle*, but with little success. She broke up the group in 1990.

A debilitating struggle with carpal tunnel syndrome sent her back to Chicago for nine months of treatment; recovered, she toured with Susannah Hoff's latest incarnation of the Bangles, before coming close to joining Courtney Love's Hole in 1994. A musical reunion with Mark E Smith, however, saw her rejoin the Fall instead, remaining on board for the next two years. Since departing, Smith has maintained a low profile, although a handful of singles, a collaboration with Future Pilot AKA, and a great version of 'Rock'n'Roll Nigger' on the Patti Smith tribute *Doppelganger* testify to her continued vitality.

SELECTED DISCOGRAPHY
ADULT NET
45 Incense and Peppermints/Searching For The Now (Beggars Banquet) 1985
45 Edie/Get Around (Beggars Banquet) 1985
45 White Night/Naughty Of Me (Beggars Banquet) 1986
45 Waking Up In The Sun/Remember (Walking In The Sand) (Beggars Banquet) 1986
45 Take Me/Sea Of Rain (Fontana) 1989
45 Where Were You/Over The Rover (Fontana) 1989
LP *The Honey Tangle* (Fontana) 1989
45 Waking Up In The Sun/August (Fontana) 1989

BRIX E SMITH
45 Happy Unbirthday (Strangelove) 1997
45 Hurdy Gurdy Man (Nettwerk)

SMITH, ELENA (keyboards January 2002-present)

WATTS, JIM (bass January 2001-present)

WILDING, NEV (guitar October 1998-December 2000)

WOLSTENCROFT, SIMON (drums June 1986-August 1997)
'Funky Si' Wolstencroft's first band, at school in Altrincham was the Patrol, alongside future Stone Roses John Squire and Ian Brown. For around a year, 1981-82, he was a member of Freaky Party, the pre-Smiths union of guitarist Johnny Marr and Andy Rourke, as they pursued a Britfunk hybrid of A Certain Ratio and Grandmaster Flash. One (unreleased) demo was recorded by the trio, 1981's 'Crak Therapy.'

Wolstencroft departed Freaky Party shortly after the arrival of vocalist Morrissey, confessing later, 'I looked on [him] as being old school, miserable Manchester and I wasn't impressed enough to jack everything in for that.' A year later, he came close to rejoining the band during a period when his replacement, Mike Joyce, looked like he wasn't going to work out. However, it didn't happen and in 1984, Wolstencroft linked with future Smiths/Adult Net guitarist Craig Gannon in ex-Special Terry Hall's infant Colour Field, appearing with them on their legendary *The Tube* showcase.

From there, he moved onto the Weeds, formed with Johnny Marr's best friend, Andrew Berry. The band cut one single for Marc Riley & the Creepers' In Tape label, and toured the UK with the Fall in spring 1986. He was recruited to the headliners months later. Since departing the Fall, Wolstencroft has continued to collaborate with Smith.

SELECTED DISCOGRAPHY
THE WEEDS
45 China Doll/Crazy Face (In Tape) 1985

APPENDIX V
Tape-ography

No full accounting of every live show the Fall have played has – or, likely, will – ever be published, with attempts at compiling one generally confined to shows either advertised/reviewed in the music press, or preserved on the several hundred live tapes circulating the Fall underground.

The following is no more complete than any other, and was based in a very large part on that compiled for the Fallnet website (see bibliography). Other material was drawn from *Punk Diary* and *Post-Punk Diary* by George Gimarc, Pollstar Online and individual issues of UK, European and US magazines.

1977
May 2?/9?/16?/23?/30? 1977 Manchester Musicians Collective, King Street.

June 3 1977 STUFF THE JUBILEE festival, the Squat Club, Devas Street, Manchester (+ the Drones, Warsaw, the Worst, the Negatives)

June 25 1977 ROCK AGAINST RACISM benefit, North East London Polytechnic, London (+ the Verbals, the Buzzcocks)

July 4 1977 The Vortex, London (+ John Cooper Clarke, the Buzzcocks, Johnny Thunders & the Heartbreakers)

July 22 1977 Hulme Labour Club, Manchester (+ the Buzzcocks)
August ? 1977 The Ranch, Manchester
September 6 1977 Barbarella's, Birmingham (+ the Worst, the Buzzcocks)

October 2 1977 Electric Circus, Manchester Source of live mini-LP *Short Circuit: Live at the Electric Circus.*

October 4 1977 The Marquee, London (+ the Buzzcocks)
October 28 1977 Rafters, Manchester (+ Magazine)
November 13 1977 Band on the Wall, Swan Street, Manchester
November 18 1977 Eric's, Liverpool (+ the Toilets, the Buzzcocks)
December 16 1977 St. John's College, Manchester (+ Manicured Noise, the Elite)
December 17 1977 Eric's, Liverpool (+ Pentration)

December 23 1977 Stretford Civic Centre (+ John Cooper Clarke, John the Postman) Source of live CD *Live 77.*

1978
January 13 1978 Huddersfield (+ The Doll, The Prefects, Sham 69)
March 3 1978 Rafter's, Manchester (+ Wayne County and the Electric Chairs)
April 7 1978 Eric's, Liverpool
May 7 1978 Greyhound, Croydon (+ Siouxsie and the Banshees)
June 25 1978 Band on the Wall, Manchester (+ Spherical Objects)

July 14 1978 UMIST, Manchester (+ the
Rich Kids)
July 23 1978 Deeplyvale Free Festival
July 28 1978 Eric's, Liverpool
August ? 1978 Band on the Wall,
Manchester
August 20 1978 Lyceum, London (+
Penetration, Ed Banger, Punishment of
Luxury)
August 21 1978 Tower Club, Oldham
August 22 1978 Mr. Pickwick's, Liverpool
Source of the live CD *Liverpool '78.*
September 8 1978 Marquee, London
September 22 1978 Harp Lounge, Belfast
September 25 1978 Music Machine, London
(+ Chelsea, the Snivelling Shits)
September 29 1978 The Factory,
Manchester (+ Chelsea)
October 5 1978 Kelly's, Manchester (+ the
Distractions, Militant Frank)
October 21 1978 Polytechnic, Manchester
October 30 1978 Band on the Wall,
Manchester (+ Rodent Enterprises)
November 3 1978 Eric's, Liverpool (+ the
Prefects)
November 21 1978 Apollo, Manchester (+ A
Certain Ratio, Grow Up)
December 2 1978 Dundee
December 7 1978 Strathclyde University,
Glasgow (+ Here & Now, Patrik Fitzgerald)
December 17 1978 Marquee, London (+
Manicured Noise)

1979
February 12 1979 Bowden Vale Youth Club,
Altrincham (two shows)
February 19 1979 Polytechnic, Manchester
February 27 1979 Lyceum, London (+
Generation X)
March 1 1979 Nashville, London (+ Staff 9)
March 17 1979 The Plough, Cheltenham
March 21 1979 Pop Club, York
March 25 1979 Lyceum, London (+ Stiff
Little Fingers, Gang Of 4, Human League, the
Mekons, the Good Missionaries)
March 30 1979 Eric's, Liverpool
April 3 1979 Barbarella's, Birmingham
April 8 1979 Sandpiper Club, Nottingham
(+ the Shapes)
April 26 1979 The Limit, Sheffield
May 9 1979 Music Hall, Aberdeen
May 10 1979 Astoria, Edinburgh
May 18 1979 Apollo, Manchester (+
Penetration, Cowboys International)
May 26 1979 Corn Exchange, Cambridge (+
Dolly Mixture, the Users)
June 16 1979 New Planet City, Lancaster
July 1979 Rochdale Technical College
July 6 1979 Eric's, Liverpool

July 20 1979 The Factory, Manchester
July 28 1979 Mayflower Club, Manchester –
Stuff the Superstars Funhouse Special
Festival (+ the Hamsters, Elti Fits, Armed
Force, the Frantic Elevators, Joy Division,
Ludus, the Liggers, the Distractions, Jon the
Postman)
July 29 1979 Marquee, London
August 6 1979 Free People's Festival,
Deeply Vale
August 9 1979 Marquee, London
August 24 1979 Funhouse, Manchester
September 1979 Futurama, Queen's Hall,
Leeds
September 1 1979 JB's, Dudley
September 15 1979 Prince of Wales
Conference Centre, YMCA Building, London
(+ Scritti Politti)
October 7 1979 London School of
Economics
October 8 1979 Eric's, Liverpool
October 24 1979 Penthouse Basement,
Sheffield
October 27 1979 Bircoats Leisure Centre,
Doncaster
Partial source of live LP *Totale's Turns.*
November 1 1979 Palm Cove, Bradford
November 2 1979 Newport Village
November 3 1979 JB's, Dudley
November 4 1979 Middlesbrough
November 7 1979 London School of
Economics
November 8 1979 Eric's, Liverpool
November 12 1979 Polytechnic, Preston
November 15 1979 Hemel Hempstead
November 16 1979 Porterhouse, East
Retford
November 17 1979 Brighton Polytechnic
November 18 1979 Marquee, London
November 22 1979 Warehouse, Preston

US TOUR
November 29 1979 Hot Club, Philadelphia,
Pennsylvania
November 30 1979 Emerald City, Cherry
Hill, New Jersey
December 1 1979 Palladium, New York
December 3 1979 The Club, Cambridge,
Mass.
December 6 1979 Madame Wong's West,
Santa Monica, California
December 13 1979 Al's Bar , Los Angeles,
California
December 14 1979 Hope Street Hall, Los
Angeles, California (+ X, the Germs)
December 14 1979 Anticlub, Los Angeles,
California

1980
UK TOUR
February 29 1980 Palm Cove, Bradford
Partial source of live LP *Totale's Turns.*
March 7 1980 MPH Building, Kings College, London (+ the Cramps)
March 18 1980 Birmingham University
March 21 1980 Electric Ballroom, London
April 17 1980 Electric Ballroom, London
May 11 1980 Finsbury Park Rainbow, London
May 14 1980 Cyprus Tavern, Manchester
May 24 1980 The Paddock, Hartlepool
May 28 1980 Beach Club, Manchester
Jun 13 1980 Effenaar, Eindhoven, The Netherlands
Jun 18 1980 ICA, London
Jun 28 1980 New Tyne Theatre, Newcastle
Jun 29 1980 Fforde Greene, Leeds
Jul 24 1980 Marquee, London
Jul 25 1980 Marquee, London
Jul 29 1980 Deeply Vale People's Free Festival (+ the Ruts, Not Sensibles, Misty, Stuffed Badgers, Distractions, Tiger Tails, Stiffs &c)

UK TOUR
September 12 1980 Cleopatra's, Huddersfield
September 27 1980 Tatton Community Centre, Chorley
October 2 1980 Polytechnic, Manchester
October 18 1980 Cork
November 1 1980 Polytechnic, Manchester
November 13 1980 Fan Club, Leeds
November 18 1980 Boat Club, Nottingham
November 19 1980 Cedar Club, Birmingham
November 21 1980 North London Polytechnic
December 11 1980 Acklam Hall, London
Source of live cassette *Live in London 1980* AKA: *The Legendary Chaos Tape – London 1980*
December 12 1980 Acklam Hall, London

1981
January 15 1981 Rafters, Manchester
January 17 1981 Sports Centre, Bolton
January 24 1981 University of East Anglia, Norwich
January 31 1981 Polytechnic, Leicester
February 5 1981 Queen Mary's College, London
February 7 1981 Cardiff University
February 20 1981 Technical College, St. Helens
February 21 1981 Brady's, Liverpool
February 23 1981 Plaza, Glasgow
February 25 1981 Paisley

February 28 1981 Sheffield University
March 17 1981 Leeds University

EUROPEAN TOUR
May 9 1981 Eksit, Rotterdam, The Netherlands
May 19 1981 Markethalle, Hamburg, Germany
May 20 1981 Jovel Cinema, Munster, Germany
May 22 1981 Alter Bahnhof, Hof, Germany
May 23 1981 SO36, Kreuzberg, Berlin, Germany
May 25 1981 Bonn, West Germany

US TOUR
May 31 1981 Oklahoma City, Oklahoma
June 3 1981 The Underground, New York (+ Fad Gadget)
June 4 1981 Maxwell's, Hoboken, New Jersey
June 5 1981 Peppermint Lounge, New York
June 6 1981 Irving Plaza, New York
June 9 1981 Bonds, New York
June 11 1981 Spit, Boston, Mass.
June 12 1981 City Gardens, Trenton, New Jersey
June 13 1981 Interferon Club, New York
June 15 1981 Mudd Club, New York
June 16 1981 Omni, Philadelphia, Pennsylvania
June 17 1981 930 Club, Washington, D.C.
June 19 1981 688, Atlanta, Georgia
June 20 1981 Antenna, Atlanta, Georgia
June 23 1981 Jimmy's, New Orleans, Louisiana
June 24 1981 Island, Houston, Texas
June 25 1981 Clubfoot, Austin, Texas
June 26 1981 Hot Club, Dallas, Texas
June 27 1981 Hot Club, Dallas, Texas
June 29 1981 El Paseo de la Luz, Santa Fe, New Mexico
July 1 1981 American Legion Hall, Phoenix, Arizona
July 2 1981 Tumbleweeds, Tucson, Arizona
July 3 1981 Los Angeles, California
July 4 1981 Al's Bar, Los Angeles, California
July 5 1981 Los Angeles, California
July 7 1981 Myron's Ballroom, Los Angeles, California (+ Blurt, the Flesheaters)
July 8 1981 Palo Alto, California
July 9 1981 The Stone, San Francisco, California
July 10 1981 Keystone, Berkeley, California
July 11 1981 The Stone, San Francisco, California
July 12 1981 Indian Center, San Francisco, California (2 shows)
July 13 1981 IBeam, San Francisco,

California
(tour also included Chicago date – apparent
source of live EP *A Part Of America Therein*).

ICELANDIC TOUR
August – 1981 Hotel Borg, Reykjavik (+ C4U)
August – 1981 Hotel Borg, Reykjavik (+ **C4U**)
August – 1981 Austerbae Javara, Reykjavik
August – 1981 unknown (+ Purkurr Pilnikk)

UK TOUR
September 4 1981 Polytechnic, Sheffield
September 30 1981 Fagin's, Manchester
October 19 1981 North London Polytechnic
October 21 1981 Xtreems, Brighton
October 23 1981 Manchester University
October 27 1981 Hofbrauhaus, Newcastle
October 29 1981 The Limit, Sheffield
October 30 1981 Northeast London
Polytechnic
October 31 1981 Totnes Civic Hall
November 1 1981 Top Rank, Plymouth
November 5 1981 Bierkeller, Leeds
November 6 1981 Imperial Cinema,
Birmingham
December 7 1981 The Venue, London (+
the Alarm)

1982
UK TOUR
March 12 1982 Polytechnic, Bristol
March 19 1982 Palm Cove, Bradford
March 24 1982 Polytechnic, Leicester
March 25 1982 Hammersmith Palais,
London
March 27 1982 Polytechnic, Manchester
April 1 1982 Night Moves, Glasgow
April 2 1982 Nite Club, Edinburgh
April 3 1982 Warehouse, Liverpool

EUROPEAN TOUR
April 10 1982 Paard Van Troje, The Hague,
The Netherlands
April 12 1982 Vera Groningen, The
Netherlands
Also one show in Belgium

UK TOUR
April 23 1982 North London Polytechnic
April 25 1982 Top Rank, Reading
April 26 1982 Scamps, Oxford
April 27 1982 Derby Hall, Bury
Source of live recordings included as bonus
discs with *Room to Live (Undiluteable Slang
Truth)* and *Palace Of Swords Reversed* CD
reissues.
April 28 1982 Blue Note, Derby
April 29 1982 Vanbrugh College, York

April 30 1982 Porterhouse, Retford
May 1 1982 Southampton University
May 2 1982 Jenkinson's, Brighton
May 3 1982 Band on the Wall, Manchester
May 4 1982 Band on the Wall, Manchester
May 5 1982 Band on the Wall, Manchester
Stated source of live recordings included as
bonus discs with *Room to Live (Undiluteable
Slang Truth)* and *Palace Of Swords Reversed*
CD reissues.
May 15 1982 666 Club, Manchester
May 19 1982 Social Club, Burnley Football
Club

AUSTRALASIAN TOUR
July ? 1982 Trade Union Club, Sydney
July 22 1982 Musician's Club, Sydney
July 29 1982 West Town Hall, Geelong
July 30 1982 Jump Club, Collingwood,
Melbourne
July 31 1982 Crystal Ballroom, Seaview
Hotel, St. Kilda, Melbourne,
August 2 1982 Prince of Wales, Melbourne
Source of live LP *Live to Air in Melbourne*.
August 5 1982 Prospect Hill, Melbourne
August 6 1982 Mt. Erica Hotel, Melbourne
August 7 1982 Crystal Ballroom, Seaview
Hotel, St. Kilda, Melbourne
August 17 1982 University of Canterbury,
Christchurch
August 18 1982 Town Hall, Christchurch
August 19 1982 Victoria University,
Wellington, New Zealand
August 20 1982 Main Street, Auckland,
New Zealand
August 21 1982 Main Street, Auckland,
New Zealand
Source of the live LP *Fall in a Hole*.
September 18 1982 Sporting, Athens,
Greece
December 2 1982 Leadmill, Sheffield
December 3 1982 Warehouse, Liverpool
December 4 1982 Manchester University
December 7 1982 Leeds University
December 9 1982 Trent Polytechnic,
Nottingham
December 12 1982 Lyceum, London
December 22 1982 Lesser Free Trade Hall,
Manchester

(incomplete)

1983
January 16 1983 Warehouse, Leeds
January 17 1983 Manhattan Club, Bradford

EUROPEAN TOUR
February 1 1983 Kino Walches, Zurich,
Switzerland

February 4 1983 Totentanz, Basel, Switzerland
February 5 1983 Lausanne, Switzerland
February 8 1983 Kombi, Amsterdam, The Netherlands
February 10 1983 Tivoli, Utrecht, The Netherlands
February 11 1983 Paradiso, Amsterdam, The Netherlands
February 12 1983 Arena, Rotterdam, The Netherlands
February 14 1983 Effenaar, Eindhoven, The Netherlands

March 21 1983 The Venue, London
Source of live recording 'Plaster on the Hands' on *Backdrop* compilation CD.
March 22 1983 The Venue, London

AMERICAN TOUR
April 4 1983 Dirt Club, Bloomfield, New Jersey
April 7 1983 Network, Island Park, Long Island, New York
April 15 1983 Danceteria, New York
April 17 1983 The Rathskeller, Boston
April 21 1983 Larry's Hideaway, Toronto, Canada
April 22 1983 Traxx, Detroit, Michigan
April 27 1983 First Avenue, Minneapolis, Minnesota
April 29 1983 Pop Shop, Cleveland, Ohio
April 30 1983 City Gardens, Trenton, New Jersey
May 4 1983 White Columns, New York Speed Trials
Source of live recordings 'Tempo House' and 'Smile' on *Speed Trials* compilation LP.

May 6 1983 Austurbae Jarbio, Reykjavik, Iceland
Source of the live CD *Austurbae Jarbio*
May 21 1983 Electric Ballroom, London (support The Smiths)

EUROPEAN TOUR
June 5 1983 Arena D, Vienna, Austria
June 10 1983 Loft Club, Berlin, Germany
June 13 1983 Markthalle, Hamburg, Germany
June 15 1983 Odeon, Muenster, Germany
July 14 1983 Tiffany's, Derby
July 15 1983 Ace, Brixton

July 27 1983 Hacienda, Manchester
Source of live recording 'Tempo House' on LP *Perverted By Language*

July 29 1983 Fforde Green, Leeds

September 4 1983 Night Club, Washington
September 21 1983 Hellfire Club, Wakefield
September 27 1983 Rock City, Nottingham
September 30 1983 North London Polytechnic
October 1 1983 Boys' Club, Bedford
October 4 1983 Buster Brown's, Edinburgh

October 15 1983 Surrey Tavern, Guildford
October 16 1983 Bowes Lyon House, Stevenage
October 19 1983 Huddersfield Polytechnic
October 22 1983 Sheffield University
October 26 1983 Concord, Brighton
October 27 1983 Concord Bar, Brighton
October 29 1983 Polytechnic, Portsmouth
November 1 1983 Madison, Middlesbrough
November 9 1983 Reading University
November 10 1983 Northeast London Polytechnic
November 12 1983 Royal Court, Liverpool
November 17 1983 Warwick University, Coventry
November 18 1983 Gala Ballroom, Norwich
November 19 1983 Leicester Polytechnic
December 8 1983 Electric Ballroom, London
December 17 1983 Hacienda, Manchester

1984
March 19 1984 Buster Brown's, Edinburgh
March 21 1984 Nite Club, Edinburgh
March 22 1984 Penthouse, Glasgow

EUROPEAN TOUR
March 31 1984 Paradiso, Amsterdam, The Netherlands
April 1 1984 Effenaar, Eindhoven, The Netherlands
April 4 1984 Alabamahalle Munich, Germany
Source of the live bootleg LP *CREEP Show*
April 5 1984 Batschkapp, Frankfurt, Germany
April 9 1984 Luxor, Cologne, Germany
April 11 1984 ICC, Hanover, Germany
April 14 1984 Odeon, Muenster, Germany

Jun 11 1984 Heaven UltraDisco, London (support The Swans)
Jun 27 1984 Loughborough University
Jun 28 1984 Surbiton Assembly Rooms
Jun 29 1984 Hacienda, Manchester
Jun 30 1984 Guildhall, Newcastle
Jul 16 1984 Rutz, Oslo, Norway
Jul 29 1984 Elephant Fayre, Cornwall (with Siouxsie & the Banshees)
August 4 1984 Brockwell Park, London
September 13 1984 Markthalle, Hamburg, Germany
September 22 1984 De Doelen, Rotterdam,

The Netherlands
October 6 1984 Woughton Leisure Centre, Milton Keynes
October 18 1984 Hacienda, Manchester
October 20 1984 Leadmill, Sheffield
October 24 1984 Dance Factory, Dundee
October 25 1984 Caley Palais, Edinburgh
October 30 1984 Lyceum, London
October 31 1984 Bristol University
November 1 1984 New Ocean Club, Cardiff
November 3 1984 Brighton Polytechnic
December 6 1984 Broadway, Louvain, Belgium
December 8 1984 Tivoli, Utrecht, The Netherlands
December 12 1984 Salle de la Cite, Rennes, France

1985
March 7 1985 Town Hall, Hammersmith, London
March 14 1985 King George's Hall, Blackburn
March 16 1985 Sunderland Polytechnic
March 17 1985 Royal Court, Liverpool

US TOUR
March 22 1985 Hollywood Palace, Los Angeles, California
March 23 1985 Oskar's Cornhusker, Azusa, California
March 25 1985 IBeam, San Francisco, California
March 26 1985 Keystone, Palo Alto, California
March 28 1985 Danceteria, New York
March 29 1985 City Gardens, Trenton, New Jersey
March 31 1985 930 Club, Washington, D.C.
April 1 1985 Agora, Columbus, Ohio
April 3 1985 Spit, Boston, Mass.
April 4 1985 Exit Club, Chicago, Illinois
April 6 1985 Peppermint Lounge, New York
Source of live recording 'Wings' on compilation *Bugs On The Wire*.

June 16 1985 Clitheroe Castle
June 19 1985 International, Manchester
July 18 1985 Underground, Croydon
July 19 1985 Mersea Island, Essex W.O.M.A.D. Festival

GERMAN TOUR
September 9 1985 Markthalle, Hamburg, Germany
September 11 1985 Schlachthof, Bremen, Germany
September 13 1985 Zeche, Bochum, Germany
September 15 1985 Batschkapp, Frankfurt, Germany

September 16 1985 Hunky Dory, Detmold, Germany

October 3 1985 Riverside, Newcastle
October 4 1985 Queen Margaret's Union, Glasgow
October 5 1985 Victoria Hotel, Aberdeen
October 7 1985 Coasters, Edinburgh
October 8 1985 Sheffield University
October 9 1985 Hacienda, Manchester
October 10 1985 Leeds Polytechnic
October 12 1985 University of East Anglia, Norwich
October 14 1985 Hexagon Theatre, Reading
October 15 1985 Rock City, Nottingham
October 16 1985 Pink Toothbrush, Rayleigh
October 17 1985 Leicester University
October 19 1985 City Hall, St. Albans
October 20 1985 Powerhouse, Birmingham
October 22 1985 Shelley's, Stoke
October 23 1985 Bournemouth Town Hall
October 25 1985 Bristol University
October 26 1985 Sussex University, Brighton
October 31 1985 Krackers, Liverpool
November 9 1985 Great Hall, Lancaster University
November 11 1985 Hammersmith Palais, London

1986
February 6 1986 Coronet, Woolwich
February 8 1986 Royal Court, Liverpool
February 10 1986 Lasers Disco, Haringay
February 11 1986 Mean Fiddler, Harlesden
February 16 1986 Underground, Croydon

US TOUR
February 27 1986 Paradise, Boston, Mass.
February 28 1986 Living Room, Providence, Rhode Island
March 1 1986 Irving Plaza, New York City
March 5 1986 9.30 Club, Washington D.C.
March 8 1986 New Century Hall, Milwaukee, Wisconsin
March 10 1986 Guthrie Theater, Minneapolis, Minnesota
March 14 1986 The Stone, San Francisco, California
March 21 1986 Lone Star Cafe, New York City
March 22 1986 Larry's Hideaway, Toronto, Canada

UK TOUR
June 5 1986 Lea's Cliff Hall, Folkestone
June 12 1986 Riverside Club, Newcastle
June 13 1986 Glasgow
July 11 1986 The Centre, Farnham Road,

Slough
July 12 1986 Town and Country, London
July 19 1986 GMex, Manchester Festival of
the 10th Summer
July 27 1986 Finsbury Park, London
August 3 1986 Sneek Festival, Sneek, The
Netherlands
August 16 1986 Waterpop Festival,
Wateringen, The Netherlands
September 6 1986 Queensway Hall,
Dunstable
September 7 1986 Albany Empire, Deptford,
London
September 8 1986 Albany Empire, Deptford,
London
Source of live recording included on sampler
Fruitcakes and Furry Collars
September 11 1986 Underground, Croydon,
London
September 13 1986 Roadmenders,
Northampton

EUROPEAN TOUR
October 8 1986 Graz, Austria
October 9 1986 Spielboden, Dornbirn,
Austria
October 10 1986 Posthof, Linz, Austria
October 11 1986 Szene, Vienna, Austria

US TOUR
October 19 1986 Roxy, Hollywood,
California 2 shows
October 20 1986 IBeam, San Francisco,
California
October 21 1986 IBeam, San Francisco,
California
October 25 1986 Ritz, New York City
October 26 1986 Revival, Philadelphia,
Pennsylvania
October 29 1986 One Step Beyond, Santa
Clara, California
October 31 1986 Amphitheatre, San Diego,
California
November 1 1986 Irvine Meadows, Laguna
Hills, California

UK TOUR
November 5 1986 Liverpool
November 6 1986 Bristol University
November 7 1986 Assembly Halls,
Walthamstow
November 8 1986 Coronet, Woolwich
November 9 1986 Powerhouse, Birmingham
November 11 1986 Folkestone
November 12 1986 Southampton University
November 15 1986 Hull University
November 16 1986 Maxwell Hall, Salford
University
November 18 1986 Nottingham

November 19 1986 Huddersfield
Polytechnic
November 20 1986 King George's Hall,
Blackburn
November 21 1986 Burton
November 22 1986 Loughton Centre, Milton
Keynes
November 24 1986 Coasters, Brighton
November 25 1986 Warwick University,
Coventry
November 26 1986 Sheffield Polytechnic
December 1986 *Hey! Luciani,* Riverside,
Hammersmith, London
December 22 1986 Free Trade Hall,
Manchester

1987
EUROPEAN TOUR
February 5 1987 Batschkapp, Frankfurt,
Germany
February 6 1987 Theaterfabrik, Munich,
Germany
February 7 1987 Theaterfabrik, Munich,
Germany
February 8 1987 Ruehrersaal, Nuremberg,
Germany
February 9 1987 Roehre, Stuttgart,
Germany
February 10 1987 Tor 3, Dusseldorf,
Germany
February 11 1987 Hanover, Germany
February 13 1987 Markthalle, Hamburg,
Germany
February 14 1987 HFT Mensa, Bremen,
Germany
Source of live recording U.S. 80's-90's on
Head Over Ears EP
February 15 1987 Metropol, Berlin,
Germany
February 18 1987 Zeche, Bochum, Germany
February 19 1987 Hunky Dory, Detmold,
Germany
February 20 1987 Kultur Fabrik, Krefeld,
Germany
February 21 1987 Paradiso, Amsterdam,
The Netherlands
February 23 1987 Weeshuis, Deventer, The
Netherlands
February 26 1987 Luxor, Arnhem, The
Netherlands
February 27 1987 Paard van Troje, The
Hague, The Netherlands
March 10 1987 Metropol, Aachen, Germany

UK TOUR
April 20 1987 International 2, Manchester
April 30 1987 Newcastle University
May 2 1987 Strathclyde University
May 5 1987 Leeds Polytechnic

May 6 1987 Keele University
May 9 1987 Leicester Polytechnic
May 11 1987 Liverpool University
May 13 1987 Astoria, London
May 14 1987 Astoria, London
May 15 1987 University of East Anglia,
Norwich
May 16 1987 Essex University, Colchester
May 22 1987 Town Hall, Cheltenham
May 25 1987 Rock City, Nottingham
Source of the live recording BBC Radio One
Live.
July 1 1987 Elland Road, Leeds (with U2)
July 25 1987 Finsbury Park, London (with
Siouxsie & the Banshees)
August 15 1987 Knopf's Music Hall,
Hamburg, Germany
August 16 1987 Biskuithalle, Bonn,
Germany
August 28 1987 Reading Festival
November 6 1987 Maxwell Hall, Salford
University
November 8 1987 Stafford University

1988
January 23 1988 Rodon Club, Athens,
Greece

UK TOUR
March 7 1988 Hummingbird, Birmingham
March 8 1988 Ritz, Manchester
March 10 1988 Exeter University
March 11 1988 Cardiff University
March 12 1988 Oxford Polytechnic
March 14 1988 Royal Court Theatre,
Liverpool
March 15 1988 Leeds University
March 17 1988 Leicester University
March 18 1988 Hammersmith Odeon,
London
March 19 1988 Corn Exchange, Cambridge
Source of the live CD Live in Cambridge
1988

EUROPEAN TOUR
April 3 1988 Grosse Freiheit 36, Hamburg,
Germany
April 4 1988 Modernes, Bremen, Germany
April 5 1988 Biskuithalle, Bonn, Germany
April 7 1988 PC 69, Bielefeld, Germany
April 8 1988 Zeche, Bochum, Germany
April 9 1988 FBZ Buergerpark,
Braunschweig, Germany
April 10 1988 Metropol, Berlin, Germany
April 12 1988 Volksbildungsheim, Frankfurt,
Germany
April 13 1988 Unterfoerhring Theaterfabrik,
Munich, Germany
April 15 1988 Fritz Club, Vienna, Austria

Source of live recording included with Sniffin'
Rock magazine June 1989/issue 9; possibly
also live LP Live Various Years.
April 22 1988 Vooruit Gonzertaal, Ghent,
Belgium
April 24 1988 Paradiso, Amsterdam, The
Netherlands

US TOUR
May 5 1988 Maxwell's, Hoboken, New Jersey
May 6 1988 Ritz, New York
May 7 1988 Chestnut, Philadelphia,
Pennsylvania
May 12 1988 The Channel, Boston, Mass.
May 13 1988 North-eastern University,
Boston, Mass.
May 15 1988 Peabody's Downunder,
Cleveland, Ohio
May 16 1988 St. Andrews Hall, Detroit,
Michigan
May 21 1988 Moore Theater, Seattle,
Washington
May 22 1988 Pine Street, Portland, Oregon
May 27 1988 John Anson Ford Theatre, Los
Angeles, California

June 11-21 1988 I Am Kurious, Oranj,
Stadsschouwburg, Amsterdam
August 17 1988 I Am Kurious, Oranj, King's
Theatre, Edinburgh
Source of live CD I Am Pure As Oranj.
August 18-20 1988 I Am Kurious, Oranj,
King's Theatre, Edinburgh
September 23-October 8 1988 I Am
Kurious, Oranj, Sadler's Wells, London
December 11 1988 Rock City, Nottingham
December 13 1988 Leeds Polytechnic
December 14 1988 Ritz, Manchester
December 15 1988 Newcastle Polytechnic
soundcheck
December 17 1988 Barrowlands, Glasgow
December 18 1988 Royal Court, Liverpool
December 20 1988 Town and Country,
London
December 21 1988 Town and Country,
London

1989
February 14 1989 Off Beat Night, Munich,
Germany
July 12 1989 Corn Exchange, Cambridge
July 13 1989 Free Trade Hall, Manchester
October 1 1989 Bradford Palace Futurama
6 Festival
October 18 1989 Music Hall, Aberdeen
November 28 1989 Philipshalle, Dusseldorf,
Germany
December 11 1989 Queen's Hall, Bradford
December 15 1989 Queen Margaret Union,
Glasgow

December 16 1989 Leadmill, Sheffield
December 18 1989 Hacienda, Manchester

1990
UK TOUR
March 1 1990 Poole Arts Centre
March 2 1990 Bristol University
March 3 1990 Coventry Polytechnic
March 6 1990 Hacienda, Manchester
March 8 1990 Liverpool University
March 9 1990 Bangor University
March 12 1990 Guildhall, Preston
March 13 1990 Leeds University
March 16 1990 Sheffield Polytechnic
March 17 1990 Barrowlands, Glasgow
March 20 1990 Hummingbird, Birmingham
March 21 1990 National Ballroom, Kilburn, London
March 22 1990 National Ballroom, Kilburn, London
March 24 1990 Essex University
March 25 1990 Trent Polytechnic, Nottingham
March 26 1990 Top Rank, Brighton

EUROPEAN TOUR
March 29 1990 Paradiso, Amsterdam, The Netherlands
March 30 1990 Polsslag Festival, Belgium
March 31 1990 Expopalis Kelcherhoef, Houthalen, The Netherlands
April 1 1990 Batschkapp, Frankfurt, Germany
April 2 1990 Biskuithalle, Bonn, Germany
April 3 1990 Zeche, Bochum, Germany
April 5 1990 Modernes, Bremen, Germany
April 6 1990 PC69, Bielefeld, Germany
April 7 1990 Docks, Hamburg, Germany
April 9 1990 Metropol, Berlin, Germany
April 10 1990 Longhorn, Stuttgart, Germany
April 11 1990 Theaterfabrik, Munich, Germany
German tour assumed source of the live CD *Live In Zagreb*.
April 12 1990 Dolce Vita, Lausanne, Switzerland
April 21 1990 Pavilion, Hanover, Germany
April 26 1990 Montmartre Elysee, Paris, France

May 14 1990 Hull University

US TOUR
May 18 1990 New Ritz, New York, New York
May 21 1990 Park Plaza Hotel, Los Angeles, California

AUSTRALASIAN TOUR
June 22 1990 East's Rugby Club, Brisbane, Australia
June 23 1990 Livid Festival, Harold Park Raceway, Sydney, Australia
June 24 1990 Canberra, Australia
June 29 1990 Old Greek Theatre, Melbourne, Australia
June 30 1990 Old Greek Theatre, Melbourne, Australia
July 5 1990 Town Hall, Auckland, New Zealand
July 10 1990 Cambridge Hotel, Newcastle, Australia
July 11 1990 Promises, Sylvania Hotel, Sydney, Australia
July 13 1990 The Venue, Dee Why Hotel, Sydney, Australia
July 14 1990 Selina's, Coogie Bay Hotel, Sydney, Australia
July 23 1990 KudanKaikan Hall, Tokyo, Japan

August 26 1990 Reading Festival
October 6 1990 Pedio Areos, Athens, Greece
October 26 1990 Waterfront, Norwich

UK TOUR
December 2 1990 Nottingham Polytechnic
December 3 1990 Fridge, Brixton, London
December 4 1990 Reading University
December 6 1990 Network, Edinburgh
December 7 1990 Strathclyde University, Glasgow
December 8 1990 The Communal Building, Bradford University
December 11 1990 Ritz, Manchester
December 12 1990 Birmingham Institute
December 14 1990 Corn Exchange, Cambridge
December 15 1990 Lancashire Polytechnic, Preston

1991
EUROPEAN TOUR
May 14 1991 Docks, Hamburg, Germany
May 22 1991 Theaterfabrik, Munich, Germany
May 23 1991 Music Hall, Frankfurt, Germany
May 24 1991 Jovel, Muenster, Germany
May 26 1991 PC 69, Bielefeld, Germany
May 27 1991 Longhorn, Stuttgart, Germany
May 28 1991 Live Music Hall, Cologne, Germany
May 30 1991 Modernes, Bremen, Germany
May 31 1991 Night Town, Rotterdam
Jun 2 1991 Metropol, Berlin, Germany
Jun 4 1991 Paradiso, Amsterdam, The Netherlands

August 2 1991 Cities in the Park, Heaton
Park, Manchester
August 20 1991 Ritz, Manchester
August 24 1991 Reading Festival

UK TOUR
December 2 1991 Coventry Polytechnic
December 3 1991 Palace Disco, Blackpool
December 8 1991 Hull University
December 18 1991 Town Hall, Stockport
December 23 1991 Town Hall, Stockport

1992
March 15 1992 Nottingham Polytechnic
Source of live CD *Nottingham 92*
March 16 1992 Leicester Polytechnic
March 17 1992 Stafford Polytechnic
March 18 1992 Manchester Academy
March 20 1992 Queen Margaret Union,
Glasgow
March 24 1992 Haigh Building, Liverpool
Polytechnic
March 25 1992 Bradford University
March 26 1992 Sheffield Polytechnic
March 29 1992 Brixton Academy, London
March 30 1992 Corn Exchange, Cambridge
April 21 1992 Waterfront, Norwich BBC
(Sound City broadcast)
May 8 1992 City Hall, Glasgow (support
Suede)
May 19 1992 Town and Country, London
May 20 1992 Event, Brighton

EUROPEAN TOUR
May 23 1992 Ancienne Belgique, Brussels,
Belgium
May 24 1992 Effenaar, Eindhoven, The
Netherlands
May 25 1992 Paradiso, Amsterdam, The
Netherlands
June 4 1992 Theaterfabrik, Munich,
Germany
June 5 1992 Live Music Hall, Cologne,
Germany
June 8 1992 Huxley's Neue Welt, Berlin
June 9 1992 Schorre, Halle, Germany
June 10 1992 Batschkapp, Frankfurt,
Germany
June 11 1992 Komm, Nuernberg, Germany
June 12 1992 Grosse Freiheit 36, Hamburg,
Germany

June 27 1992 Glastonbury Festival
July 27 1992 Slough Festival
August 3 1992 Pyramid Centre, Portsmouth
September 15 1992 Ritz, Manchester
September 22 1992 Town and Country,
London
October 3 1992 Free Trade Hall, Manchester

GREEK TOUR
October 15 1992 Milos Club, Salonica,
Greece
October 16 1992 Rodon Club, Athens,
Greece
October 17 1992 Rodon Club, Athens,
Greece

November 19 1992 Town Hall, Birmingham
December 18 1992 Queen Margaret Union,
Glasgow

1993
UK TOUR
April 7 1993 Hallam University, Sheffield
May 6 1993 Newcastle University
May 7 1993 Manchester University
May 8 1993 Methodist Central Hall,
Liverpool
May 9 1993 University of East Anglia,
Norwich
May 10 1993 Junction, Cambridge
May 12 1993 The Road Mender,
Northampton
May 13 1993 Leeds University
May 15 1993 Clapham Grand, London
May 16 1993 Clapham Grand, London
May 17 1993 Wolverhampton
May 18 1993 Pyramid Centre, Portsmouth
May 19 1993 The Rainbow Club, Victoria
Rooms, Bristol

US TOUR
August 19 1993 Trocadero, Philadelphia,
Pennsylvania
August 20 1993 The Grand, New York
August 21 1993 Axis, Boston, Mass.
August 23 1993 Agora Ballroom, Cleveland,
Ohio
August 24 1993 Opera House, Toronto,
Canada
August 25 1993 St. Andrews, Detroit,
Michigan
August 27 1993 Bogarts, Cincinnati, Ohio
August 28 1993 Cabaret Metro, Chicago,
Illinois
August 29 1993 Barrymore Theater,
Madison, Wisconsin
August 30 1993 First Avenue, Minneapolis,
Minnesota
September 2 1993 Backstage, Seattle,
Washington
September 4 1993 Slim's, San Francisco,
California
September 5 1993 Slim's, San Francisco,
California
September 7 1993 Roxy, Hollywood,
California

September 10 1993 Trees, Dallas, Texas
September 11 1993 Liberty Lunch, Austin,
Texas
September 13 1993 Masquerade, Atlanta,
Georgia
September 14 1993 40 Watt Club, Athens,
Georgia
September 16 1993 Black Cat, Washington,
D.C.
September 17 1993 Academy, New York,
New York
Source of material included on live LP *Live
Various Years*.

EUROPEAN TOUR
October 1 1993 Grosse Freiheit 36,
Hamburg, Germany
October 4 1993 Vier Linden, Hildesheim,
Germany
October 5 1993 Wartesaal, Cologne,
Germany
October 7, 1993 Live Station, Dortmund,
Germany
(tour also included date in Munich, source of
material included on live LP *Live Various
Years*.)
October 8, 1993 L'Arapaho, Paris, France
October 17 1993 Paradiso, Amsterdam, The
Netherlands
October 19 1993 Kentish Town Forum,
London

UK TOUR
October 23 1993 Tivoli Theatre, Dublin
October 24 1993 Limelight, Belfast
December 6 1993 Roadhouse, Manchester
December 7 1993 Roadhouse, Manchester
December 8 1993 Roadhouse, Manchester
December 9 1993 Roadhouse, Manchester
December 27 1993 Al's Music Cafe,
Manchester

December 28 1993 Almada, Portugal

1994
UK TOUR
January 20 1994 Lomax, Liverpool
January 21 1994 Lomax, Liverpool
January 22 1994 Lomax, Liverpool
January 28 1994 The Fridge, Brixton, London
January 29 1994 Oxford Venue, Oxford
January 30 1994 Oxford Venue, Oxford

March 8 1994 ICA, London
April 29 1994 Shepherds Bush Empire,
London
May 24 1994 The Venue, Penzance
May 25 1994 University of Exeter, Exeter
May 26 1994 Trinity Centre, Bristol

May 28 1994 Vilnius Rock Festival,
Lithuania
May 31 1994 The Anvil, Basingstoke
Jun 1 1994 Queen Elizabeth Hall, Oldham
Jun 3 1994 Riverside, Newcastle
Jun 5 1994 Assembly Rooms, Derby
Jun 6 1994 Riley Smith Hall, Leeds
University Union
July 15 1994 Main Stage, Phoenix Festival,
Stratford-Upon-Avon
August 13 1994 Glasgow Arena
August 15 1994 The Volcano Tent,
Edinburgh
August 15 1994 The Acropolis, Carlton Hill,
Edinburgh

UK TOUR
September 1 1994 Roadhouse, Manchester
September 2 1994 Roadhouse, Manchester
September 3 1994 Leadmill, Sheffield
US TOUR
September 7 1994 Club Babyhead,
Providence, Rhode Island
September 8 1994 Axis, Boston, Mass.
September 9 1994 Black Cat, Washington DC
September 10 1994 Tramps, New York
September 11 1994 Trocadero,
Philadelphia, Pennsylvania
September 13 1994 RPM Club, Toronto,
Canada
September 14 1994 Blind Pig, Ann Arbor,
Michigan
September 15 1994 Bogart's, Cincinnati,
Ohio
September 16 1994 Cabaret Metro,
Chicago, Illinois
September 17 1994 First Avenue,
Minneapolis, Minnesota
September 20 1994 The Starfish Room,
Vancouver, British Columbia, Canada
September 21 1994 Backstage, Seattle,
Washington
September 22 1994 La Luna, Portland,
Oregon
September 24 1994 Fillmore, San
Francisco, California
September 25 1994 The Palace, Los
Angeles, California
November 24 1994 Bradford University
December 19 1994 Al's Music Cafe,
Manchester
December 20 1994 Northwick Theatre,
Worcester
December 21 1994 Lomax, Liverpool
December 22 1994 Barbican, York

1995
March 10 1995 Forum, London
March 20 1995 Roadhouse, Manchester

March 21 1995 Roadhouse, Manchester
March 22 1995 Roadhouse, Manchester
Source of live LP *The Fall In The City*.

EUROPEAN TOUR
April 28 1995 Salle de la Cite, Rennes,
France
May 8 1995 Student Festival, Portugal
May 13 1995 St. Lo Festival, Brittany
May 19 1995 Lisbon, Portugal
May 20 1995 Lisbon, Portugal
(tour also included Prague, Tel Aviv dates –
source of material included on live LP *The 27
Points*).
July 14 1995 Phoenix Festival
July 22 1995 Szene Music Theater,
Salzburg, Austria
September 17 1995 The Hague,
Netherlands Mark spoken word

UK TOUR
October 8 1995 Caledonian University,
Glasgow
October 23 1995 Astoria, London
October 24 1995 Junction, Cambridge
December 12 1995 Mean Fiddler, Dublin

December 31 1995 Volksbuehne, Berlin,
Germany

1996
May 30 1996 Hacienda, Manchester
June 26 1996 Astoria, London
June 28 1996 Leadmill, Sheffield
June 30 1996 Roskilde Festival, Denmark
July 21 1996 Phoenix Festival
September 21 1996 Barcelona, Spain

UK TOUR
September 25 1996 Zodiac, Oxford
September 27 1996 Prince of Wales Centre,
Cannock
September 28 1996 Corn Exchange, King's
Lynn
September 29 1996 Waterfront, Norwich
October 1 1996 Ritz, Manchester
October 3 1996 Civic Centre, Aylesbury
October 4 1996 Town Hall, Cheltenham
October 5 1996 Concert Hall, Motherwell
October 8 1996 Assembly Rooms, Worthing
October 11 1996 Forum, London
December 24 1996 Volksbuehne, Berlin,
Germany

1997
January 28 1997 Bierkeller, Bristol
Source of material included on live LP *Live
Various Years*.

January 29 1997 Level 3, Swindon
January 30 1997 Guildhall, Gloucester
February 26 1997 Astoria 2, London
May 13 1997 Jilly's Rockworld, Manchester
May 14 1997 Jilly's/Rockworld, Manchester
July 27 1997 Cooper's Field, Bute Park,
Cardiff
August 2 1997 Bangor Rugby Club
August 9 1997 Edinburgh
September 24 1997 Dingwall's, London

UK TOUR
November 5 1997 Sir Henry's, Cork
November 6 1997 Mean Fiddler, Dublin
November 13 1997 Sankey Soap's,
Manchester
November 19 1997 Riverside, Newcastle
November 20 1997 Lemon Tree, Aberdeen
November 21 1997 The Venue, Edinburgh
November 23 1997 The Garage, Glasgow
November 24 1997 Fat Sam's, Dundee
November 26 1997 Tivoli, Buckley
November 27 1997 Zodiac, Oxford
November 30 1997 Stage, Stoke
December 1 1997 Irish Centre, Leeds
December 2 1997 Krazy House, Liverpool
December 4 1997 Wedgewood Rooms,
Portsmouth
December 5 1997 Kentish Town Forum,
London
December 7 1997 Junction, Cambridge
December 8 1997 Waterfront, Norwich
December 9 1997 Bierkeller, Bristol

1998
US TOUR
March 30 1998 Coney Island High, New
York City
March 31 1998 Coney Island High, New
York City
April 2 1998 Loop Lounge, Passaic Park,
New Jersey
April 3 1998 Middle East Restaurant &
Nightclub, Cambridge, Mass
April 4 1998 Trocadero, Philadelphia,
Pennsylvania
April 5 1998 Black Cat, Washington, DC
April 7 1998 Brownies, New York City
April 8 1998 Brownies, New York City

April 27 1998 Dingwalls, London
April 28 1998 Dingwalls, London
April 30 1998 Alleycat, Reading
August 11 1998 Manchester University
August 12 1998 Astoria 2, London
October 21 1998 St. Bernadette's Club,
Whitefield
October 22 1998 St. Bernadette's Club,
Whitefield
December 14 1998 Fleece and Firkin,

Bristol
December 16 1998 Astoria 2, London
December 29 1998 Ritz Ballroom,
Manchester
1999
February 28 1999 Ashton Witchwood
March 1 1999 Ashton Witchwood
March 2 1999 Ashton Witchwood
April 15 1999 Sound Republic, London

UK TOUR
May 3 1999 Princess Charlotte, Leicester
May 4 1999 Irish Centre, Leeds
May 5 1999 Foundry, Birmingham
May 6 1999 Brighton Centre
May 7 1999 Salisbury Arts Centre
May 8 1999 The Crypt, Hastings
May 9 1999 Sheffield University
May 10 1999 The Attic, Cheltenham
May 11 1999 The Junction, Cambridge
May 12 1999 Chinnery's, Southend
May 13 1999 Venue 21, Luton
May 14 1999 Kentish Town Forum, London

June 20 1999 Meltdown Festival, Queen
Elizabeth Hall, London (spoken word)
August 20 1999 Planet K, Manchester
August 22 1999 Flux Festival, Queen's Hall,
Edinburgh
August 27 1999 Reading Festival
August 28 1999 Leeds Festival

DUTCH TOUR
September 14 1999 Doornroosje, Nijmegen,
The Netherlands
September 15 1999 Paradiso, Amsterdam,
The Netherlands
September 16 1999 Vera, Groningen, The
Netherlands
September 17 1999 013, Tilburg, The
Netherlands
September 18 1999 V.K., Brussels, Belgium
September 19 1999 L.V.C., Leiden, The
Netherlands
October 20 1999 Dingwalls, London
December 2 1999 Planet K, Manchester
December 19 1999 Victoria Inn, Derby
December 20 1999 Boardwalk, Sheffield
December 21 1999 Ashton Witchwood
December 22 1999 Ashton Witchwood

2000
March 21 2000 Yales, Wrexham
March 22 2000 Leopard, Doncaster
March 23 2000 Fibbers, York
March 24 2000 Duchess of York, Leeds
May 24 2000 LA2, London
UK TOUR
Jun 12 2000 Witchwood, Ashton

Jun 13 2000 Adelphi, Hull
Jun 14 2000 Cornerhouse, Middlesbrough
Jun 15 2000 King Tut's Wah Wah Hut,
Glasgow
Jun 16 2000 Liquid Room, Edinburgh
Jun 17 2000 West Bar, Dundee
Jun 18 2000 Glow 303, Aberdeen

August 8 2000 Festival de Arcos de
Valdevez, Portugal
August 13 2000 Water's Edge Festival,
Castlefield, Manchester
September 22 2000 Royal Festival Hall,
London
October 6 2000 StAnza Poetry Festival, St.
Andrews

UK TOUR
November 15 2000 HMV Records, Oxford
Street, London
November 21 2000 Rock City, Nottingham
November 22 2000 Dingwalls, London
November 24 2000 Lomax, Liverpool
November 25 2000 Liquid Room, Edinburgh
November 26 2000 The Garage, Glasgow
November 27 2000 Sheffield University
November 29 2000 Music Box, next to
Jilly's Rock World, Manchester
November 30 2000 Irish Centre, Leeds
December 1 2000 The Dome, Whitley Bay
December 2 2000 Princess Charlotte,
Leicester

2001
February 24 2001 Red Box, Dublin, Ireland

DUTCH TOUR
April 5 2001 Bolwerk, Sneek, The
Netherlands
April 6 2001 Patronaat, Haarlem, The
Netherlands
April 7 2001 Melkweg, Amsterdam, The
Netherlands

April 12 2001 Trinity College, Dublin,
Ireland (spoken word)

UK TOUR
April 16 2001 TJ's, Newport
April 17 2001 Concorde 2, Brighton
April 18 2001 Union Bar, Maidstone
April 19 2001 Arts Centre, Colchester
April 20 2001 Arts Centre, Norwich
April 21 2001 Woughton Centre, Milton
Keynes
April 22 2001 Zodiac, Oxford
April 23 2001 Mean Fiddler, London
April 24 2001 Academy 2, Birmingham
April 25 2001 Bar Cuba, Macclesfield

August 11, 2001 The Bulldog Bash, Long Marston Airfield, Warwickshire

UK TOUR
October 8 2001 Cockpit, Leeds
October 9 2001 The Cluny, Newcastle
October 10 2001 Liquid Room, Edinburgh
October 11 2001 The Limelight, Belfast
October 12 2001 Temple Bar, Dublin
October 13 2001 University of Liverpool Student Union, Liverpool
October 15 2001 The Park, Peterborough
October 17 2001 The Bierkeller, Bristol
October 18 2001 Princess Hall, Aldershot

EUROPEAN TOUR
October 19 2001 VK, Brussels, Belgium
October 20 2001 Zall Spuugh, Vaals, The Netherlands
October 22 2001 De Kade, Zaandam, The Netherlands
October 23 2001 Kantine, Cologne, Germany
October 24 2001 Logo, Hamburg, Germany
October 25 2001 Vega, Copenhagen, Denmark
October 26 2001 Sticky Fingers, Gothenburg, Sweden
October 27 2001 KB, Malmo, Sweden
October 28 2001 Festival@Berns, Stockholm, Sweden MES spoken word
October 28 2001 Kagelbanan, Stockholm, Sweden MES spoken word
October 30 2001 Maria Am Ostbahnhof, Berlin, Germany
November 10 2001 The Forum, London

US TOUR
November 13 2001 The Knitting Factory, Los Angeles, California (MES spoken word)
November 14 2001 The Knitting Factory, Los Angeles, California
November 15 2001 The Knitting Factory, Los Angeles, California
Source of material included on live CD 2G+2
November 19 2001 Great American Music Hall, San Francisco, California
November 20 2001 Crocodile Cafe, Seattle, Washington
Source of material included on live CD 2G+2
November 23 2001 The Knitting Factory, New York City
Source of material included on live CD 2G+2
November 24 2001 The Knitting Factory, New York City
November 25 2001 The Knitting Factory, New York City
Source of material included on live CD 2G+2

November 29 2001 Footage and Firkin, Manchester

2002
EUROPEAN TOUR
January 26 2002 Club 22, Athens, Greece
February 19 2002 Palace Akropolis, Prague, Czech Republic
February 20 2002 Szene, Vienna, Austria
February 21 2002 Rockhouse, Salzburg, Austria
February 22 2002 Hafen/Crash, Innsbruck, Austria
February 23 2002 Conrad Sohm, Dornbirn, Austria
February 24 2002 Schüür, Luzern, Switzerland
February 25 2002 Tunnel, Milan, Italy
February 26 2002 Covo, Bologna, Italy
February 27 2002 Brancaleone, Rome, Italy
February 28 2002 Velvet, Rimini, Italy
March 1 2002 Interzona, Verona, Italy
March 2 2002 Reitschule, Bern, Switzerland
March 4 2002 FZW, Dortmund, Germany
March 7 2002 Deli, Berlin, Germany
March 8 2002 Haus der Judend, Dusseldorf, Germany

April 19 2002 North Cafe Bar, Blackburn
April 20 2002 The Garage, London
April 21 2002 All Tomorrow's Parties, Camber Sands, East Sussex
April 28 2002 All Tomorrow's Parties, Camber Sands, East Sussex
May 19 2002 11th Annual WaveGottikTreffen festival, Leipzig, Germany
May 21 2002 Starclub, Dresden, Germany
May 24 2002 Loppen, Christiana, Copenhagen, Denmark

UK TOUR
September 22 2002 King George's Hall, Blackburn
September 25 2002 Rock City, Nottingham
September 27 2002 Zodiac, Oxford
September 28 2002 Arts Centre, Colchester
September 30 2002 Concorde 2, Brighton
October 2 2002 Irish Centre, Leeds
October 3 2002 Guildhall, Gloucester
October 5 2002 University of Liverpool Student Union
November 4 2002 Electric Ballroom, Camden

Bibliography

BOOKS & MAGAZINES

GENERAL REFERENCE
British Hit Albums (6th ed) (Guinness World Records)
British Hit Singles (15th ed) (Guinness World Records)
In Session Tonight: The Complete Radio One Recordings by Ken Garner (BBC Books)
Indie Hits 1980-89: comp Barry Lazell (Cherry Red Books)
Invisible Jukebox: ed Tony Herrington (Wire)
NME Book of Modern Music (*New Musical Express* supplement 1978)
Post-Punk Diary: George Gimarc (St Martin's Press)
Punk Diary: George Gimarc (St Martin's Press)
The Great Rock Discography (6th ed): Martin C Strong (Canongate)

BIOGRAPHIES & MEMOIRS
Head On by Julian Cope (Magog Books)
Joy Division To New Order: The Factory Story by Mick Middles (Virgin)
Morrissey & Marr: The Severed Alliance by Johnny Rogan (Omnibus Press)
Paintwork: A Portrait of the Fall by Brian Edge (Omnibus Press)
The Fall Lyrics (in German!) by Mark E Smith (Lough Press, Berlin)

In addition to sources directly cited in the text, multiple individual issues of the following proved helpful: *Alternative Press* (USA), *Boston Phoenix* (USA), *City Life*, *Creem* (USA), *Goldmine* (USA), *Melody Maker*, *Mojo*, *New Musical Express*, *New York Times* (USA), *Pandemonium* (USA), *Q*, *Record Collector*, *Record Mirror*, *Select*, *Sounds*, *Trouser Press* (USA), *Vox*, *Zig Zag*

WEBSITES
All links current as of December 31, 2002

http://www.visi.com/fall/ – the official Fall website, edited by Stefan Cooke and Conway Paton. Your first stop on the web for all things Fall, including the most up-to-date news, a huge archive of old print articles, the internet's largest band disc- and gigography.

http://liquid2k.com/fall/lyrics/lyrics.html – the Fall lyrics parade. Painstaking transcriptions of (almost) every song, by Jonathan Kandell and Jeff Curtis.

http://members.tripod.com/~the27points/lineups.html – the legendary Fall Bandmember-ography. Seems to have been down for most of 2002, but this is where it should be.

http://members.tripod.com/~GColeman/index.html – The Biggest Library Yet, for close to a decade the #1 source of Fall thoughts, news and info.

http://homepage.ntlworld.com/s.bending/ – excellent page of multimedia content.

http://www.wes.ukgateway.net/Fall/FallIndex.html – a fascinating collection of memorabilia.

http://www.voiceprint.org.uk/ – home page of Cog Sinister's parent label.

Acknowledgements

And, finally, for no reason whatsoever, a dozen great Fall songs that just keep on getting greater...

Big New Prinz
Blood Outta Stone
Chiselers/Chilinist/Interlude/Chilinism
Eat Y'self Fitter
Glam Racket
Hostile
Living Too Long
Marquee Cha-Cha
Mr Pharmacist
Repetition
Telephone Thing
The Man Whose Head Expanded

Other Titles available from Helter Skelter

Coming Soon

Steve Marriott: All Too Beautiful – The Definitive Biography   Spring 2004
by Paolo Hewitt and John Hellier £20.00
Marriott was the prime mover behind 60s chart-toppers The Small Faces. Longing to be treated as a serious musician he formed Humble Pie with Peter Frampton, where his blistering rock 'n' blues guitar playing soon saw him take centre stage in the US live favourites. After years in seclusion, Marriott's plans for a comeback in 1991 were tragically cut short when he died in a housefire. He continues to be a key influence for generations of musicians from Paul Weller to Oasis and Blur.

Pink Floyd: A Saucerful of Secrets   Spring 2003
by Nicholas Schaffner £14.99
Long overdue reissue of the authoritative and detailed account of one of the most important and popular bands in rock history. From the psychedelic explorations of the Syd Barrett-era to 70s superstardom with *Dark Side of the Moon*, and on to triumph of *The Wall*, before internecine strife tore the group apart. Schaffner's definitive history also covers the improbable return of Pink Floyd without Roger Waters, and the hugely successful *Momentary Lapse of Reason* album and tour.

The Big Wheel   Spring 2003
by Bruce Thomas £10.99
Thomas was bassist with Elvis Costello at the height of his success. Though names are never named, *The Big Wheel* paints a vivid and hilarious picture of life touring with Costello and co, sharing your life 24-7 with a moody egotistical singer, a crazed drummer and a host of hangers-on. Costello sacked Thomas on its initial publication.
    "A top notch anecdotalist who can time a twist to make you laugh out loud." *Q*

Hit Men: Powerbrokers and Fast Money Inside The Music Business
By Fredric Dannen £14.99
Hit Men exposes the seamy and sleazy dealings of America's glitziest record companies: payola, corruption, drugs, Mafia involvement, and excess.
    "So heavily awash with cocaine, corruption and unethical behaviour that it makes the occasional examples of chart-rigging and playlist tampering in Britain during the same period seem charmingly inept." *The Guardian*.

I'm With The Band: Confessions of A Groupie
By Pamela Des Barres £14.99
Frank and engaging memoir of affairs with Keith Moon, Noel Redding and Jim Morrison, travels with Led Zeppelin as Jimmy Page's girlfriend, and friendships with Robert Plant, Gram Parsons, and Frank Zappa.
    "Miss Pamela, the most beautiful and famous of the groupies. Her memoir of her life with rock stars is funny, bittersweet, and tender-hearted."
Stephen Davis, author of *Hammer of the Gods*

Psychedelic Furs: Beautiful Chaos
by Dave Thompson £12.99
Psychedelic Furs were the ultimate post-punk band – combining the chaos and vocal rasp of the Sex Pistols with a Bowie-esque glamour. The Furs hit the big time when John Hughes wrote a movie based on their early single "Pretty in Pink". Poised to join U2 and Simple Minds in the premier league, they withdrew behind their shades, remaining a cult act, but one with a hugely devoted following.

Bob Dylan: Like The Night (Revisited)
by CP Lee £9.99
Fully revised and updated B-format edition of the hugely acclaimed document of Dylan's pivotal 1966 show at the Manchester Free Trade Hall where fans called him Judas for turning his back on folk music in favour of rock 'n' roll.

Currently Available from Helter Skelter

Marillion: Separated Out
by Jon Collins £14.99
From the chart hit days of Fish and "Kayleigh" to the Steve Hogarth incarnation, Marillion have continued to make groundbreaking rock music. Collins tells the full story, drawing on interviews with band members, associates, and the experiences of some of the band's most dedicated fans.

Rainbow Rising
by Roy Davies £14.99
The full story of guitar legend Ritchie Blackmore's post-Purple progress with one of the great 70s rock bands. After quitting Deep Purple at the height of their success, Blackmore combined with Ronnie James Dio to make epic rock albums like *Rising* and *Long Live Rock 'n' Roll* before streamlining the sound and enjoying hit singles like "Since You've Been Gone" and "All Night Long." Rainbow were less celebrated than Deep Purple, but they feature much of Blackmore's finest writing and playing, and were one of the best live acts of the era. They are much missed.

Marc Bolan and T Rex: A Chronology
by Cliff McLenahan £13.99
Bolan was the ultimate glam-rock icon; beautiful, elfin, outrageously dressed and capable of hammering out impossibly catchy teen rock hits such as "Telegram Sam", and "Get It On". With their pounding guitars and three chord anthems T Rex paved the way for hard rock and punk rock.

Back to the Beach: A Brian Wilson and the Beach Boys Reader REVISED EDITION
Ed Kingsley Abbott £14.00
Revised and expanded edition of the Beach Boys compendium *Mojo* magazine deemed an "essential purchase." This collection includes all of the best articles, interviews and reviews from the Beach Boys' four decades of music, including definitive pieces by Timothy White, Nick Kent and David Leaf. New material reflects on the tragic death of Carl Wilson and documents the rejuvenated Brian's return to the boards. "Rivetting!" **** *Q* "An essential purchase." *Mojo*

Harmony in My Head
The Original Buzzcock Steve Diggle's Rock 'n' Roll Odyssey
by Steve Diggle and Terry Rawlings £14.99
First-hand account of the punk wars from guitarist and one half of the songwriting duo that gave the world three chord punk-pop classics like "Ever Fallen In Love" and "Promises". Diggle dishes the dirt on punk contemporaries like The Sex Pistols, The Clash and The Jam, as well as sharing poignant memories of his friendship with Kurt Cobain, on whose last ever tour, The Buzzcocks were support act.

Serge Gainsbourg: A Fistful of Gitanes
by Sylvie Simmons £9.99
Rock press legend Simmons' hugely acclaimed biography of the French genius.
"I would recommend *A Fistful of Gitanes* [as summer reading] which is a highly entertaining biography of the French singer-songwriter and all-round scallywag" – JG Ballard
"A wonderful introduction to one of the most overlooked songwriters of the 20th century" (Number 3, top music books of 2001) *The Times*
"The most intriguing music-biz biography of the year" *The Independent*
"Wonderful. Serge would have been so happy" – Jane Birkin

Blues: The British Connection
by Bob Brunning £14.99
Former Fleetwood Mac member Bob Brunning's classic account of the impact of Blues in Britain, from its beginnings as the underground music of 50s teenagers like Mick Jagger, Keith Richards and Eric Clapton, to the explosion in the 60s, right through to the vibrant scene of the present day.
'An invaluable reference book and an engaging personal memoir' – Charles Shaar Murray

On The Road With Bob Dylan
by Larry Sloman £12.99
In 1975, as Bob Dylan emerged from 8 years of seclusion, he dreamed of putting together a travelling music show that would trek across the country like a psychedelic carnival. The dream became a reality, and *On The Road With Bob Dylan* is the ultimate behind-the-scenes look at what happened. When Dylan and the Rolling Thunder Revue took to the streets of America, Larry "Ratso" Sloman was with them every step of the way.
"The *War and Peace* of Rock and Roll." – Bob Dylan

Gram Parsons: God's Own Singer
By Jason Walker £12.99
Brand new biography of the man who pushed The Byrds into country-rock territory on *Sweethearts of The Rodeo*, and quit to form the Flying Burrito Brothers. Gram lived hard, drank hard, took every drug going and somehow invented country rock, paving the way for Crosby, Stills & Nash, The Eagles and Neil Young. Parsons' second solo LP, *Grievous Angel*, is a haunting masterpiece of country soul. By the time it was released, he had been dead for 4 months. He is 26 years old.
"Walker has done an admirable job in taking us as close to the heart and soul of Gram Parsons as any author could." **** *Uncut* book of the month

Ashley Hutchings: The Guvnor and the Rise of Folk Rock – Fairport Convention, Steeleye Span and the Albion Band
by Geoff Wall and Brian Hinton £14.99
As founder of Fairport Convention and Steeleye Span, Ashley Hutchings is the pivotal figure in the history of folk rock. This book draws on hundreds of hours of interviews with Hutchings and other folk-rock artists and paints a vivid picture of the scene that also produced Sandy Denny, Richard Thompson, Nick Drake, John Martyn and Al Stewart.

Hang On To A Dream: The Story of The Nice
by Martyn Hanson £13.99
Formed to back singer PP Arnold, Keith Emerson's band prior to ELP, The Nice, outgrew this purpose to become one of the most exciting bands of the era – paving the way for acts like ELP by ripping apart songs like Bernstein's "America" and mixing rock with jazz and classical elements. Recently reformed for a series of live dates, it is time to credit The Nice with their role as a key pioneering act in the evolution of progressive rock.

Al Stewart: True Life Adventures of a Folk Troubadour
by Neville Judd £25.00
Authorised biography of the Scottish folk hero behind US Top Ten hit "Year of The Cat". This is a vivid insider's account of the pivotal 60s London coffee house scene that kickstarted the careers of a host of folkies including Paul Simon – with whom Al shared a flat in 1965 – as well as the wry memoir of a 60s folk star's tribulations as he becomes a chart-topping star in the US in the 70s. Highly limited hardcover edition!

ISIS: A Bob Dylan Anthology
Ed Derek Barker £14.99
Expertly compiled selection of rare articles which trace the evolution of rock's greatest talent. From Bob's earliest days in New York City to the more recent legs of the Never Ending Tour, and his new highly acclaimed album, *Love and Theft*, the ISIS archive has exclusive interview material – often rare or previously unpublished – with many of the key players in Dylan's career: his parents, friends, musicians and other collaborators.

The Beach Boys' Pet Sounds: The Greatest Album of the Twentieth Century
by Kingsley Abbott £11.95
Pet Sounds is the 1966 album that saw The Beach Boys graduate from lightweight pop like "Surfin' USA", *et al*, into a vehicle for the mature compositional genius of Brian Wilson. The album was hugely influential, not least on The Beatles. This the full story of the album's background, its composition and recording, its contemporary reception and its enduring legacy.

King Crimson: In The Court of King Crimson
by Sid Smith £14.99
King Crimson's 1969 masterpiece *In The Court Of The Crimson King*, was a huge U.S. chart hit. The band followed it with 40 further albums of consistently challenging, distinctive and innovative music. Drawing on hours of new interviews, and encouraged by Crimson supremo Robert Fripp, the author traces the band's turbulent history year by year, track by track.

A Journey Through America with the Rolling Stones
by Robert Greenfield UK Price £9.99: Featuring a new foreword by Ian Rankin
This is the definitive account of their legendary '72 tour."Filled with finely-rendered detail ... a fascinating tale of times we shall never see again" *Mojo*

Razor Edge: Bob Dylan and The Never-ending Tour
by Andrew Muir £12.99
Respected Dylan expert Andrew Muir documents the ups and downs of this unprecedented trek, and finds time to tell the story of his own curious meeting with Dylan. Muir also tries to get to grips with what exactly it all means – both for Dylan and for the Bobcats: dedicated Dylan followers, like himself, who trade tapes of every show and regularly cross the globe to catch up with the latest leg of The Never Ending Tour.

Calling Out Around the World: A Motown Reader
Edited by Kingsley Abbott £13.99
With a foreword by Martha Reeves, this is a unique collection of articles which tell the story of the rise of a black company in a white industry, and its talented stable of artists, musicians, writers and producers. Included are rare interviews with key figures such as Berry Gordy, Marvin Gaye, Smokey Robinson and Florence Ballard as well as reference sources for collectors and several specially commissioned pieces.

I've Been Everywhere: A Johnny Cash Chronicle
by Peter Lewry £12.99
A complete chronological illustrated diary of Johnny Cash's concerts, TV appearances, record releases, recording sessions and other milestones. From his early days with Sam Phillips in Memphis to international stardom, the wilderness years of the mid-sixties, and on to his legendary prison concerts and his recent creative resurgence with the hugely successful 2000 release, *American Recording III: Solitary Man*.

Sandy Denny: No More Sad Refrains
by Clinton Heylin £13.99
Paperback edition of the highly acclaimed biography of the greatest female singer-songwriter this country has ever produced.

Emerson Lake and Palmer: The Show That Never Ends
by George Forrester, Martin Hanson and Frank Askew £14.00
Drawing on years of research, the authors have produced a gripping and fascinating document of the prog-rock supergroup who remain one of the great rock bands of the seventies.

Animal Tracks: The Story of The Animals
by Sean Egan £12.99
Sean Egan has enjoyed full access to surviving Animals and associates and has produced a compelling portrait of a truly distinctive band of survivors.

Like a Bullet of Light: The Films of Bob Dylan
by CP Lee £12.99
In studying in-depth an often overlooked part of Dylan's oeuvre.

Rock's Wild Things: The Troggs Files
by Alan Clayson and Jacqueline Ryan £12.99
Respected rock writer Alan Clayson has had full access to the band and traces their history from 60s Andover rock roots to 90s covers, collaborations and corn circles. Also features the full transcript of the legendary "Troggs Tapes."

Waiting for the Man: The Story of Drugs and Popular Music
by Harry Shapiro UK Price £12.99
Fully revised edition of the classic story of two intertwining billion dollar industries.
   "Wise and witty." *The Guardian*

Dylan's Daemon Lover: The Tangled Tale of a 450-Year Old Pop Ballad
by Clinton Heylin UK price £12.00
Written as a detective story, Heylin unearths the mystery of why Dylan knew enough to return "The House Carpenter" to its 16th century source.

Get Back: The Beatles' Let It Be Disaster
by Doug Sulpy & Ray Schweighardt UK price £12.99
No-holds barred account of the power struggles, the bickering, and the bitterness that led to the break-up of the greatest band in the history of rock 'n' roll.
   "One of the most poignant Beatles books ever." *Mojo*

XTC: Song Stories – The Exclusive & Authorised Story
by XTC and Neville Farmer £12.99
"A cheerful celebration of the minutiae surrounding XTC's music with the band's musical passion intact ... high in setting-the-record-straight anecdotes. Superbright, funny, commanding." *Mojo*

Born in the USA: Bruce Springsteen and the American Tradition
by Jim Cullen £9.99
"Cullen has written an excellent treatise expressing exactly how and why Springsteen translated his uneducated hicktown American-ness into music and stories that touched hearts and souls around the world." *Q*****

Bob Dylan
by Anthony Scaduto £10.99
The first and best biography of Dylan. "The best book ever written on Dylan" *Record Collector* "Now in a welcome reprint it's a real treat to read the still-classic Bobography". *Q******

Firefly Publishing: An Association between Helter Skelter and SAF

Coming Soon from Firefly Publishing:

The Nirvana Recording Sessions
by Rob Jovanovic £14.99
Drawing on years of research, and interviews with many who worked with the band, the author has documented details of every Nirvana recording, from early rehearsals, to the *In Utero* sessions. A fascinating account of the creative process of one of the great bands.

Currently Available from Firefly Publishing

The Music of George Harrison: While My Guitar Gently Weeps
by Simon Leng £20.00
Often in Lennon and McCartney's shadow, Harrison's music can stand on its own merits. Santana biographer Leng takes a studied, track by track, look at both Harrison's contribution to The Beatles, and the solo work that started with the release in 1970 of his epic masterpiece *All Things Must Pass*. "Here Comes The Sun", "Something" – which Sinatra covered and saw as the perfect love song – "All Things Must Pass" and "While My Guitar Gently Weeps" are just a few of Harrison's classic songs.
   Originally planned as a celebration of Harrison's music, this is now sadly a commemoration.

The Pretty Things: Growing Old Disgracefully
by Alan Lakey £20
First biography of one of rock's most influential and enduring combos. Trashed hotel rooms, infighting, rip-offs, sex, drugs and some of the most remarkable rock 'n' roll, including landmark albums like the first rock opera, *SF Sorrow*, and Rolling Stone's album of the year, 1970's *Parachute*.
   "They invented everything, and were credited with nothing." Arthur Brown, "God of Hellfire"

The Sensational Alex Harvey
By John Neil Murno £20
Part rock band, part vaudeville, 100% commitment, the SAHB were one of the greatest live bands of the era. But behind his showman exterior, Harvey was increasingly beset by alcoholism and tragedy. He succumbed to a heart attack on the way home from a gig in 1982, but he is fondly remembered as a unique entertainer by friends, musicians and legions of fans.

U2: The Complete Encyclopedia
by Mark Chatterton £14.99

Poison Heart: Surviving The Ramones
by Dee Dee Ramone and Veronica Kofman £9.99

Minstrels In The Gallery: A History Of Jethro Tull
by David Rees £12.99

DANCEMUSICSEXROMANCE: Prince – The First Decade
by Per Nilsen £12.99

To Hell and Back with Catatonia
by Brian Wright £12.99

Soul Sacrifice: The Santana Story
by Simon Leng UK Price £12.99

Opening The Musical Box: A Genesis Chronicle
by Alan Hewitt UK Price £12.99

Blowin' Free: Thirty Years Of Wishbone Ash
by Gary Carter and Mark Chatterton UK Price £12.99

www.helterskelterbooks.com

All Helter Skelter, Firefly and SAF titles are available by mail order
www.helterskelterbooks.com, along with all music books in print in the world.
These titles are also kept in stock at the world famous Helter Skelter
bookshop.

You can either phone or fax your order to Helter Skelter on the following
numbers:

Telephone: +44 (0)20 7836 1151 or
Fax: +44 (0)20 7240 9880

Office hours: Mon-Fri   10:00am – 7:00pm,
                  Sat: 10:00am – 6:00pm,
                  Sun: closed.

Postage prices per book worldwide are as follows:
  UK & Channel Islands   £1.50   Europe & Eire (air)   £2.95
  USA, Canada (air)   £7.50   Australasia, Far East (air) £9.00
  Overseas (surface)   £2.50

You can also write enclosing a cheque, International Money Order, or
registered cash. Please include postage. DO NOT send cash. DO NOT send
foreign currency, or cheques drawn on an overseas bank. Send to:Helter
Skelter Bookshop,4 Denmark Street, London, WC2H 8LL, United Kingdom.

If you are in London come and visit us, and browse the titles in person!!

Email: info@helterskelterbooks.com